T0125025

THE LETTERS OF JACOB BURCKHARDT

JACOB BURCKHARDT

THE LETTERS OF

JACOB BURCKHARDT

Selected, edited, and translated by

ALEXANDER DRU

LIBERTY FUND

INDIANAPOLIS

This book is published by Liberty Fund, Inc.,
a foundation established to encourage study of the ideal of a society
of free and responsible individuals.

𒀫𒄀

The cuneiform inscription that serves as our logo
and as the design motif for our endpapers is the earliest-known
written appearance of the word "freedom" (*amagi*), or "liberty."
It is taken from a clay document written about 2300 B.C.
in the Sumerian city-state of Lagash.

© 1955 Routledge and Kegan Paul.
Published in 1955 by Pantheon Books Inc., New York, N.Y.
Foreword © 2001 Liberty Fund, Inc.
All rights reserved
Published by arrangement with Taylor & Francis Limited,
11 New Fetter Lane, London EC4P 4EE, UK

Printed in the United States of America

05 04 03 02 01 C 5 4 3 2 1
05 04 03 02 01 P 5 4 3 2 1

Library of Congress Cataloging-in-Publication Data

Burckhardt, Jacob, 1818–1897.
[Briefe. English]
The letters of Jacob Burckhardt / selected, edited, and translated by Alexander Dru.
p.   cm.
Originally published: London: Routledge and Kegan Paul, 1955.
Includes bibliographical references and index.
ISBN 0-86597-122-6 (alk. paper)—ISBN 0-86597-123-4 (pbk.: alk. paper)
1. Burckhardt, Jacob, 1818–1897—Correspondence.
2. Historians—Switzerland—Correspondence I. Dru, Alexander.

D15.B8 B87   2001
907'.202—dc21
[B]   2001038018

Liberty Fund, Inc.
8335 Allison Pointe Trail, Suite 300
Indianapolis, Indiana 46250-1684

FOR GABRIEL

CONTENTS

List of Illustrations	ix
Foreword to the Liberty Fund Edition	xi
Preface	xix
Introduction	xxiii
The Letters	3
Biographical Notes	251
Principal Editions of Burckhardt's Letters	255
Index	257

ILLUSTRATIONS

1   Jacob Burckhardt in 1843   37
    A drawing attributed to Franz Kugler
2   A view of Cologne, 1843   38
3   Pont des Arches, Liége, 1843   58
4   Ponte Rotto, Rome, 1847   59
5   St. Peter's, 1847   100
6   A street in Rome, 1848   101
7   Burckhardt on his way to the University (undated)   120
8   Burckhardt, photographed by Hans Lendorff, *c.* 1890   121

FOREWORD TO THE

LIBERTY FUND EDITION

IN THE OPENING YEARS of the twenty-first century, why should anyone bother to read the letters of an art history professor from the late 1800s? Whatever answer one gives, the reason has something to do with the qualities of Jacob Burckhardt's mind and its capacity to illumine some of the best and most beautiful things in Western civilization. To the contemporary reader, Burckhardt speaks as convincingly about the value of beauty, contemplation, and freedom as he did to his increasingly harried age. In many ways, we need his voice today even more urgently than we did a century ago.

The core of Burckhardt's life was his love of beauty. Indeed, one of his signal contributions to the tradition of freedom in Western civilization, and to conservative thought, was the line he drew between beauty and freedom. Like another great contemporary conservative, Fyodor Dostoevsky, Burckhardt recognized that man's love of, and impulse toward, beauty is a powerful force that ultimately leads man to affirm the worth of his spirit, his individuality, and the existential necessity of freedom. The strongest roots of freedom, and of human liberty, are spiritual.

Burckhardt's life spanned the nineteenth century (1818–1897). After a careful study of the entire corpus of Burckhardt's extensive correspondence, Professor Alexander Dru published in 1955 this selection covering his life from the age of twenty until a few months before his death. The selected letters give the reader a comprehensive view of Burckhardt's life, the evolution of his thinking, and his chief concerns. Reading these letters, one is impressed by the remarkable continuities in Burckhardt's outlook and the consistent themes that undergird this outlook.

He was deeply conservative by nature. Even in his youth, when along with his friends he was captivated by the strong currents of romanticism and idealism, he never succumbed to democratic liberalism or the modern belief in progress. While studying for the ministry he ceased to be an orthodox Christian, but to the end of his life he retained an appreciation for the Christian message of original sin, combined with utter contempt for liberal theologians who kept teaching at seminaries and leading congregations long after they had stopped believing. Burckhardt was proud to be, as he put it, "an honest heretic." His main quarrel with the churches throughout his lifetime was that they, along with everyone else, had succumbed to the optimistic illusions of the nineteenth century.

But Burckhardt's conservatism was neither ideological nor extreme. He despised extremes of every kind. When he was asked to become the editor of the local conservative newspaper, he accepted the job, in his own words, "mainly in order to exterminate by slow degrees the odious sympathy that exists among the ruling clique here for absolutism of every kind (e.g., the Russian) and on the other hand to come out against our raucous Swiss Radicals, which last I find precisely as repellent as the former." In keeping with his dislike of abstractions and ideologies, he wrote to a friend that he wanted to get away from "the 'ists' and 'isms' of every kind."

His conservatism often slipped into pessimism, and Burckhardt is often described, even by many of his admirers, as one of the great "pessimists" in the modern Western tradition. This characterization must be applied to him with care, but it is not far off the mark. It is true that he enjoyed life, especially the pleasures of aesthetic contemplation. He loved few things more than his long walks in the woods and mountains of Switzerland and Germany; his recurring pilgrimages through Italy, where he relished exploring the ancient architectural and artistic glories; and a hearty meal followed by a good wine and his favorite cigar. Although he never married, he was fond of his nephews and nieces and their children, and he believed that, in spite of the crisis that was about to shake European civilization, the younger generations would survive and manage to build a new order.

But in discussing politics Burckhardt was unabashedly pessimistic and unwilling to give modernity or modern liberalism credit for anything good. He was viscerally opposed to mass suffrage, modern public education, women in scholarship, and public health insurance, and he thought little about alternatives for dealing with the massive social problems developing in the second half of the nineteenth century. As he advanced in years, Burckhardt became more alarmed at the catastrophe he foresaw looming in the not-too-distant future. Unlike the pro-Enlightenment Edward Gibbon, who argued that the collapse of the Roman Empire coincided with "the triumph of barbarism and religion," Burckhardt thought that the decline of European civilization would be accompanied by the triumph of barbarism, commerce, and science.

While Burckhardt's distrust of modern liberalism may have gone too far, his general pessimism about the future of Western civilization and the consequences of modern mass society were not unwarranted. He believed that the combination of mass politics, the growth of democracy and egalitarianism, the collapse of the authority of the Church and the aristocracy, and the domination of modern life by the demands of economics, science, and technology would produce in the course of time a brutal and barbaric tyranny with a horrifying grip on political power. And indeed, only four short decades separated Burckhardt's life from the construction of Auschwitz, Bergen-Belsen, and Dachau in the heart of civilized Europe.

As annoying as Burckhardt's persistent critique of egalitarianism, liberal democracy, and industrial progress is bound to be for many readers, his legacy is squarely in the tradition of ordered liberty and aristocratic liberalism we associate with the names of Edmund Burke, Alexis de Tocqueville, José Ortega y Gasset, and Wilhelm Roepke. He distrusted the masses as inherently intolerant of individual greatness and hostile to culture. He noted that the most significant historical developments at the end of the eighteenth century were the advent of mass politics and the belief that every man's opinion was of equal worth. The long-term results of this would be the destruction of every vestige of traditional authority, the cheapening of culture, the enthronement of mediocrity at all levels of public life, and the eventual rise of *"terribles simplificateurs"*: the ruthless demagogues who would ride the waves of mass politics and culture to set up a tyranny armed with all the instruments provided by large-scale industrial capitalism, science, and technology.

Burckhardt also distrusted large institutions of every sort as inherently dehumanizing and hostile to individual freedom. Any institution, religious or secular, that became large and powerful enough fell, sooner or later, into the grip of what he called one of the ghastliest *idées fixes* in history: the desire for unity and conformity. Burckhardt loved small cities, small republics, and loose private associations as nurturing of pluralism and liberty. His love of pluralism was driven by his aesthetic recognition of the intrinsic beauty and wonder of diversity, and the belief that freedom could thrive more easily in the soil of diversity and decentralization than in uniformity.

Burckhardt was shocked by the ravages wrought on the created order by industrialization, modern technology, and economic progress. He believed that Western civilization since the seventeenth century had become dominated by acquisitiveness, and that this acquisitiveness was the force behind the appalling despoliation of Europe's forests, rivers, and ancient towns. The new cities, with their large, impersonal size, industrial squalor, and high cost of living, were the antithesis of a humane way of life. To the last, he retained a longing for a vanishing world in which beauty would dominate the natural as well as the man-made landscape.

A lifelong bachelor who was inherently shy with women, Burckhardt considered himself "a secular monk." He loved and praised the contemplative life at a time when modern society was becoming inhospitable to it. One of his quarrels with modernity was that its emerging mass society, and its acquisitive economic system focused on efficiency and speed, was crowding out opportunities for solitude and contemplation. He drew a sharp distinction between rational philosophy or "speculation," connected with thinking about abstract ideas, and contemplation, deriving from love of and wonder at the beauty and complexity of human beings and their deeds. He saw himself as a contemplative historian rather than a philosophical one. At the age of twenty-four, he confided to a friend,

> You must long ago have recognized the one-sided bent of my nature towards contemplation. My whole life long I have never yet thought philosophically, and never had any thought at all that was not connected with something external. I can do nothing unless I start out from contemplation. . . . What I build up historically is not the result of criticism and Speculation, but on the contrary, of imagination, which fills up the lacunae of contemplation.

Unlike many of his colleagues, Burckhardt did not see himself as mainly a technician. In his view, the historian needed to master the technical fundamentals of historical research and to be a specialist about at least one particular field. But he also enjoyed taking a more comprehensive view of things even at the risk of being accused of "amateurishness." As he was to admonish his students in the lectures that were later published as *Reflections on History*, "[a man] should be an amateur at as many points as possible. . . . Otherwise he will remain ignorant in any field lying outside his own specialty and perhaps, as a man, a barbarian." Many of these letters reflect that comprehensiveness, and they reveal a capacious mind that, in spite of the prejudices of time and place (Burckhardt never traveled outside Western Europe), was capable of immensely thoughtful insights about times and places far removed from his own. Ultimately, all of these insights flowed from his love of freedom and beauty and his deeply humanistic appreciation for the mystery of human greatness and the worth of individuals.

Although he founded the discipline of art history, and his *Civilization of the Renaissance* is still considered a most perceptive work, Burckhardt is hardly popular with today's art historians and their deconstructionist colleagues. He believed that not all art was equal, that great art was capable of expressing universally valid truths, and that art and beauty were companions. Rather than simply pouring out his or her feelings, the artist could aim "to transform all suffering, all excitement into sheer beauty," even if one devoted "all one's strength to doing so." Ultimately, the artist's greatest impulse was love. As he advised a young friend, "Stick to the old idealist line; only a scene that has somehow or other been loved by an artist can, in the long run, win other people's affection."

In the course of these letters, as Burckhardt's life moves along, the reader follows him in his successive peregrinations to the Italy he loved so profoundly, tracing thereby the growth of the malaise affecting European civilization. In the course of half a century the towns grew in wealth and size, the roads became busier, many beautiful old buildings were demolished to make room for newer ones, and the socialists became more numerous and radical. It hardly seemed an improvement, but as Burckhardt noted, most Europeans — capitalists and socialists alike — were eager to sacrifice the intangible cultural and aesthetic goods of the older civilization for the sake of "sleep-through trains." In the midst of these tumultuous changes in society, Burckhardt searched for an anchor, "an Archimedean point" of existential detachment and serenity, and he found it in the cultural and artistic treasures of the past. He was unsure how many of these would survive the cataclysmic wars and upheavals he saw coming soon, but he thought that enough might be left to inspire the human spirit to build anew.

So, how is one to think of Jacob Burckhardt and read his letters today? In spite of the calamities of world war, revolution, and every other upheaval that Burckhardt feared coming to pass in the first half of the twentieth century, at the opening of the successive century the West has experienced another of its periodic bouts of runaway optimism. The fall of communism, globalization, the information revolution, and unparalleled advances in scientific and genetic research all promise to bring about a radically new era of uninterrupted peace and prosperity. In the midst of our heightened expectations we will want to consider two questions posed by Burckhardt throughout these letters. First, can man ever find permanent rest and equilibrium in history? And, second, how are two of the fundamental qualities of a humane existence, beauty and freedom, to be preserved in the midst of mass democracy, egalitarianism, and the worship of economic growth? However we grapple with these two questions, Burckhardt's writings will help to keep them constantly before us lest we forget their vital importance.

ALBERTO R. COLL

NAVAL WAR COLLEGE, 2000

PREFACE

IN MAKING THIS SELECTION and translation I have been fortunate in being able to rely on the first volume of the new and complete edition of the letters which Dr. Max Burckhardt, assisted by the printing of Benno Schwabe & Co., has made a delight to read and a comfort to depend upon. For the remaining years I have used the original editions of the letters, except in cases where they are virtually unobtainable under present conditions—many of the letters were published in periodicals—and here I have again been fortunate in having before me Dr. Fritz Kaphahn's excellent selection published by the Kröner Verlag. Dr. Kaphahn's volume embraces very many more letters than I have been able to include, and I have rarely found it possible to depart from his choice except of course where new material has come to light in the interval, or when certain letters seemed of special interest to the English-reading public. Dr. Kaphahn's edition must have introduced so many readers to Burckhardt that it is a pleasure for one at least to be able to acknowledge so agreeable a debt.

But in making the selection and preparing the Introduction my principal support and guide has been Professor Werner Kaegi's *Jacob Burckhardt: eine Biographie,* vols. i and ii, published by Benno Schwabe in Basle. I have made such continual use of the invaluable quotations and the judicious interpretations and in particular of the complete picture of the background of Burckhardt's life which is to be found nowhere else either so complete or so finely drawn, that I had to abandon giving references and must content myself with stressing the extent of my debt. Of course, the emphasis in the Introduction is mine; but allowing for its incompleteness I think I may say that it is in general agreement with Professor Kaegi's authoritative work.

The selection of the letters has been made in order to show Burckhardt the man as his friends knew him, the "Arch-dilettante" with all his interests, foibles and enthusiasms. It does scant justice to his professional side, and only aims to reveal the personality which gives his work as an historian and as an art historian its value and its charm. More than this could hardly have been achieved in so short a compass, nor would a more scholarly approach have served much purpose until the works to which his letters often add a useful gloss or explanation have been translated.

The notes have been kept to a minimum. An asterisk after the name of the recipients of the letters refers to the brief biographical notes on pages 251–53.

The illustrations, equally, I owe to the kind offices of Professor Kaegi, who made it possible for me to use some of the unpublished sketches made by Burckhardt in Rome in 1848 and procured all the photographs for me. And in conclusion, to cut short my gratitude, I should like to recall the repeated hospitality which I have enjoyed at the Münsterplatz in Basle.

It only remains for me to say that in spite of straying far beyond the bounds set for it, the Introduction is not complete in any one respect. Whole aspects of Burckhardt's activities, such as the history of art, have simply been omitted. My wish is to provide enough information about his life and a sufficiently sharp outline of his point of view to enable the reader to enjoy the letters as letters — not simply as an interesting source, but as the letters of a figure already known in a generally familiar period. Except where the letters seemed to require it, I have said little about Burckhardt's personality, believing that the letters speak convincingly for themselves, at any rate if they can be read and enjoyed without too many obstacles and hindrances.

And finally, I have to thank the translator and publishers (Messrs. Allen & Unwin, London, and Pantheon Books Inc., New York) of the *Reflections on History* for permission to quote at some length from the English version of Burckhardt's most important work.

INTRODUCTION

BURCKHARDT'S *Civilization of the Renaissance in Italy* was published in 1860 and translated into English in 1878. Thirty years after its first appearance Lord Acton described it in a well-meant phrase as "the most instructive of all books on the Renaissance." Since then Burckhardt has continued in a state of suspended animation, imprisoned in his one successful, though by no means representative, book.

In 1943 the *Weltgeschichtliche Betrachtungen* (Reflections on History) appeared in an excellent translation, to be followed in the next few years by *The Age of Constantine the Great* and *Recollections of Rubens.* These translations cannot be said to have modified the accepted estimate of Burckhardt's importance substantially, though they may be the forerunners of a new interest in his work and personality. It is not after all impossible that Burckhardt's reputation should undergo the same metamorphosis in English-speaking countries which overtook him posthumously in his own and in Germany.

At first sight so very complete a change seems improbable: Burckhardt appears to belong among the historians Acton once summed up as "living quietly in a small way, with a dim political background." His career was uneventful and conventional and he deliberately warded off success. His *Cicerone* and the *Renaissance,* after a slow start, went into several editions; his reputation as an historian of art won him more than one offer to teach in German universities, but he would never give a single lecture outside Basle. In 1874, on Ranke's retirement, he was invited to succeed his master in the Chair which Ranke had made the most distinguished appointment in the academic world in Germany. He was in no two minds about refusing: "In Basle," he said, "I can say what I like." The salary was then slightly lowered, and the post accepted by Treitschke.

Although Burckhardt's lectures in the University—where he was plagued by the presence of visiting scholars—and his lectures for the general public were regarded as his outstanding achievement, he would never allow them to be published on the grounds that they would look "like carpets the wrong side up." But in the end he agreed that his nephew, Jacob Oeri, might edit them after his death. Oeri published Burckhardt's longest work, the *Griechische Kulturgeschichte,* in three volumes (1902 ff.) and the *Reflections on History* in 1906.

Burckhardt's letters began appearing in the following decade, though the most interesting collections—in particular those to von Preen—were not published until 1924. A collected edition of his works, the *Gesamtausgabe,* edited by Wölfflin, Emil Dürr and others, was issued between 1929 and 1934. This was followed by a cheap edition of his principal works and the selection of his letters prepared by Dr. Kaphahn.

Burckhardt's work was slow to mature, slow to appear and slow to be understood. The final stage in the process of his inclusion in the canon of German thought and literature was brought about by circumstances. In the light of the Nazi revolution, when his books first became easily obtainable, the element in his work which had formerly been overlooked suddenly assumed profound significance. The "practical and therefore the political element" which Acton—knowing only the *Renaissance*—regarded as the weakest, stood out as his greatest claim to be heard. The prophecies which his earliest editors felt it tactful to leave aside or gloss over were fulfilled by events and followed by catastrophes, and Burckhardt came to be regarded as one of the great representatives and guardians of the European tradition, not only because he foretold the nature of the threat that endangered its continuity, but because the terms in which he did so seemed strikingly relevant and not without hope for the future.

The key to this sudden vogue for his lectures and letters and the continued interest in his personality and thought is his faith in man and tradition, never falsified or bolstered up by any form of optimism—in his eyes the most disintegrating compound of thought and feeling produced by the thinkers of the eighteenth century. In this he has much in common with Lord Acton, whose reputation was heightened and consolidated for the same reasons and under similar auspices. In everything else, in temperament, outlook and gifts, they differed widely, but they were both liberal in Acton's sense of the word, and with the collapse of "liberalism" their views seemed to offer a new point of departure.

Burckhardt's letters are anything but an extension of his lectures—as Acton's often are. They lead back to the source and reveal another dimension of Burckhardt, and in doing so even some of the thoughts which Nietzsche, not altogether without reason, complained that he concealed. They do so indirectly, simply through the form and style and finish of the letters—in a sense his most finished work. For he seems to have adopted the form almost deliberately in later life, writing to one correspondent about the European situation and to another about art and architecture, rather as Horace Walpole selected his correspondents. Unfortunately he destroyed all the letters that came into his hands, and certainly never dreamed of appearing in the *cortège* of Madame de Sévigné—the subject of his last public lecture. Even after he had "given up all thought of literary success" and had published his last short volume of poetry, he admits he could not put down his pen, and so went on to express himself and his thoughts in the form that suited him best. With his attention always focused on the outside world, on men and things, art, politics and morals—he was temperamentally averse from philosophical speculation and introspection—he was at his happiest and best in his letters, in a form which lies half-way, as it were, between a Journal and the formal historical work circumstances prevented his writing.

The letters fall roughly into two groups: those which were written during his youth and the period of uncertainty before his return to Basle; and the letters in which he had fully come into his own. "Originality," he says in the *Reflections,* "must be possessed, not acquired," but though he was no phoenix, as he said, he had what Nietzsche calls *Oberfläche,* "a natural skin for his content and depth," and the letters which move so lightly and easily on the surface reveal as much again of him and his thought as the clearest and most penetrating lectures.

★   ★   ★

Jacob Burckhardt was born on 25th May 1818 and died in 1897. Shortly before his death he prepared, according to custom, a short curriculum of his life which was read at his funeral. "The family circle in which he grew up," he there says, "was altogether happy; though while he was still quite young he encountered his first sorrow, the death of his mother on 17th March 1830. . . . Thus very early in life, notwithstanding an otherwise cheerful temperament, in all likelihood inherited from his mother, he received an indelible impression of the great frailty and uncertainty of all earthly things, and this determined his view of life."

The Burckhardts and the Schorndorffs—his mother's family—had both settled in Basle at the close of the fifteenth century. The Burckhardts in particular proved themselves able and worthy of the leading positions which they occupied so consistently as to give the impression that Basle was a patrician city, like Berne or Venice. They were talented, industrious, prolific and successful, and their prominence is adequately expressed by the fact that for more than a century and a half one of the two Burgomasters was invariably a Burckhardt. As merchants, doctors and divines, or at the Rathaus, they contributed largely to the prosperity of Basle and to the continuity which marks its growth; for at the time of Burckhardt's birth it was still in many respects the town in which the oecumenical Council had met in the fifteenth century: it had kept its walls, its guilds, its democratic structure and even the arms of its former episcopal rulers. During Burckhardt's life the surrounding country, Land-Basel, asserted and won its independence, while the city, partly through the railways, quadrupled in size and wealth. The temptation to think of Basle as a backwater from which Burckhardt surveyed the modern world has little basis in fact: when he went to the University it had less members than attended his lectures in his later years.

Burckhardt's father came of a minor and poorer branch of the clan, some of whom lived in style, the sober style of a free city, while others took Holy Orders. His father had studied theology in Heidelberg when Schleiermacher's influence was in the ascendant, and never departed from the tolerant and humane teaching of the "Second Reformer." He was attached to the Minster at the time of his son's birth, and was so well liked as a man and as a preacher that the congregation elected him Antistes, a position corresponding to Dean, and *primus inter pares*. He appears to have been a pleasant, conventional figure, the author of one or two plain books on history and theology, whose talent for sketching perhaps first inspired his son. Unfortunately, Burckhardt destroyed all his letters to his father, and their absence lends a false air of isolation to Burckhardt's life which was so deeply rooted in Basle.

There were certainly times when he found it stifling, but in the end he derived a genuine satisfaction from being known as *"ce vieux monsieur au portefeuille"* carrying a vast portfolio of photographs to his lectures on Art—till age obliged him to engage a servant. There was nothing of the *déraciné* about him. He automatically formed part of the closely knit society into which he was born, participated naturally in the legacy of the past, in the responsibilities of the present and hopes for the future. He looked with misgivings on many of the changes that occurred in his lifetime, and saw clearly how much which seemed to him of inestimable value would be sacrificed by a utilitarian world, but "the more vital and developed one's feeling for man's utter inadequacy," he writes, "the less the temptation to take sides: once one knows that there never has been and never will be a Golden Age in any fantastic sense, one is rid of the foolish desire to overvalue some period in the past, to despair of the present, or to nourish absurd hopes for the future." Of course, he adds, "we may keep our preferences, for these are matters of taste"—and

Burckhardt made full use of his saving clause, without which detachment tends to claim the privileges of a disembodied spirit, if not of the World Spirit.

Burckhardt's "Archimedean point outside events" was the traditional view of life he describes as determined by his upbringing, by an inner harmony and security which was sustained by his sense of "the frailty of earthly things," and a mature feeling for man's insufficiency in all things. Basle was the soil in which Burckhardt's conception of tradition grew and developed.

*   *   *

The letter with which this selection begins gives a sort of summary of the interests and enthusiasms which Burckhardt wove into his life without dissipating his energies or narrowing his sympathies. At school, he says in his *curriculum vitae,* he had acquired a knowledge of the classics which "enabled him at all times to live on terms of familiarity with antiquity," though without having been made to work so hard that he "took against learning." Between leaving school and going to the University he spent nine months in the French-speaking town of Neuchâtel, where he discovered in French literature (which he had been taught in Basle by Alexandre Vinet) "a second spiritual home." On his return, he brought with him an almost completed essay on some of the Gothic churches of Switzerland, a sketch-book in which he had noted architectural or decorative features that interested him or a view that pleased him, his first poems, the *Compositione di Jacopo Bucardo,* and the memories of a visit to Italy.

In the same letter, written in August 1838, Burckhardt confesses with some emotion that he has been led by his Professor of Theology, Dewette, to the point at which he too can only regard the life of Christ as a myth. The letter was addressed to Johannes Riggenbach, who, with Alois Biedermann and later von Tschudi, were his closest friends at this period. All three were studying for Holy Orders, and it was with them that Burckhardt carried on the argument set in motion by Dewette's views. He did not discuss the question with his family except on one occasion when he was carried away, as he admits, in conversation with his eldest sister. The letter which she sent him on the following day moved him deeply, but apart from this incident his relations with his family were undisturbed; the theological disputes in which he was so unhappily involved were distinct from the deeper beliefs which he shared with them. When he gave up theology, Professor Kaegi says, he did not give up Christianity in its deeper sense. Nor was he made to feel that he had broken with tradition or rebelled against the past. And once he had reached a clear understanding of his position in terms of theology and the Church, and began to consider his religious position and disposition, it was to his sister Louise that he confided his belief in Providence, and "in the sum of Christ's teaching . . . the law of love and sacrifice for others." The *ressentiment* of men like Nietzsche and Overbeck was entirely foreign to him.

Most of Burckhardt's friends were numbered at first among the "orthodox," but were soon swept along by the prevailing rationalism, though some of them returned at a later date to more conservative views. Burckhardt sided with neither party, and while admitting the force of the rationalist criticism of the "orthodox" position never accepted the reinterpretation of Christianity which followed, and one of the lasting consequences of his discussions at this time was a lifelong aversion for liberal theologians and a contempt for their Hegelian philosophies of faith.[1] It is in opposition to them that he speaks of remaining an "honest" heretic. The intellectual honesty of his position freed him for the future and is reminiscent of Kierkegaard's rejection of the "orthodox" and the Rationalists, the subject of so many of the early entries in his *Journal*.

In a little more than a year, and while Burckhardt was finishing his theological studies in Basle, events in Zürich confirmed him finally in the correctness of his attitude. David Friedrich Strauss, the author of the *Life of Jesus*, was given an appointment in Zürich, where his radical views so offended public opinion that the insult which his presence as a teacher

---

1. See the letter to von Preen written in 1878, p. 179, bottom.

seemed to offer to Christianity ended in a rising. The conservative element were temporarily successful in cancelling the appointment, but not until the dead and wounded remained to embitter the conflict between the liberal intelligentsia and the Church party. Biedermann was by then an ardent supporter of Strauss and Riggenbach a convert to Hegel, and from then on Burckhardt's relations with his Swiss friends became difficult. To Burckhardt the *Züriputsch* proclaimed the opening of a long and bitter feud between the intelligentsia and the Church, an extension of the theological argument into the realm of politics where the theological issues were often no more than party slogans. He had no more wish to be involved in this conflict, which seemed to him disruptive of tradition, than to side with the Rationalists or the "orthodox."

Christianity, he held, at least in its theological and institutional forms, had seen its best days. The controversies and conflicts symbolized in the Strauss affair seemed to him profoundly misdirected and contrary to the interests of religion itself—though in what form religion would once again appear the future alone would tell. "Burckhardt," Biedermann wrote not long after, "often attached himself to us [to him and to Riggenbach], sometimes to the one, sometimes to the other, often disturbing our relations with his affected jealousy, which seemed in time to become almost natural. . . . But he did not really belong among us, and gradually drifted away." Burckhardt's friendships in these years fluctuate with his moods and the demands which he makes on his correspondents, on his desire to fit in with others. He was conscious of the criticism, perhaps, and speaks of his resolve "to give up all sentiment"—a resolve which reappears in later life when his relations with others were canalized and given a somewhat formal mould. The lasting friendships of his life were stilted, and the little he says about himself leads one to think that if he never married, the reason must have been bound up with the same temperamental limitation which disturbed his friendships. When his sister Louise wrote in 1841 to break the news that Maria Oser, with whom he had been in love, had become engaged in his absence, Burckhardt answered that knowing the man she was to marry, he could only resign

himself and felt obliged to recognize that he was too "passionate" a character to make her happy. It was more than a conventional phrase, and the
emotional tone of many of the early letters, after making every allow-
ance for the overripe romanticism of the period, is pitched high and was
only very gradually controlled so that his natural spontaneity and originality could find expression.

"What happened in Zürich the day before yesterday," he writes to
Schreiber, "once again reminds me how dangerous and sinful it would be
in times such as these, when the position of the Church is so unsettled,
to dedicate one's life to theology without the clearest inner call." It was
Schreiber, in the end, himself "a deserter *ex theologorum castris,*" who gave
Burckhardt a helping hand and showed him the way out of the wood.
Heinrich Schreiber was a respected historian for whom Burckhardt had
done some work in the Basle archives. He was born in 1792 in Freiburg
im Breisgau, studied for the priesthood in Meersburg on the lake of
Constance and returned to Freiburg as Professor of Moral Theology. In
Meersburg he met Dalberg, the Primate, and learnt his theology in the
school where Catholicism was most deeply affected by the doctrines of
the Enlightenment, largely owing to the influence of Dalberg and Wes-
senberg. The religion which he was taught and which he taught in turn
as Professor of Moral Theology was a thin, ethical version of the Gospels,
free from miracles and mystery and aiming to be free from Rome and
the clerical vow of celibacy. His views met with considerable opposition
in Freiburg, but this scholarly Vicaire Savoyard retained his appointment
for ten years before being elbowed into the Philosophical Faculty of the
University where he lectured on History. Finally in 1844, when he gave
his formal adherence to Ronge's "German Catholic Church," he was ex-
communicated. But he was soon disillusioned by Ronge's Church, retired
into private life, married and lived peacefully until 1872, working at his
histories. Schreiber was a plump, cheerful, painstaking character, a philosopher in the eighteenth-century sense who coupled an enlightened
outlook with a romantic enthusiasm for the Middle Ages. He appears to
have been without ambition, except to reform the Church. It was Schrei-

ber's example which helped Burckhardt to find the practical solution to his difficulties and to find in the study of history an alternative to "devoting his life to theology."

Burckhardt did not interrupt his theological studies, and took his degree in the following year. When his father agreed that he might read History, it followed naturally that he should go to Berlin and work under Ranke.

He left Basle in the late summer of 1839 with Jacob Oeri, the same travelling-companion who attended him to Italy three years earlier and who was later to marry his sister Louise. They took five weeks over the journey, stopping at Munich, Regensburg, Nuremberg and Bamberg, leaving only a few hours for the gallery in Dresden and ignoring the town of Augustus the Strong that was to impress Burckhardt so favourably two years later: "it was high time to be in Berlin." But when he got there it seemed hardly less flat and uninteresting than the sandy plain in which it was set, where the *"soi-disant* hills" only reminded Burckhardt of the scenery he might have been enjoying in the Alps and beyond them. But Berlin was redeemed by the museums and by the excellence of the opera. Fifty years later he recalled *Armide* and the polyphonic music he first heard in Berlin. The deepest impression and his most lasting gain was, however, "the historical school," and he sat wide-eyed with astonishment through Ranke's first lectures and the conception of history, of historical method and of presentation which they revealed to him.

Among the half-dozen names that had made Berlin famous — Ranke, Grimm, Böckh and others — Ranke was the one he admired most, and liked least. He never misses a chance of telling a story against him. Droysen, too, he classed among the great, but Droysen soon left for Kiel. But their influence, Ranke's in particular, passed wholly, he says, through the medium of the intellect, and he began to feel the lack of a "fatherly friend" like Schreiber. *Viri doctissimi,* he discovered, were jealous, and greatly given to intriguing for promotion.

Almost as he was uttering his complaints to Schreiber and regretting the distance which separated him from Freiburg, he met Franz Kugler, who was to become to him all and much more than Schreiber could ever have been. As Professor of the History of Art—a newfangled subject which left him free from the too close interest of his colleagues—Franz Kugler could go very much his own way. As a young man he had lived a Bohemian existence and only settled down, took his degree and joined the University when his marriage obliged him to earn a steady income. And when Burckhardt called on him he found what he wanted, a guide who had kept the freshness of outlook and the enthusiasm of an amateur, and who shared his dominant interests. In no time Burckhardt was accompanying his fat friend on his walks and on the piano, and learning from him "to stand on his own feet." It was Kugler who gave him the courage to embrace his love of the arts in his love of history, to recognize his "enormous thirst for contemplation" as the fundamental trait in his spiritual make-up, and led him to history as "the highest form of poetry."

During the winter of 1840 Burckhardt gradually drifted away from his Swiss friends and found himself at last among a group of young men who no longer questioned the colour of his patriotism or of his theology. The "wonderful clique" by which he was taken up, was fired by the last rays of romanticism, still literary and aesthetic in tone but with a budding political interest that was to grow and finally cast shadows between them. They revered the past and revelled in the Middle Ages, its cathedrals, its sagas and poetry, but their love of "Teutschland" had little anchor in the present and swung between the distant past and a glorious future, when it would fulfil its cultural destiny and resurrect its national fortunes and unity on the firm foundation of constitutional liberties. Their outlook was a last echo of the mood of 1813, with its political literature and its literary politics. Nationalism and socialism were to go easily hand in hand.

All this "enthusiasm" and the emotional bonds which carried them along together gave Burckhardt a new sense of freedom, of entering the great world. Only two of his new acquaintances were studying in theology; Eduard Schauenburg, who became a school-master, and Siegfried Nagel, were classical scholars; Hermann Schauenburg was reading Medicine in Leipzig, and the attitude of one and all was liberal. For a time, Burckhardt, no doubt with Ranke's lectures in mind, "had the courage to be conservative," but though he came to speak of his liberal principles it was in no strictly political sense. Moreover, Burckhardt, it was agreed, was *eine künstlerische, goethesche Natur,* and his Goethean superiority entitled him to conservative opinions in tune with those of the poet and sage.

★   ★   ★

The centre of Burckhardt's new world was Gottfried Kinkel, who imposed upon them all by his presence, his energy, his fluency and a roving, superficial intelligence. When Burckhardt left Berlin in the early summer of 1841 he did so, to his astonishment, with regret. He was bound for Bonn with a letter to Eduard Schauenburg's brother in Leipzig and another to Kinkel. He had chosen Bonn in order to be near Cologne, which he needed to visit for an essay he was writing for Ranke's seminar, and for the sake of Wolter's lectures on Canon Law. On the road he visited Hildesheim, Leipzig and Frankfort, paused to study and sketch the "Byzantine" churches as he travelled down the Rhine, and after an ecstatic day in Cologne retraced his steps to Bonn in a state of enthusiasm for everything German that drowned all consideration for his academic duties and prepared him for his meeting with Kinkel.

Gottfried Kinkel was the first Rhinelander to join the University which the Prussian Government had sited in Bonn in order to maintain their control over university education and prevent its falling into the hands of the Archbishop of Cologne. Kinkel was a Lutheran by upbringing and a theologian by training, but all his sympathies lay with the Catholic population, whose anti-Prussian feelings he shared. He was "already a socialist without knowing it," he confesses in his autobiography, and his indignation was aroused by the gauche administration of the province and echoed the rebellious mood which was growing among the people.

Two years earlier Kinkel had met Johanna Matthieux in Cologne and fallen in love at first sight. The romantic affair was the beginning of the tragi-comedy which involved them both. Johanna had been married for a short time to a Catholic publisher in Cologne, whom she divorced on grounds of cruelty. Her position after the divorce was made easier through the generosity of Bettina von Arnim, Burckhardt's "benefactress" in Berlin. Bettina's fame and connections were sufficient, as Johanna's were not, to enable her to treat with indifference the conventions of a Catholic milieu already at loggerheads with Prussia over the Marriage Laws. As a girl, Bettina Brentano had thrown herself at Goethe's head and the old man responded with letters which she had built into a story, certain scenes of which appalled her brother Clemens, the poet, now converted and reformed, and surprised even Sainte-Beuve. The success of her book was repeated when she dealt in the same way with the letters of her friend Karoline Günderode, who put an end to her hopeless love affair with the historian Creuzer by throwing herself into the Rhine. Bettina moved shortly afterwards to Berlin, living with her sister, the widow of Friedrich von Savigny, next to Ranke the brightest ornament of the historical school.

On Bettina's return to Berlin, Johanna followed Kinkel to Bonn, where she lived with her mother and earned her livelihood giving music lessons, organising and conducting concerts (she is spoken of as the Directrix in the letters) and even on occasions an opera by Handel. She was amusing and a welcome diversion in the society of Bonn, but Kinkel's tactlessness in advertising his attachment, while they were still legally unable to marry, involved them in difficulties, for he was still, at the time, lecturing on Theology in Bonn, preaching at a church in Cologne and teaching in a girls' school. But though he could not afford to lose his appointments, both he and Johanna felt under compulsion to force their position down the throats of their friends and colleagues. They founded a poetry club—the *Maikäferbund* of the letters—held musical evenings and organized expeditions into the surrounding country, where they picnicked, sang their songs, recited their poems and declaimed their plays. It was while returning from one of their outings that the skiff in which the party was recrossing the Rhine was rammed and sunk by a paddle-steamer which they had failed to see in the darkness. Kinkel managed to support Johanna to the shore, and the rest of the party was saved. In the emotional tension which followed their narrow escape they decided to publish their engagement. The fact that Johanna combined being a divorcée and a Catholic caused the maximum of pain to Kinkel's superiors. He was peremptorily dismissed by his congregation and by the school where he taught, and only prolonged negotiations saved him from having to resign from the University. In the end the affair was patched up: he was allowed to transfer to the Philosophical Faculty and call his lectures what they had been for some time past, lectures on the History of Art. Johanna eased the position by becoming a Protestant, but they continued to feel persecuted by the "philistines" and wished to be emancipated without being ostracized.

It was at this point in Kinkel's career that Burckhardt arrived in Bonn. For the moment they had, or appeared to have, everything in common, and Burckhardt could study in his expansive acquaintance a dramatized version of some of his own moral and intellectual conflicts, under the illusion that they were leading in the same direction. Their friendship was sealed by mutual admiration, and Kinkel, who had begun to think of himself as the poet of the national revival—before becoming the spokesman of the revolution—found in Burckhardt all the gifts and talents he longed to possess. Burckhardt, he wrote, a few years later, "was a virtuoso in the enjoyment of life, a connoisseur in all aesthetic matters who had plundered the world's culture for his own enrichment. He knows everything; where the sweetest grapes grow on the shores of Lake Como, and can tell you offhand the best sources for a life of Nostradamus. . . . Then he will throw himself down on a sofa, smoke half a dozen of the best Manilla cigars and write you a fantasy on the love of one of the Prince Bishops of Cologne for an alchemist's daughter." But by the time he composed his somewhat fanciful picture of Burckhardt, he was in prison in Spandau for his revolutionary activities, and the conclusion of his letter gives a generous interpretation of their parting. "Who could ask that a life of such rich enjoyment should be willingly thrown between the bayonets of modern history?"

Burckhardt spent the summer in Bonn and returned in the spring of 1844 to be best man at Kinkel's wedding. When they next met, in the autumn of 1847, Kinkel was already fully launched on his political escapades. In 1848 Kinkel came out on the Republican side and after taking part in several risings, joined the revolution in the Palatinate, where he was wounded on 29th June 1849 and taken prisoner. The death sentence, after a plea by H. Schauenburg, was commuted to life imprisonment.

Kinkel had a knack of getting himself talked about, and a simple, personal conception of the technique of revolution that exasperated Karl Marx. Rescued from prison by his wife and Carl Schütz, he fled to England with Johanna and their three children, where he became the leader, as Herzen remarks, of "one of the forty times forty German sects." Always clerical in manner, patronizing and self-satisfied, he reminded Herzen of a butler in a large house: "the head of Jupiter on the shoulders of a German Professor." His vanity was apparently the only excuse for Johanna's growing jealousy, though Herzen had also noticed his absurd, uxorious manner, but under the stress of exile and impoverishment Johanna finally lost her reason and threw herself out of the window of their London house.

Eight or nine years later, when Kinkel was lecturing at the Polytechnique in Zürich on the History of Art, he called on Burckhardt in Basle. But although the call was never acknowledged, he spoke of him in the highest terms in his autobiography as the most gifted man he had ever met, and of their friendship as the greatest loss which exile had cost him—showing a generosity which Herzen failed to detect. Burckhardt had certainly admired Kinkel in return quite as uncritically, until he proved to be all that Burckhardt most disliked, a left-wing don who meddled in politics without an elementary understanding of the practical questions, or a real grasp of the deeper problems involved.

★   ★   ★

Burckhardt attended Kinkel's wedding in May 1844 and spent six months in Paris before returning to Basle. After the freedom of his life in Germany he found his social duties irksome and the company snobbish, philistine and a nest of gossip. Johanna wrote encouraging him to flaunt his views and snub the philistines, as she and Kinkel would have done, but he answered that he only wished to live and let live: he was no phoenix, he wrote, to impose his views on others, and settled down to lecturing at the University (without an appointment), and supplemented his fees by revising the articles of the *Brockhaus Encyclopaedia* which Kugler handed on to him, and writing in the *Kölnische Zeitung*. For the rest he kept himself to himself as far as he could, though Johanna would have liked to hear that he was in love. But he only answered that he had no intention of "tying himself to the money bags of an industrialist" by making a *mariage de convenance,* and hints that marriage was not to be for him, the price, he adds, that fate made him pay for the gifts and good fortune which had been showered on him in other respects.

Burckhardt's gifts had not in fact gone unobserved. Early in the following year the owner and editor of the most important conservative paper, the *Basler Zeitung,* Andreas Heusler, asked him to edit the paper under his direction. Heusler was a lawyer, a wealthy man of considerable attainments with a finger in every pie in Basle and a position of considerable influence in Switzerland. He felt that a promising young man should be encouraged and eased gently into the career which his standing and talents demanded. Burckhardt's undoubted academic attainments needed to be flanked by practical experience in politics and administration so that in time he would conform to pattern and play his part in the administration and the University. Burckhardt accepted without enthusiasm mainly for the sake of the financial advantages which the post offered, slender though these now appear. He was already saving for a journey to Italy and had no more intention of being caught by the State than by the Church.

The eighteen months during which Burckhardt edited the *Basler Zeitung* were more than he bargained for. He was thrust head first into the conflict he saw coming in 1839 and compelled to follow at close quarters the arguments, the agitators and the events which led to civil war three years later. It was an ample corrective for the airy views which he had heard for four years in Germany, from Kinkel or in Bettina's salon. The ostensible grounds of the dispute between the Radicals and the conservative and Catholic Cantons was the return of the Jesuits to teach in the schools. The Radicals seized on the Jesuit question to the discomfort of their Protestant opponents, and the *Basler Zeitung*, for example, had to combat the Radicals without supporting the Jesuits, remain staunchly conservative without being tarred with the clerical brush. Burckhardt was not invariably successful in his attempts to steer a middle course, and his hope of teaching both Radicals and Absolutists a lesson was not fulfilled.

But if he failed on some occasions to deal with a difficult situation, the experience was invaluable and crystallized his attitude in a way which nothing else could have done. His knowledge of the past was from then on backed by familiarity with the technique of demagogy, of agitation and the use of idealistic slogans and half-truths. Burckhardt's experience of the clericals and anti-clericals and of the confusion of religion and politics that ended in the *Sonderbundkrieg* might be compared to Péguy's experience in the Dreyfus affair: he learnt to look behind the ideas and phrases to the leaders, and to see what was meant by power.

Although he complains that the *Basler Zeitung* took him all his time, Burckhardt went on lecturing and in 1844 was given the honorary title of Professor at the University where there was still no vacancy for him. The "disgusting métier" of journalism apart, he began to appreciate the agreeable side of life in Basle, which was the only University, he says, where there was still some sort of collegiate life and where the lecturers did not fight like cat and dog.

In 1845 he announced a series of lectures on the History of Painting, and encouraged by the success of his venture he decided to follow it up with a second series. But when he tried to re-engage the hall he found that his criticism of the "Christian" school of painting, the Nazarener, had offended some of his audience, and that the "pietists," as he calls them, were intriguing to prevent him continuing in the same "worldly" vein. He also suspected that Heusler was privy to the cabal. But in spite of the difficulties he persevered, made his second series "more worldly still," and having resigned from the paper with enough money saved, prepared to leave for Rome. He could hardly wait to leave all the "ists" and "isms" of politics and ideology behind him and plunge into the past. His German friends, he knew, would accuse him of running away and wanted him to take part in the revolution. The letter to Schauenburg dated 5th May 1846, almost the last written from Basle, gives his answer and ends with a hint of the practical view of his future work which was already in his mind, his hope to return to Basle "to teach the old culture of Europe during the inevitable lulls in the revolutionary process."

⋆   ⋆   ⋆

"I shall never be happy away from Rome," he wrote to Kinkel soon after his arrival. He was happy as he had only been in Bonn, though inexplicably so, for he was neither in love nor surrounded by friends. He could only say that "he felt the harmony of every faculty" as he had never tasted it before, and would find himself overwhelmed by this sense of happiness for no apparent external reason, on the first landing of the staircase in the Palazzo Farnese, for example, or standing near the Trevi Fountain. But his raptures had hardly begun when he heard from Kugler, who offered him work at a good salary in the Academy of Art in Berlin. Partly for Kugler's sake, largely because he had to think of his career, he accepted and tore himself away from Rome. A week or two in Naples, in Florence and in Venice, and he retraced his steps across the Alps to Basle, and travelling via Bonn to see the Kinkels, went straight to Berlin.

There is no indication that Burckhardt tried to take up the threads of his former life in Berlin. He does not mention his "benefactress" Bettina and assures Kinkel that he saw no one except Kugler and the poets, Paul Heyse and Geiger, friends of Kugler whose poetry so outshone his own that he felt quite discouraged. But work did not normally prevent Burckhardt from seeing his friends, and it is more than probable that he deliberately avoided the circles in which he had formerly moved. Both Kinkel and Schauenburg were known to hold dangerous views, and his own opinions were too definite now to allow him to make all the concessions he had formerly consented to. As soon as his work was done he made his way south again, travelling via Vienna and Trieste and so skirting Switzerland, where the civil war would have made movement difficult. He only returned to Basle in the early summer of 1848.

For the next decade or so Burckhardt's life swings between Basle, where he remained till he could bear it no longer, and Italy, where he lived as long as his money held out. But even in Basle he did not sacrifice himself entirely to a career and refused the invitation to become curator of the Museum, in order to leave time for work of his own. He was already thinking of *The Age of Constantine the Great*.

It was in Basle, in 1849, that Burckhardt learnt of Kinkel's imprisonment. The news was far from unexpected, but it meant the final severance of their friendship; Kinkel is never mentioned again. He at once sent Schauenburg some money for Johanna and the three children, who he thought must be in difficulties. Kinkel had never earned much money. With the exception of Eduard Schauenburg, all his German acquaintances drifted away. He made no attempt to prevent the break, but confessed to Schauenburg that he could never replace the friends of his youth and that he would never have believed how lonely life could be at thirty. Schauenburg had just become engaged, and Burckhardt was in love; but the parents of the girl did not regard the match as a suitable one. The anonymous volume of poetry which he published at the end of the year in the Basle dialect, *E Hämpfeli Lieder,* touches with genuine feeling on his unhappy love affair. It was the last time, and perhaps the only one, when he forgot, or tried to forget, that it was not to be his destiny to marry. A note of melancholy creeps into his letters, and although he concealed his state of mind it was some time before his natural cheerfulness reasserted itself.

Burckhardt remained in Basle teaching and lecturing until 1852, when he resigned from the staff of the school in a moment of irritation and, against Schreiber's advice, escaped to Italy. The reorganization of the curriculum threw some additional work on him, and seeing no immediate prospects of a University appointment, he felt the need of a change. The result of his journey was the *Cicerone,* "a guide to the enjoyment of art in Italy," compiled and finished in little more than a year. Later in life he pretended to be horrified at the speed and *insouciance* with which he undertook the work, covering the whole history of painting, sculpture and architecture in Italy. In fact, he was proud of the "Tchitch," and left others to wrestle with the problem of correcting its errors or omissions and retaining its charm, till the publishers found that Burckhardt's book conveyed his likes and dislikes much better in the original form. Nietzsche recommended it as a good substitute for a journey to Rome.

Largely on the strength of the "Tchitch," Burckhardt was among those invited to launch the new Polytechnique which was to open in Zürich in 1855. Zürich offered two advantages: its libraries were particularly rich in material for the work on the Renaissance he wished to write, in order to still the "complaint" which he had brought back from Italy; and he thought that the staff of the new college would set some store on making themselves known in society and that his presence in the crowd would not be missed. Everything fell out as he hoped. He found some congenial company, he could get into beautiful country in a matter of five minutes and he found ample time, in addition to his lectures on the history of art, to prepare the *Renaissance.*

Burckhardt's life began to take shape in Zürich, and the letters to one of his pupils, Albert Brenner, written at the time, are among those which come nearest to speaking about himself. Not that they go for one instant behind the scenes, or explore "the crevasses and chasms which lie so close beneath the surface" and which he warns Brenner against exploring. On the contrary, he would not have him trapped by the world of necessity and chance, to the exclusion of that "excellent daily bread, good and evil." The little sermons—the sort he would never have listened to himself he admits—take up the theme of the letters to his sister Louise written in 1842, and express Burckhardt's traditional philosophy of life in the simplest manner possible. At the same time they reveal plainly enough why he broke with so many of "the friends of his youth."

He had not always been fortunate in his choice, and a naturally cheerful and sociable temperament led him to see his relations with others in simple terms that could not last. Kinkel was not the only case. Burckhardt had encouraged and helped the Basle painter Böcklin financially and befriended him in Rome in 1848. Not long after, Böcklin accused Burckhardt of intriguing to prevent him getting a commission in Basle. Burckhardt's relations with Paul Heyse, too, were interrupted, and only resumed on a more formal basis. The fact that his attempt to get married came to nothing and was allowed to do so, suggests that he was at the time very uncertain of himself and his future—though little or nothing has ever been published about this episode in his life. His instructions that *Literaten* should not be allowed to grub about in his papers after his death has been respected, and until more facts are available, explanations are worthless. But it seems as though the characteristic which Nietzsche noted, his tendency not to falsify but certainly to conceal the truth, extended to his relations with others, and as though the Socratic note which irritated some of his critics like Dilthey and Overbeck, gave his personal relationships a certain inconclusiveness. He demanded too much or too little. As an old man Burckhardt reproached himself with having failed to do all he might have done for his pupils. He was not ungenerous with his time or his money or his books, but perhaps with himself, and at one point "don't bother about others" tended to become don't bother with others. When the illusion of his friendship with the Kinkels was exposed he took fright and for ever after kept people at arm's length. Shyness, reserve, modesty and restraint were mingled with a dislike of closer attachments and the play of feeling and emotion that had ended badly in the past.

There was a very real change between the Burckhardt of the first period, down to about 1850, and the figure who emerges in Basle, and it is characteristic that the deliberate break with the past which then occurred should be reflected in his outward appearance. In the photograph taken at the Palais Royal in 1844 Burckhardt is dressed in the fashion of 1830, with his hair long, like Gauthier, a loose cravat, a ring on his forefinger, in marked contrast to the subdued, inconspicuous figure of the later period, quite contemporary in appearance, with his hair *en brosse,* a neat black suit and a soft black hat. As a young man he thought of himself as a poet; in one of the letters of the middle period he refers to himself and his cronies — that is the impression he wished to give — as cheerful philistines; but finally, when he saw himself among the *viri doctissimi,* he saw himself as an "arch-dilettante" whose vocation was teaching. "The word amateur," he says in the introduction to the *Reflections,* "owes its evil reputation to the arts. An artist must be a master or nothing. . . . In learning, on the other hand, a man can only be a master in one particular field, namely as a specialist, and in some field he *should* be a specialist. But if he is not to forfeit his capacity for taking general views or even his respect for general views, he should be an amateur at as many points as possible. . . . Otherwise he will remain ignorant in any field lying outside his own speciality and perhaps, as a man, a barbarian."

*   *   *

In 1858 the Professorship of History became vacant in Basle and Burckhardt readily accepted the appointment, happy to find himself reinstated where he felt he belonged while his father was still alive. "The decades which he spent in this office," he writes in his *curriculum vitae,* "were to be the happiest in his life. A sound constitution enabled him to devote himself undisturbed to his task without having to postpone a single lecture until obliged to do so as the result of an accident in May 1881. In other respects too his existence flowed on almost undisturbed. During the first years after his arrival he put the finishing touches to works already on the stocks,[2] and subsequently lived exclusively for his work as a teacher, in which the constant effort was more than balanced by a real feeling of happiness. In conformity with the requirements of a small university, he regarded his task as Professor of History as consisting less in the communication of special knowledge than in generally encouraging an historical outlook. A second occupation, teaching in the school (first of all in the two top classes, subsequently in the top class only), equally became a source of continual pleasure to him. It was given up—unwillingly—first of all in part and finally altogether, in order to undertake a course as complete as possible on the history of art, simultaneously with his lectures on history. Thus during the years 1882 to 1886 his academic duties amounted to ten hours weekly. And finally the writer of these lines often lectured to the general public, first of all with his own cycle of lectures and later taking part in the series of this kind organized by the University.

"May the friendly recollection of his former students at the University, the pupils at the high school and the audiences at his winter lectures, be assured him beyond the grave. He always valued his office highly in all respects, and gave up all thought of literary success with a whole heart. A modest competence preserved him in later years from having to write for money and from living in servitude to publishing ventures.

"The warnings of approaching old age obliged him to request the authorities to release him from his Professorship of History in 1885; at his own wish he still retained the Chair of the History of Art. Asthmatic troubles finally compelled him to retire altogether in April 1893."

For almost the whole of this period Burckhardt lived in two rooms above a baker's shop in the old part of the town, not far from the Minster. When Heinrich Wölfflin, his pupil and successor, first visited him there he was astonished at the simplicity and bareness of the rooms. Most of his visitors were similarly struck, and remarked on the bare table, the

---

2. The two books on the Renaissance begun in Zürich.

Piranesi prints and the upright piano. Wilhelm Bode, who came from Germany to express his indebtedness to Burckhardt, was thrown off his guard by the unexpectedness of the surroundings and began by mistaking him for the baker. "If you must speak to Jacob Burckhardt," he was told, "you must make do with me." He was entirely successful in not looking like the professors for whom he had little sympathy, and the photographer whose studio he had at last been persuaded to visit (he had an unaccountable aversion for being photographed) sent him politely away, explaining that he was expecting a famous professor.

Burckhardt settled down comparatively early in life to a rather *voulu* old age, noting with a mild clinical interest the slow disintegration of "the machine" and adapting himself resignedly so as to carry on his work. He liked to attribute his excellent health to his week-end walks in the country round Basle, and to the low collars which he always affected. Moreover, teaching, he held, was one of the healthiest of occupations, while "learned authorship" was among the unhealthiest: he would not even allow *viri doctissimi* good health, and noted that each revision of the *Cicerone* cost the editor his life.

From about 1864, when Burckhardt arranged to absent himself for the summer term, his life was regulated by the rhythm of the academic year and punctuated by a journey abroad, where he renewed and pursued his work in the galleries and the cities of Italy, Germany or France, and on two occasions London. By the end of the 'sixties he had begun to enjoy life as he had never done before. The letters to von Geymüller begin in 1867, those to von Preen and Max Alioth, though there are one or two of an earlier date, in 1870, and among his new circle of correspondents some like von Salis were former pupils. Geymüller was an Austrian architect educated in France and in England, whose work on St. Peter's first brought them together. Von Preen whom he met on one of his walks in the neighbourhood of Lörrach in the Black Forest, in 1864, was Prefect of the district, a *Beamter* of the old school, in appearance correct and rigid, with a grasp of administration in the new Germany and of its immense implications for the future and in other hands than Bismarck's that evidently fascinated Burckhardt, whose complementary contribution to the same theme is the subject of so many of their letters. But on his holidays, writing in a café and describing his day, Burckhardt turned most often to Max Alioth, a round-faced old Bâlois with his pince-nez slightly askew, the very reverse of von Preen, cheerful, feckless, incapable of sticking to anything, fond of food and wine and of the sort of joke that was not made to Preen.

A few of his correspondents lived in Basle, and these, apart from his family, formed the nucleus of the friends whom he met regularly in the evening at a café or *Weinstube*. He always put his pen down at eight o'clock, though as he grew older he grew more attached to his solitude and his piano "as old people do." The friends who called were warmly welcomed and made to share his favourite wine, *Château-neuf,* and if he felt in the mood were given a lively performance of an opera or operetta, or a Mass by Haydn or Mozart in which he took all the parts in turn with such a feeling for the music and the scene that Geymüller was entranced and entirely forgot the technical imperfections. Richard Wagner was never mentioned. Later again he began going to concerts and operas in Basle as he did abroad, though a visiting virtuoso was treated as coldly as the *viri doctissimi.*

★   ★   ★

The one interlude in these almost undisturbed years was the arrival of the new Professor of Classical Philology, the young Friedrich Nietzsche. Too much has sometimes been made of their meeting, but the very unexpectedness of the encounter throws Burckhardt's moral and intellectual features into relief in a way that the quiet background of his life in Basle does not. Moreover, Nietzsche has come to represent the nihilistic trend in his age so completely that his presence in Burckhardt's life sets off the traditional character of Burckhardt's thought, and in a sense he provides a measure with which to gauge its significance.

In his old age Burckhardt would have liked, I think, to be allowed to forget Nietzsche, and he tended to gloss over the ties which brought them together. When von Pastor offered to contradict the suggestion that Burckhardt's *Renaissance* put forward the same view of tyrants and power as Nietzsche's *Zarathustra,* Burckhardt answered that he had always regarded such figures as *flagella Dei,* that he had never talked to Nietzsche on the subject and that anyway Nietzsche had become "a publicity stunt"—in the hands, he meant, of his sister. Frau Förster-Nietzsche had in fact called on Burckhardt with the intention of pumping him for the garbled life of her brother which was being prepared, but Burckhardt guessed her intentions and gave, according to Wölfflin, a very good imitation of a senile old gentleman. Frau Förster-Nietzsche went away empty-handed.[3]

Burckhardt and Nietzsche had long since ceased to have anything in common. But when Nietzsche first arrived in Basle—he was twenty-four—Burckhardt at once recognized the originality of his gifts, and Nietzsche found in the older man a harmony of qualities which aroused his lasting admiration.

"Yesterday evening," he wrote to von Geersdorff in 1870, "I had the pleasure which I should have liked you above all people to have shared, of hearing Jacob Burckhardt lecture. He gave a lecture without notes on Historical Greatness which lay entirely within the orbit of our thoughts and feelings. This very unusual middle-aged man does not, indeed, tend to falsify the truth, but to concealments, though on our confidential walks and talks he calls Schopenhauer 'our philosopher.' I am attending his weekly lectures at the University on the study of history,[4] and believe I am the only one of his sixty hearers who understands his profound train of thought with all its strange circumlocutions and abrupt breaks wherever the subject fringes on the problematical. For the first time in my life I have enjoyed a lecture: and what is more, it is the sort of lecture *I* shall be able to give when I am older."

3. Her account of the interview is given in volume iii of Nietzsche's letters.
4. *Reflections on History.*

Burckhardt's skill in keeping people at a distance prevented Nietzsche's admiration going sour and turning into Nietzsche contra Burckhardt—as with Wagner—and he went on sending his books to Burckhardt to the end, hoping for a word of encouragement even though the replies became more formal after Nietzsche had got beyond that "excellent daily bread, good and evil." It has been suggested that there are traces of "our great teacher" Burckhardt in *Zarathustra*, but he was more nearly "the perfect opponent" for whom Nietzsche looked in vain among his contemporaries and found in Pascal and Fénelon—one of the many revealing passages of *Sanctus Januarius* that Burckhardt was quick to recognize as one of Nietzsche's most personal works.

But at the period when they met not infrequently the ideas which later separated them were only grumbling in Nietzsche's mind. Schopenhauer, Greece and the European situation provided enough common ground. Both were haunted by the fear of war, or rather by the era of wars which they foresaw bringing about a destruction of the monuments and art of the past on a scale to match and further the spiritual disintegration which they felt spreading around them. During the Commune the rumour spread in Basle that the Louvre and all its contents had gone up in flames. They both rushed out in search of one another, Burckhardt to find Nietzsche and Nietzsche to find Burckhardt, and when they at last met on the street, returned speechless to Nietzsche's rooms at the other end of the town.

They agreed, in fact, upon the dangers threatening, and to a large extent in their analysis of the causes of the European sickness. But when Nietzsche began to unfold his cures[5] Burckhardt withdrew into polite generalities—have you ever thought of the drama?—which made Nietzsche smile. For however Nietzsche twisted and turned in the course of his kaleidoscopic flight from despair, his despair was the constant: he only believed in this world, *Diesseits,* and the multifarious cures which might

---

5. Nietzsche hoped that a powerful and threatening Russia would draw Europe together.

be drawn from that assumption, and which are only superficially contradictory. And perhaps when he complains of Burckhardt's circumlocutions it was because Burckhardt observed a Socratic restraint whenever his thought fringed the "problematical question" of immortality. For although his work as a whole, and his life, leads towards belief in immortality and certainly demands that doctrine for its fulfilment, he was careful never "to talk beyond his means"; tact and conviction went hand in hand. At the end of his life, for example, in a letter to von Geymüller who must sometimes have fished if not pressed for an answer, Burckhardt explains to his Catholic friend that he has not got his grounds for belief—the grounds offered by revelation—but that nevertheless he faced death without fear or horror and "hoped for the undeserved." Again, in the *Griechische Kulturgeschichte,* a somewhat critical and ironical appreciation of Socrates concludes with the reflection that whatever his faults he stood for the immortality of the soul, "the one basis of true morality," and in *Constantine* the strength and creative power of Christianity at that period is seen to spring from the central Christian conviction, the revelation of eternal life.

"True scepticism," he says in the *Reflections,* "has its indisputable place in a world where beginning and end are all unknown, and the middle is in constant flux, for the amelioration offered by religion [Revelation?][6] is here beyond our scope. At certain times the world is overrun by false scepticism, and that is no fault of ours; and then it will suddenly go out of fashion again. Of the true kind there can never be enough."

---

6. Elsewhere in the introduction to the lectures on the study of history Burckhardt says that "History from the religious standpoint has its special rights. Its great model is St. Augustine's *City of God.*" He uses the word religion in several senses, but it seems clear in this case that beginning and end are unknown and unknowable except through revelation. Burckhardt's standpoint seems to me close to Vico's, who speaks of history as the "new science" because, as in Burckhardt, it is man's knowledge of man, whereas man's knowledge of nature, being God's creation, is imperfect and cannot be complete.

Nietzsche, in the end, believed that Burckhardt's quiet scholarly life in Basle was a mask. He was unable to reconcile Burckhardt's acceptance of everyday reality with his pessimism; he could not understand the traditional and Christian view which Burckhardt had described as determined by his happy family life and his indelible impression of the frailty and uncertainty of earthly things, which taken together form the ground of his "true scepticism."

Nietzsche was not alone in finding Burckhardt's form of expression fugitive; Dilthey[7] too complained of his refusal "to follow up the causal nexus in abstract terms," a "caprice" as it seemed to him which could only awaken opposition and doubts. From first to last Burckhardt acknowledged his incapacity for Speculation, and writing to Karl Fresenius ("although you are a philosopher") asks him whether he is not after all justified in clarifying the most important questions of his life and studies "in the way that comes naturally to him. My surrogate," he concludes, "is *Anschauung, contemplation*," a word which is more easily understood than defined, which Goethe had used in the same general sense and that means looking, seeing, vision, insight, intuition, contemplation, and is neither rationalistic nor irrationalistic. Burckhardt, therefore, denies that he has any philosophy of history to offer, since the alpha and the omega are mysteries and we can never know the origin or beginning of anything, of the State, of Religion, of Culture. What he has to say is about man "as he is and was and ever shall be," since as man, man is never altogether strange to him. And with that humanistic opening, closer to Vico than to his contemporaries, Burckhardt begins his *Reflections on History*.

* * *

In the summer of 1868 Burckhardt went for three weeks to the lake of Constance to escape the heat of Basle and to prepare his lectures on history. During the morning and until the late afternoon, with a pause for

7. In his review of the *Renaissance, Ges. Schr.,* vol. xi.

his siesta, coffee and cigar, Burckhardt worked at his table, reading and making notes. In the evening he walked to an inn about an hour away from his hotel, where he drank a glass of wine and enjoyed the view. It was on these walks, he afterwards told Heinrich Wölfflin, that all his ideas fell into place, and from that time on he held that the best ideas came to one in the evening, when the work of the day was done. There is, in fact, an echo of his experience in the opening pages of the *Reflections,* where he says that "beyond the labour we expend on sources, the prize beckons in those great moments and fateful hours when, from things we have long imagined familiar, a sudden intuition dawns."

The *Reflections* (the lectures on the study of history) are not a philosophy of history, nor a method, nor are they, as he pretends, merely a way of "linking up a number of historical observations and enquiries to a series of half-random trains of thought." The modesty of the proposal is only carried out in its tone and mood. The lectures are best regarded as the insight or vision which his study of history had revealed, and may be linked to his earliest moral and intellectual thoughts when, after giving up theology, he began to see in history the form in which his poetry (his philosophy of life) would be expressed.

It was not until a year or two after he had formally given up theology that Burckhardt began to consider his relation "to God and the world," distracted as he had been both by the discovery of his "new science" and by his new friends and acquaintances. When he did so, he wrote that the choice for him lay between "complete worldliness in the manner of seeing and doing everything" and, as he says to his sister, "the sum of Christ's teaching, the law of love and sacrifice." The traditional terms in which he expresses his choice, the alternative between worldliness and unworldliness, disappears for a time from his letters to reappear in all its clarity in his work. Silently, and perhaps almost unbeknown to him, the alternative became the fabric of his thought and the two poles by which his life and his work were orientated—the common basis of both. And to understand the letters, no less than the works, it is necessary to see what he meant by worldliness and unworldliness and how his point of view illuminates both past and present.

"Let us begin," he writes in the *Renaissance*, "by saying a few words about the moral force which was then the strongest bulwark against evil. The highly gifted men of that day thought to find it in the sentiment of honour. This sentiment was an enigmatic mixture of conscience and egoism which often survived in modern man after he had lost, whether by his own fault or not, faith, love and hope. This sense of honour is compatible with much selfishness and great vices, and may be the victim of astonishing illusions; yet nevertheless all the noble elements that are left in the wreck of a character may gather around it, and may draw strength from this source."

This "worldly" morality, he goes on to say, was to become, in time, faith in the goodness of human nature, the optimistic doctrine which inspired the men of the second half of the eighteenth century and thus helped to prepare the way for the French Revolution.

Roughly ten years later, in the *Reflections,* which are marked throughout by Burckhardt's fear of a Europe entirely given up to "mundane affairs," he returns to the function of the sense of honour in his own time. "We may well ask," he writes in a note added to his lectures in 1871, "how long 'the last mighty dam' will hold against the general deluge?" The "strongest bulwark against evil" has, in the interval, become "the last mighty dam," and the sense of honour no longer offers much hope. The real character of the "present crisis," only then emerging, is indicated by a further question. "Are we at the beginning of a religious crisis? Who can tell? We shall be aware of ripples on the surface very soon, but it will be many years before we know whether a fundamental change has taken place."

This "fundamental change" is compared at one point in the *Reflections* to the change which took place in the third and fourth centuries, and the undercurrents of Burckhardt's thoughts are revealed if we turn to the analysis of the change given in *The Age of Constantine* written in 1852. The

Renaissance was in fact a sort of pendant to *Constantine* and Burckhardt originally intended to link the two with a series of studies of the Middle Ages. More precisely, the description of the moral force which played a preponderant part in the culture of the post-Renaissance period is balanced in *Constantine* by a description of the spiritual force which then came into being as an active influence, the significance of which is such for the whole of Burckhardt's work that it may be quoted at length.

"The anchorites' way of life premises a not wholly healthy state of society and the individual, but belongs rather to the periods of crisis, when many crushed spirits seek quiet, and at the same time many strong hearts are puzzled by the whole apparatus of life and must wage their struggle with God remote from the world. But if any man possessed by the modern preoccupation with activity and its immoderately subjective view of life would therefore wish to place the anchorites in some institution for enforced labour, let him not regard himself as particularly healthy minded; he is no more so than the multitudes in the fourth century who were too weak or too superficial to have any comprehension of the spiritual forces which drove those towering personalities into the desert. . . . It was these anchorites who communicated to the clerical order of succeeding centuries the higher ascetic attitude toward life or at least the claim to such an attitude; without their pattern the Church, which was the sole pillar of all spiritual interests, would have become entirely secularized and have necessarily succumbed to crass material power." [8]

The importance of this passage lies in the fact that it brings out Burckhardt's point of view so clearly, the alternative between spiritual interests and crass material power which is again and again the theme of the *Reflections* and of the letters to von Preen. It is at this point that Burckhardt's attitude divides sharply from so many types of humanism, and more particularly those which derive, as a rule consciously, from the Renaissance.

8. I have quoted the American translation of *The Age of Constantine the Great*, p. 323, published by Routledge & Kegan Paul (London) and Pantheon Books, Inc. (New York).

And since his emphasis on asceticism and spiritual interests may suggest that Burckhardt's "unworldliness" is open to the usual criticism that a pure religion either despairs of practical and political affairs or is indifferent to them, one more quotation from the same remarkable chapter will not be out of place.

"To the needs of the ancient world, which the Roman rule of force had brought to despair in politics, Christianity offered a new State, a new democracy, even a new civic society, if it could have been kept pure"[9] —pure from worldliness.

The relation between asceticism and the creative spirit which is implied in this quotation and runs through the whole of Burckhardt's work is explained clearly and simply in the lecture on Pythagoras which forms part of the *Griechische Kulturgeschichte*. In that lecture he discusses the meaning of the spontaneous outburst of communism among the followers of the sage. The obvious parallel, he says, is "the *great 4th chapter of Acts*," where the first group of Christians sold all they had and laid it at the apostle's feet: "There was one heart and soul in all the company of believers; none of them called any of his possessions his own, everything was shared in common." But instead of this example, Burckhardt chose another from the Middle Ages in Switzerland, drawing certain conclusions which illuminate his whole attitude. In all these cases, he concludes, men shared their possessions in common:

". . . not with the object of attaining certain ends, not as a consequence of the hate which the Hellenic idea of the State reserved for the individual, nor did the desire spring from theoretical political ideas and least of all was it an expression of an envious equalization of the enjoyment of life—it arose for the sake of a heightened and more exalted *Stimmung* or mood."

The expression which Burckhardt uses here, *"for the sake of* a more exalted mood," has two layers of meaning, I think. It means that the sharing of goods is both an expression of the mood when there is one

9. Ibid, p. 127.

heart and one soul in the community, and equally that the mood is encouraged and preserved by dispensing with worldly possessions. The *Stimmiung* itself releases the spontaneity which to Burckhardt seemed so lacking in his own time and which on one occasion, writing from London, he calls "leisure, the mother of contemplation and of the inspiration that springs from it." For one of the points on which he agreed with Nietzsche was that "hard work" as a doctrine was destructive of the religious instinct. But leisure, he adds, has become the privilege "of the *happy few,*" invaded by luxury and equated with idleness, so that it ceased to be the occasion of that exalted mood which needed to be freed through asceticism from the oppressive entanglements of a worldly society. All that Burckhardt writes against security and in favour of war and the emphasis placed on "the crises of history" should be understood in the light of faith in the creative spirit. It is this faith which ultimately separates him from Nietzsche and from the determinist views of so many of his contemporaries. His pessimistic view of the immediate future is lightened and clarified by his hope.

"With regard to the failure of spontaneity in Germany," he wrote to Preen in 1872, "things can only be changed by ascetics, by men who are independent of the enormously expensive life of the great cities, who are far removed from the atmosphere of company promoting and the horrific luxury to which official art and literature are falling victim, by men that is who will be able to help the national spirit and the popular soul to express themselves." And in another letter written in 1871 he tells Preen this can only come about through "a new art, a new society, a new religion—I say religion, because without an *Übernatürliches Wollen,* a supernatural will, the thing can't be done."

The expression *Übernatürliches Wollen* means no more than that degree of "other-worldliness" without which the creative faculties in man succumb to utilitarianism and grow desiccated, incapable of producing a new art, a new society or a new religion. It is in this sense too that Burckhardt speaks of the characteristic of all higher civilizations as being the capacity for renaissances. The only part of the world where that capacity is fully developed up to the present time is the West, and the West is therefore the central theme of history.

The West, Burckhardt says,[10] is a living unity, at one time more or less coextensive with the Roman Empire when it embraced the Middle East.[11] "It is only there," he continues, "that the postulates of the spirit were realized; only there that development and transition became the rule, instead of absolute decline." The history of cultures which contributed little or nothing to that unity are beyond his scope; for though valuable in themselves they are not the great central theme of history. It was only a question of time, he held, before the "passive cultures" were penetrated and transformed by the more vital, spiritual culture, since it is only in the West that the essential character of all higher cultures was fully developed and "renaissances" became the rule.

It should be unnecessary to say that Burckhardt did not regard material progress as identical with "activity." On the contrary, the material aspect, the technical aspect may even become the specific form of decadence in the West, and the source of spiritual sclerosis, the occasion of a

---

10. See the opening sections of the *Historische Fragmente*.

11. The passage on Rome in the *Reflections* is characteristic of his attitude and gives an example of Burckhardt's emphasis on the spirit of institutions.

"Rome then *salvaged* all the cultures of the ancient world, in so far as they were still in existence and in any condition to be salvaged. Rome was primarily a State, and the study of it stands in no need of commendation, for here at last the πόλις was created which did not only, like fifth-century Athens, rule a clientèle of fifteen to eighteen million souls, but in course of time dominated the world, and that not by virtue of the *form* of the State (which was poor enough in the century preceding Caesar), but by virtue of the *spirit* of the State, and the overwhelming prejudice of the individual in favour of citizenship of a world power. The question at issue here is not whether world monarchies are desirable institutions, but whether the Roman Empire actually fulfilled its own purpose, namely, to subsume the ancient cultures and to spread Christianity, the only institution by which means the main elements could be saved from destruction by the Teutons."

crass materialism which stifles the source of spontaneity—and then only "ascetics," men who had not succumbed to the material luxury of the age would lead it back to "contemplation."

⋆   ⋆   ⋆

In 1893 Burckhardt was finally compelled to give up his lectures on the history of art and his pupil Heinrich Wölfflin came at short notice to take on the course.

Wölfflin's first impressions had not been propitious; the simplicity of Burckhardt's rooms took him by surprise, and the simplicity of his lectures, the absence of systematic philosophy, disappointed him. *"Das viele Schauen ermüdet,"* he complains in his diary, *"Anschauungsunterricht,"* to do nothing but look at things was fatiguing; the lecture was simply a lesson in contemplation. But a year later he was more disposed to listen and admitted that Burckhardt was perhaps right to refuse to call history a science. Gradually he accustomed himself to the unfamiliar perspective and he began to note their conversations with rising approval.

"Listen to the secret of things. The contemplative mood." Or again "What tastes good *is* good." "How is the collector of inscriptions to find time for contemplative work? Why, they don't even know their Thucydides! Don't bother about others." The really important thing is teaching, and that could be best done by remaining at a small university and not by moving around from job to job and going to the assemblies of the learned, "where they go to sniff one another, like dogs." And above all, beware of the specialist who spends his life correcting the attributions of pictures, the *Attributzler.* "A teacher cannot hope to give much. But in the first place he can keep alive belief in the value of spiritual things. And secondly he can awaken the conviction that there is real happiness to be found in such things."

Wölfflin had fallen under Burckhardt's spell and they agreed on all but one point. "I have begun to absorb his philosophy of life almost imperceptibly and I am beginning to think about work, relations with colleagues and friends just as he does. He has never yet unbosomed himself on the subject of women, though he enjoys collecting examples of un-happy marriages. And at this point I mean to keep the remnant of my freedom of choice." But in everything else the conversations which Wölf-flin noted give an attractive picture of Burckhardt's serene and happy old age.

But even in his retirement he could not at first resign himself to aim-less reading and went on touching up his lectures, and then, though it was thirty years since he had thought of writing a book, he wrote his *Recollections of Rubens,* a short essay full of the recollections of the happi-ness which painting had given him, grouped round the personality and work of Rubens to whom he had always felt particularly drawn. "It is an exhilarating task to evoke the life and personality of Rubens," he begins, and his sense of wonder and appreciation flows on to the last sentence, de-scribing "one of the most splendid pictures in the Pitti Palace" (the Land-scape, with Ulysses and Nausicaa) as spontaneously as though it were his first book: "and so they meet, the Ionian and the Fleming, the two great-est story-tellers our earth has ever known—Homer and Rubens."

No one reading *Rubens* or the letters of the last years would describe Burckhardt as a pessimist, and if he did so himself it was in his impatience with the optimism he regarded as among the greatest threats to the fu-ture. "Happiness," he writes in the *Reflections,* "is a mere absence of pain, at best associated with a faint sense of growth"—an echo of Schopen-hauer which bears no relation to his life and work. Burckhardt's pessi-mism was of a different order:

"According to Christian doctrine, the Prince of this world is Satan. There is nothing more un-Christian than to promise virtue a lasting reign, a material reward here below, as the early Church writers did to the Christian Emperors. Yet evil, as ruler, is of supreme importance; it is the one condition of selfless good. It would be a horrible sight if, as a result of the consistent reward of good and punishment of evil on this earth, all men were to behave well with ulterior motives, for they would continue to be evil men and to nourish evil in their hearts. The time might come when men would pray for a little impunity for evil-doers, simply in order that they might show their real natures once more. There is enough hypocrisy in the world as it is."

The lecture from which this passage is taken, the last in the *Reflections*, "On Fortune and Misfortune in History," forms the conclusion to Burckhardt's work. He had begun by excluding the possibility of a philosophical explanation of history, since beginning and end are unknown, and went on to the rejection of the categories fortunate and unfortunate which imply a knowledge of the end. In one of the letters written from Berlin in 1840, Burckhardt speaks of "his new subject *history*" as the shock which unseated his fatalism and the worldly view of life he had begun to build upon it. His short-lived fatalism gave way to a renewed belief in Providence and he "found himself back at the old and much misunderstood saying that the Lord is the supreme poet."

The form in which his belief in Providence survived is marked by the detachment and hope of the lecture on fortune and misfortune, the belief that there is meaning in history even if it is not wholly within our grasp, and that it is grasped best in the contemplative mood.

"Everything depends on how our generation stands the test. It may well be that frightful times are ahead, and an age of deepest misery. We should like to know on which wave we are driving forward — only we form part of it. But mankind is not destined to perish yet, and nature creates as liberally as before. But if happiness is to be found in the midst of our misfortunes, it can only be a spiritual one: to be turned facing the past so as to save the culture of former times, and facing the future so as to give an example of the spiritual in an age which might otherwise succumb entirely to the material."

That is the happiness which sounds through all the "pessimism" of the letters and made Burckhardt, even in Nietzsche's eyes, "our great teacher."

THE LETTERS OF JACOB BURCKHARDT

To Johannes Riggenbach *

Basle, 28 August 1838. In the afternoon

To mark the anniversary of Goethe's death,[1] I am enclosing a setting of *Wanderers Nachtlied*. As a matter of fact Alois[2] read me your letter, which arrived yesterday, and at your mention of the poem it occurred to me to send you my setting of it. Let me have a few words about it (criticism, and no compliments). I am really sorry to hear you are feeling so lonely, but you will find that nothing so strengthens one's character and gives one such independence as being thrown upon one's own resources. And who knows how soon I shall be with you. Your letter put me utterly to shame; for while I was set on the highest of all concrete enjoyments, the enjoyment of Italy, you were suffering, and wrestling with your convictions. Nothing, indeed, nothing in the world, appeals more to the lazy than orthodoxy, and provided a man keeps ears, eyes and mouth shut, he can be sure of peaceful slumber. Moreover, the recent reaction in theology has been towards orthodoxy and comes partly from the fact that few sensitive people have had the courage to keep pace with the giant steps theology took in the last century and continues to take in this. With convictions such as mine (if I may so call them) I could never take a living with a clear conscience, not at any rate while the present views on revelation prevail—and they are unlikely to change very soon. Hence my final decision to become a teacher. That miserable *juste-milieu* 'twixt supernaturalism and rationalism, "the Prophet,"[3] is a terrible example of the position theologians sometimes reach trying to be enlightened and orthodox at the same time. (I won't laugh at or even think of his stupidities; they are so frequent and so disgustingly crass; he gossips all over the shop about the job he has been offered at Göttingen, explaining why he did

---

* See Notes on p. 251.
1. Burckhardt meant to say Goethe's birth.
2. Biedermann, see note, p. 251.
3. J. J. Stähelin, Professor of Theology.

not accept it, and how, if he had accepted it, he would have arranged matters with Papa.)

If I am to accept responsibility, then at least I want to bear it for myself alone and not for others. In my eyes, Dewette's[4] system grows in stature every day; one simply *has* to follow him, there is no alternative; but every day a part of our traditional Doctrine melts away under his hand. Today, finally, I realized that he regards the birth of Christ simply as a myth—and that I do too. And I shuddered as a number of reasons struck me why this almost *had* to be so. The divinity of Christ consists, of course, in his pure humanity. But it is not quite so easy to deal with the *Logos;* and John is so explicit on the Incarnation. All this reminds me of the Sardinian cleric who, one heavenly evening on the citadel in Novi,[5] wanted to make a Catholic of me, and at my objections finally rounded on me with a penetrating look and said: *et si tu morieris in hoc statu animae tuae?* Under this kind of assault I sometimes take refuge in the idea that a pure moral life might compensate for one's scepticism and transform it into Pelagianism. A proven remedy is to fix one's thoughts firmly on Providence, and for the time being that still holds good for me; but then I take far less account of philosophy than you do. Perhaps there is a department in the Theological Faculty where one can leave dogma and revelation on one side and study antiquity and languages, and as I have a talent and a bent for both, I am trying to keep the door open. For the moment I cannot look the ruins of my convictions in the face. Dewette is certainly on his guard against getting too deeply involved in the conclusions of his argument and I can only follow his example in not merely demolishing, but also in rebuilding, though the result is less reassuring

4. Burckhardt's Professor of Theology.
5. Novi is situated on the north side of the Ligurian Apennines. The conversation is mentioned in the *Gesamtausgabe,* I, 16: "So as to lose no time I climbed up to the ruined citadel with the priest (earlier called the Jesuit) from whence one could see the greater part of Piedmont. We walked up and down for an hour and a half in the cool of the evening; it was a clear starlight evening; every quarter of an hour we were interrupted by the chimes of the Cathedral."

than what has been destroyed. Alois will be able to explain everything to you far better; though he has not been to the lectures on Dogma this term. In any case I have no wish to importune others with my doubts, for as it is an acknowledged fact that I am anything but a born thinker, and am muddle-headed, I should only bore people. I observe, however, that clear thinkers are no better off. Nor have I any desire to communicate my opinions on Dewette to all and sundry, for people have assured me so often of my incapacity to think, that in the end I have come to believe it myself, and at times even *console* myself with the thought; though to have to consider myself *a priori* incapable in any respect, particularly in this one, is a hard nut for my vanity to crack!

You have taken the words out of my mouth, telling me people often think they must either be methodists or fools, and that it is more honest to be a fool. Cases of desperate methodism are common enough in the pulpit, and in the lecture room; people are often intolerant because they fear that a new religious idea might sound like a clap of thunder in their consciences and wake them from their sleep. This being the case, what are we to do, my dear Johannes? Prayer is still open to me, but there is no revelation, that I do know. If I come upon anything encouraging, I will let you know; please do the same! And from now on let there be a still closer bond between the two of us and Alois! I must really talk the whole thing over with him, and perhaps he will have some encouragement to offer. What a comfortable time the orthodox have! They deafen one another mutually, and enjoy universal recognition and inward peace simultaneously. Of course, anyone who determines to set his mind at rest will have no trouble in doing so; but I simply cannot make up my mind to do it. Let's be honest heretics! I need your company more than ever, and fate has parted us. How will things stand, I wonder, when we meet and embrace in Berlin? Adieu, dear friend, and in your trials and tribulations think of one who is struggling inwardly far away from you, and who loves you.

To Johannes Riggenbach

Basle, Friday, 9 November 1838

Read this letter *after* Biedermann's.

I cannot tell you how your letter of 11th Sept. (I quail at the date!) affected me. There is no question as yet of my convictions being firm, but I am in a much better, more cheerful mood, thanks to your letter — so rejoice! My last letter, as you must have noticed, was written in a moment of quite special discouragement. And now I must push ahead, struggling and fighting slowly on; I have at last accustomed myself to theological and philosophical disputations, and certainly begin to feel the benefit. But my transitional period is by no means over: though Religion is going better, there are many other things which are, for the time being, going far worse, e.g., the Bible. So for the moment I cannot possibly let you into my theological lumber room; but I am *thinking* more, and my next letter will bring you circumstantial news. You know, if you have read Alois' letter, what has happened since then; you will have heard of my foolish and, thank God, unsuccessful attempt to renounce all *sentiment;* I have abandoned it and now feel a new-found joy, like seeing friends again; you will probably hardly understand me. If you could see deep within me, you would, in part at least, excuse the attempt, for it was no mere whim.

Italy to me (listen and marvel) is a land of painful memories; I dared not let myself enjoy even a tithe of the whole corpus of nature and art; for the moment my heart and feelings — still profoundly emotional — rather than my mind were opened to the touch of the divine south, everything was transmuted into longing for vanished friendship, such as I never wish to feel again on earth. I believe you know what I mean; the pain with which we are both familiar, of longing for absent friends, is child's play by comparison. What I suffered one heavenly evening in Pisa will remain for ever in my memory. I stood sketching on the beautiful green meadow where Duomo, Campanile, Baptistry and Camposanto rise, leaning against the wall of the Seminary. Looking at the Byzantine arches of the Duomo, I inevitably thought of you and by a natural association of ideas had to think of you all, so that I was in no fit condition to go on drawing. (Camuph[6] was asleep at the time in a near-by café.) I walked quickly along, following the old walls of the town and passing across the Arno, where I was able to delight in a sunset that every artist in the world would have envied me. The whole sky was deep blue; the Apennines were violet in the evening light; the Arno flowed at my feet, and I could have cried like a child. All my heroism evaporated, and were Alois to have joined me, I should have fallen into his arms. Much the same thing happened three days later as we watched the sunset from the dome of the Cathedral in Florence. It seemed to me at times as though I were *Faust,* full to overflowing with yearning, with Camuph as my *Wagner.* (Not to be used or pressed in depreciation of Camuph!)[7] Before me lay the riches of nature and art, as though the Godhead had passed through the land like a sower. *Und alle Näh und alle Ferne befriedigt nicht die tiefbewegte Brust.* But all that's near and all that's far can't satisfy the troubled heart. Forgive my impudence! How often I have envied Camuph, be it said *sub rosa,* so independent and free from passions high and low, armed with practical good sense and prudence, stumping his way calmly through life! But things are going better now: you are reading the words of a happy man who knows how to tackle life. Like the Catholic Church which attributes to itself a *thesaurus perpetuus* of good works, I attribute to you, whom I have so often offended, a treasure of love, a love *"quand même"* as Laube says: and on the strength of this belief I once again beg you to forget the past, for I too have forgotten much.

The deserted Palace in Genoa is the Palazzo Sauli. The sheen on the sea (*il grasso del mare,* sea-fat!) consists of bright shining patches four to

6. Camuph: the nick-name of Johannes Jakob Oeri, Burckhardt's cousin, who later married his eldest sister Louise.

7. *Wagner* plays Watson to Faust's Holmes. The next quotation is from Faust: in a letter to Albert Brenner, written in 1855, p. 104, Burckhardt refers to his "Faust period," and many of the things he says to Brenner may be applied to him.

eight inches in diameter, that one sees in large numbers in the foam (especially near the wheels of steamships, and behind them, in the wake of the steering-gear). You must see it for yourself. Do you ever see Fritz Godet?[8]

Addio, dearest friend; I see you quite clearly before me at this very moment, and embrace you more warmly than ever.

To Johannes Riggenbach

Basle, 12 December 1838

I am writing after spending a wonderful night in conversation with Alois. The front door at home, as it happened, was bolted when I got back from an interesting meeting of the Zofinger Society, so I went at once to the Barfüsserplatz—it was already midnight. Alois! I shouted up, and was as soon let in. There was little thought of sleep.

Once again I talked to him about my home-made little System he finds so unsatisfactory. You, too, I suppose. Now listen: The end which Providence has set before mankind is the conquest of selfishness and the sacrifice of the individual for the sake of the universal. Hence man's most necessary attribute is Resignation; each hour preaches abnegation, and our dearest wishes remain unfulfilled. We are obliged to give up a thousand things for the sake of the whole and a thousand others simply as a result of external circumstances. Man grows old fighting his desires; his highest aim is to forgo his wishes *lovingly,* never to yield to misanthropy for a single moment, and to die at peace with the world. On no account must he grumble at mankind, or withdraw from life; he must hold out to the end. My life has not been so altogether cloudless as it seems to you; *I*

8. Fritz Godet, the younger brother of Burckhardt's tutor in Neuchâtel, recently appointed tutor to Prince Frederick of Prussia in Berlin. Neuchâtel was a Prussian enclave.

would exchange my life against never having been, at any moment, and, were it possible, return to the womb—although I am not guilty of any crime and grew up in favoured circumstances. I now see that the aim of life is to bear existence as best one can, and to try to do as much as possible for others. I have given up all thought of high endeavour and every sort of ambition (believe it or not). Poetry means more to me than ever, and I have never before felt its beneficent powers so active within me. But I have quite given up any idea of literary fame; *aut Caesar aut nihil,* and I have no wish to be lost in the crowd. I have no fears for my future; I have talents enough, but do not mean to rest satisfied with them. *Edel sei der Mensch, hülfreich und gut,*[9] and I will do what I can for others.

O, I am still so sleepy, and in no condition to gather my thoughts together; and yet these pages are written in a really cheerful mood, though half dulled by sleep. Another time, when I have all my wits about me, I will send you the philosophical basis my System certainly needs badly. Though it is not really a System, and is only so described for want of a better word. I have got along with it for some time now, and my decision to deaden myself to all feeling was the mistaken outcome of resignation; a devilish *consilium!*

If only you could have gazed, at the time, into my storm-swept mind, so much in need of affection!

13 December

Yesterday and today I saw the first ice; it reminded me vividly of the time, a year ago, when we tried to arrange a journey to Milan. Had anyone told me then, in black and white, that I was to see Milan this summer, I should have been royally pleased. As it is, I have seen far more than I

---

9. The first two lines of Goethe's poem *Das Göttliche: Edel sei der Mensch, Hülfreich und gut! Denn das allein Unterscheidet ihn Von allen Wesen, Die wir kennen.* Man must be honourable, helpful and good, for that alone distinguishes him from all other beings known to us.

dared hope; though the gloomy thought of having seen it all as a hermit hangs over my recollection of many places, and the more beautiful the thing I saw, the more bitter the pain! If only I could travel with the two of you, and wipe away the melancholy flora of recollection from Genoa, Pisa and Florence!

By the way, I have just set something by Wackernagel[10] to music, and as my custom is, the last strophe. It includes some stolen goods. The piano accompaniment is easy to figure out. We are singing Beethoven's *Christ on the Mount of Olives* in the Choral Society—unspeakably beautiful, like everything of Beethoven's I have heard; and what power it has! Last Friday I went to the Opera. The *Magic Flute* was bungled, but as you know I have acquired the gift, picked up from looking at buildings, of imagining things to myself as they should be, and really it gave me the greatest delight. If you have not seen it you must go sometime; you will certainly not regret it, and no doubt it will be given better than here. I have done with Ehrenberg's *Architectural Journal;* the fellow never respected my anonymity, and put my name to any trash. By the by, he paid up. And anyway with the *Minster at Zürich* I had come to an end of my material. . . .

Now, at last, the recollection of my journey is beginning to rise up before me in all its grandeur, transfigured and half idealized. One forgets disagreeable things on the whole, and only the wonderful, great impressions remain, to become my very own inheritance. Now and then I dream at night of what I have seen, and see it on a monstrous scale, more marvellous than ever. Not long ago I saw Milan Cathedral in my dreams, though quite six times as large as life; moreover, it looked quite different, and when I awoke I realized that I had imagined a wonderful building which, had I been a draughtsman, I should have been able to put down on paper on waking. The same thing has happened to me before now with pictures. Perhaps you dream about the Hamburg churches? Though they would need a good deal more idealizing than Milan Cathedral.

10. Wilhelm Wackernagel, Professor of German in Basle.

Here and there in Italy one meets with sights that make a more than normal impression on the stranger. On those occasions my heart beats faster—was it timidity, or was I overcome? or did my feeling for beauty, more sensitive than at other times, suspect an affinity with the beauty of the outer world? One such moment was the descent from the village of Vezzia towards Lugano; the entry into Genoa—we were driving along the shore towards the harbour; and above all the Piazza del Duomo in Pisa, the Piazza della Signoria in Florence and the loveliest place on earth, Fiesole! You will see it all some day; for I believe it is an essential part of your nature, as of mine.

Yet another place where I felt the need of an affectionate friend: the Monastery Al Monte, to the south-east above Florence. I had discovered that beautiful spot the very day after our arrival, and on the last glorious afternoon of our stay I climbed the steep rock and sketched the quarter of the town one sees so superbly from there, with the surrounding mountains and villages. I felt utterly alone and realized how little the outer world counts if the inner world is not in harmony. That is the point where resignation is most painful: to do without the company of someone who loves us. And those who are not loved must at least love, and hope until death to find their affection returned.

Do you see now why I always take up Platen's defence so fervently? In him I find obscure and undeveloped feelings clearly expressed:

Wo ist ein Herz, das keine Schmerzen spalten?[11]

At other times, to be sure, he gives way to a boundless hatred of mankind, and unfortunately most of his poems originated in that mood. More about this another time, and then more *theologica*.

---

11. The sense of the lines quoted by B. are as follows: Where is the heart untorn by pain? Those who would fly to the ends of the earth are ever followed by the illusions of life. Only one consolation remains: to use the whole strength and dignity of my soul to counterbalance the burden of my pain.

I am now attending Beck's lectures on Ephesians; the clarity with which he proceeds is extraordinary; things that in Dewette's hands remained as dark as night are presented with a clarity and profundity that can only be equalled by few lecturers in Berlin. Beck tries to find a comprehensive whole in each detail, so that from his discussion of Chap. I, 1–10 (for that is as far as we have reached) we got to know a good deal about Pauline doctrine. There is one fatal flaw: being a supernaturalist he does not admit any variations within the N.T.; Corinthians, 1 Peter, Hebrews, the Apocalypse are all quoted alongside each other, and quite dissimilar things are often pounded into a dogmatic porridge. He will force the sense of a particular word till one is positively alarmed, inserting his own meaning into it. Or again link up passages that have nothing to do with one another, in order to prove something; yet not to such a degree as to outweigh the merit of his method in illuminating some point or other with all his might. Occasionally he is sarcastic in his controversy, specially about Harless.[12] Dewette on Corinthians is boring, confused and long drawn out; his Christian Doctrine almost always so; though of course we are only at the beginning: God, the world, etc. All the old rot is trotted out in unintelligible terms, and as a result sometimes looks new. Dewette's real *forte* seems to be criticism. Hagenbach's *History of Dogma* is sometimes very interesting. (Alois cuts at least *one* of the four lectures every week, and says they are nothing special.) Stähelin on the Psalms is magnificently dull. *À propos,* a few days ago we improvised a serenade for Stähelin, which in the eyes of any reasonable person could only have been taken as a charivari. Gsell played a little dance on the fiddle and made a ridiculous speech; we were invited in and regaled with wine, *Basler Läckerli*[13] and a speech by the old boy. I was honestly ashamed, though Camuph thought it a splendid joke.

Adieu, dear Hans, and cheer me soon with a letter.

12. Harless, 1806–1879, theologian.
13. A sort of *pain d'épice.*

To   Friedrich von Tschudi★

Basle, 29 May 1839

Your confidence in me is not misplaced, and as I know you have never readily confided your thoughts to anyone, it shall not go unrewarded; and I know that you number reserve among the finest virtues at your age.

O, when love and friendship beckon, do not repel them with cold maxims! You have qualities that must make many people long to be near you—I am not begging on my own behalf, for you will probably not see me for years to come, and moreover I know you are not altogether indifferent to me: I am begging on behalf of those who look to you for sympathy and find none, simply because you prefer to play the marble statue. But why waste my breath on that score? A heart as sensitive as yours will not endure the burden of self-sufficiency for long; give it free rein, and see that you store up memories you will one day be able to look back upon with pleasure! (Saturday last I was twenty-one years old, and yet I already live intensely in my memory.) See that you allow your inmost self the innocent delight of Epicureanism, of being happy in your affections, and realize that if you do not need others, others, perhaps, need you!

Let me conduct you into the most secret chamber of my life. My family knows, or at any rate suspects, the nature of my religious convictions. I told you once about my eldest, married sister;[14] in her goodness she is the living image of my mother, who lived and died a saint. Not long ago I argued somewhat fierily with her in favour of freedom of belief, though one ought never to do so with women because, unlike us, they cannot fight with the weapons of learning, so that we only cause them grief. That same evening I got a letter from my dear, loving sister, a letter she had begun some days before, but had only just finished, with

14. Margarethe Salome, married Melchior Berri, the architect of several buildings in Basle in the classical style.

an enclosure containing my beloved mother's last words of farewell to us. Ten years before she died, she knew she would probably die suddenly, which in fact happened, on 17th March 1830, and what is more at midnight, without anyone being able to take leave of her. So she had written something down for us. And so, dear Fritz, bear with me while I tell you my story. I cannot pour out my complaints to anyone else, Biedermann has become a stranger to me; Widmer and Wirz are the one a rationalist, the other a child—though I am very fond of both of them. Listen sympathetically to me now, and one day, perhaps, someone will repay you.

Now for the content of my sister's letter! She is one of those rare souls who is always cheerful their whole life long, though in her heart of hearts she sympathizes with every form of suffering; she is one of those characters who are both gentle and strong, cheerful, happy and at the same time deeply religious. O, how shall I conclude! She begs me on her knees, as it were, to recollect my mother's words: to cherish my father's life; she conjures me by my father's health to alter the course of my life. "O, do not let yourself be cheated of your childlike faith, they will give you nothing, absolutely nothing in return." She tells me how my mother prayed with us as children, how once, when I was not a year old and dangerously ill, she fell on her knees, and that she is now praying for her children before the Eternal God. She mentions with reserve her great longing for her mother, and ends by asking me not to take her letter amiss! She wrote to me, she says, because it would have been difficult to talk to me about such things.

The enclosure is carefully copied in her own fair hand (my father has the original). It is the farewell of one who kept faith and suffered, of one already standing on the frontiers of the beyond, a simple, loving and deeply moving message. Above it she had written the text she wanted preached on at her funeral.

What is the use of my writing all this to you—not I admit, without tears? You will find, my dear Fritz, that you too will have to pass through similar experiences, and drink them to the dregs.

Next autumn, it has now been decided, I go to Berlin; but I am thankful to say that it is now quite clear to me that I shall not make theology, nor indeed find in it, my life's work. Don't forget to write to me if and when you decide to go to Berlin.

To   Heinrich Schreiber *

Basle, Sunday, 8 September '39

Next Thursday week I set off for Berlin with the same friend who went with me to Italy.[15] Before I go I would like to send you a few words to express my gratitude and my lasting affection.

Were I ever to achieve anything of any importance in the field of history, the honour would be mainly due to you; without your encouragement—even though you were not perhaps aware of it—and but for the stimulus you gave me on hearing of my decision, and lastly, without your shining example, it would probably not have occurred to me to seek my vocation in the study of history, although very early on I was determined never to lose sight of history my whole life long. One day I very much hope to tender my thanks to you personally.

Should you want excerpts or copies from the treasure house of Berlin for any research you may have in hand, I most sincerely hope you will apply to me (unless you have a better agent in Berlin); that sort of thing is now my business, and no longer a parlour trick (thanks to you!).

How I should love to stop off at your heaven-blessed Freiburg on my way! But five weeks is far too short a time even to see the veriest essentials in Munich, Nuremberg and Prague. However, though I cannot pay you a visit, you will be constantly in my thoughts, and in moments of dejection that will help to sustain me.

What happened in Zürich the day before yesterday[16] once again re-

15. J. J. Oeri, "Camuph."
16. The September disturbances in Zürich, the so-called *Züriputsch*. See Introduction, pp. xxix–xxx.

minded me how dangerous and sinful it would be, in times such as these, when the position of the Church is so unsettled, to dedicate one's life to theology without the clearest inner call. Dr. Gelzer, whom I recently consulted about my work, drew my attention to the advantage which my theological studies would be to me in judging of a thousand historical matters. Unless I am much mistaken, I believe he himself is a deserter *ex theologorum castris*. The day before yesterday, while the bullets whistled round the Rathaus in Zürich, we had our Disputation in Latin for the Doctorate (*philosophiae*), in fact that of a friend of mine, Candidate Streuber. (Fortunately he too is going to Berlin, principally for the sake of the historical faculty.) After Gerlach's speech, I disputed about Tell's arrow-shot for something over half an hour, denying it. Everything went fairly well, at any rate without grammatical or other howlers, though I was not sorry when the turn of the other two disputants came. One of whom, like me, spoke on one of the themes offered, the other disputing with the Candidate on his dissertation (*de Horatii Arte Poetica ad Pisones*). My public appearance did something to make my apostasy more acceptable to my father, and that was my principal object. He has now been able to take a certain pride in me, though at bottom it doesn't mean much.

I am being formally embalmed in letters of introduction. Among them are some really useful ones, e.g., a special family recommendation to Hofprediger Sack. I should much prefer a note to Ranke! Though he is said to be fairly approachable. On the way I mean to keep my eyes open and sketch as much as possible. I shall pay special attention, in all the galleries, to your Hans Baldung cognomine Grien Gamundianus, and then communicate my collected notes to you, i.e., if there are any to collect. I will also ask Professor Kugler in Berlin for advice.

Fare you well! Do me the honour of a commission very soon! In many respects Berlin is my Patmos; and more than one book there will make my belly bitter (Apoc. x, 10). A page from you will always be a great comfort.

I am tortured by a great longing and impatience for my new work, and yet know so little about it! I am certainly not jumping light-heartedly into it; I know what I am doing, why I am doing it, and will do it with all my might. Whenever I want to award myself a "Bene" in the sandy desert of Brandenburg, I shall take some Laterna Magica slides from the store of memory and let them float past me, among others those of your lovely, mild, sunny Freiburg; but the best of all cures, and the greatest encouragement will always be my recollection of you.

PS. The printing of my description of the Minster proceeds at a snail's pace. The art dealer now wants the illustrations to be engraved on copper by a very skilful engraver who has settled here.

To **Friedrich von Tschudi**

Berlin, 1 December '39

I felt as happy as a child in my last letter at the thought of talking to you of Flemish painting, and giving you my views about Jan van Eyck and Rubens, or rather of submitting them to your judgment. But I am no longer in a condition to talk to you about them. Your last letter, you see, was like a heavy-laden table, where one could choose light or heavy dishes to taste; you placed three or four different subjects before me for discussion, beginning with the highest. You did so in your earlier letters too, but I only answered the first page briefly. Things are different now.

You must be familiar by now with my fantastic reveries, having taken a certain interest in them, listening willingly, among other poetic beatifications of my situation, to a lover's complaints. It is true that I barely hinted at the fact that I was living in a state of great discord regarding the highest questions of life. Do not blame me for not admitting the fact, for I hardly admitted it to myself, and drove away each crisis as it threatened, with violent distractions, sometimes of a studious order, at other times in society. I had a whole army of figures in reserve with which to distract my imagination from the ever more pressing problem of my condition, of my relation to God and the world. Read my last letter again, it was written when that mood was on the wane, when I had decided to cling once again to love, and to find my peace therein.

And now here I am grubbing about in the ruins of my former view of life, trying to discover what is still usable in the old foundations, though in a different way—though whether I shall succeed in the undertaking alone, God knows, for I should hardly have dared begin the work by myself; but there is someone by my side whose future relation to me is hinted at in my previous letter,[17] and with whose letter my own is enclosed. Abyss after abyss opens at my feet, and I should despair were I not sustained by the encouragement which he gives me. And this makes me all the more conscious of your solitary worries, which Zwicki has told me about. O, if only you were already in Berlin! The only thing that can give you companionship is hope, and I do know that left to myself I should be without hope, and should once again become the victim of my old life of reverie and fantasy, though it would satisfy me less and less.

I am overcome with shame as I write, and feel that I ought to keep silent for a long time. Had I but emerged from scepticism, in itself a great step, I could speak from my heart, as you have the right to do. At the same time there are other demons to overcome, and to put it in a word, complete worldliness in the manner of seeing and doing everything. One remedy against this I have found in my main subject, *History,* which was the first shock that unseated my fatalism and the view of life I had based upon it. But that does not diminish the debt I owe to one whom I shall continue to hold in affection till I die—and gradually I shall come to recognize all that I owe him; at the moment I only dimly suspect it, for the greater part is still in seed.

Do not expect a System from me yet; building is slow work. But, together with my affectionate farewell, believe me when I say that I shall be worthy of your company when we meet in the spring.

17. Zwicki, mentioned below. See Notes, p. 252.

To Heinrich Schreiber

Berlin, 15 January 1840

I do not deserve the affection you show me in the least, and I feel very ashamed that my negligence should be brought home to me by a third person.[18] If I owe an account of my life to anyone in the world, I owe it to you, and what is more a punctual account, so I beg your forgiveness for despatching it so late.

My eyes were wide with astonishment at the first lectures I heard by Ranke, Droysen and Böckh. I realized that the same thing had befallen me as befell the Knight in *Don Quixote:* I had loved my science on hearsay, and suddenly here it was appearing before me in gigantic proportions — and I had to lower my eyes. Now I really am firmly determined to devote my life to it, perhaps at the cost of a happy home life; from now on no further hesitation shall disturb my resolve.

I have summoned up all my courage and chosen a special field of research — Asia Minor. For a long time the Middle Ages in Germany and Italy tempted me! But owing to the enormous expansion of historical studies one is obliged to limit oneself to some definite subject and pursue

18. Probably Theodor Meyer mentioned in the *PS.* In a letter to Jacob Oeri, written at the end of November, Meyer wrote about Burckhardt: "I have had far from satisfactory accounts of Köbi, specially from Jaqui, and it seems all too probable that things are as he reports them. However, I think that in this case more is to be done with care and patience than by any other means, and that you owe him as much for the sake of your former friendship; also on account of his family and of the fact that you come from the same country."

There is another reference to Köbi's behaviour in a letter from Biedermann, in which he is said to have thrown himself into a dissolute life now that he is "free from the restraints of social and family life." Burckhardt's own letter to von Tschudi seems the more credible account of his brief *Sturm und Drang* period. The letters to Brenner are the best commentary on his state of mind at this time.

it single-mindedly, otherwise one runs the risk of dispersing all one's efforts. It will perhaps pain you to hear that I have not turned my attention to the Middle Ages; and if one could act to please others in such matters I would certainly have done so for your sake.

I am working at Arabian, attending Ritter's lectures on Geography, Böckh's on Greek Antiquity, Droysen on History, Kugler on the History of Architecture, Panofka's introductory lectures on Archaeology, Homeyer on the history of the German Länder (so as to be able to form some kind of opinion on the present age, only *one* hour a week). I should attend Ranke on Modern History without hesitation, only his classes coincide three times a week with Kugler's, so that I can only go from time to time, as an outsider. Unfortunately Ranke never lectures on Ancient History; nevertheless, I shall go to all his lectures, for even if one learns nothing else from him, one can at least learn the art of *presenting* material. I am keeping up my Hebrew, and have now finished the minor prophets. I have also begun to make excerpts from the classics with reference to the East. As a matter of fact, I have not got beyond the third book of Herodotus; I have already finished Berosus. Furthermore, I am reading the Greek poets—in a word, much too much to be able to do anything properly. As to Asia Minor, I am particularly pleased because it is still to all intents and purposes a *tabula rasa,* which is more than can be said for Greece and Rome. For the immediate future I am planning a brief study of Greek dialects and a revision of Hebrew Grammar; next term I mean to take Greek as well, but there is no time at the moment. Arabian takes up a lot of time. O Lord! I am almost only reporting on all I want to do! When will the time come when I can report what I have done?

Moreover, the History of Art will always draw me like a magnet—just as literature will always figure among the principal aspects of my philological and historical work. On my journey through my beloved Germany I gathered all manner of artistic data, and absorbed all kinds of fermenting matter. I see that at many points even the experts are only feeling their way, e.g., in their criticism of Byzantine[19] architecture. I talked about it with several people, with Schäfer, the architect in Bamberg, with an archaeologist in Regensburg, etc., and began to notice that none of them had any definite criterion. And then along comes Professor Kugler and insists that Bamberg Cathedral was built in the year 1200, and the famous doorway of St. Jacob in Regensburg too, as indeed most of the graceful Byzantine buildings. In fact, Kugler sets to work more conscientiously than any of them, compares mouldings, cornices and pilasters carefully, and then, after establishing the date where manuscript evidence is available, draws his conclusions with regard to the others. But he puts everything too late!

I spent two whole days sketching in the heavenly town of Regensburg; only one, unfortunately, in Bamberg. Except for the Frauenkirche, Munich is only interesting for its modern buildings.

Talking of Gmünd, there is something more I can tell you about Hans Baldung Grien. I have not found anything in the German galleries to compare with his painting in Freiburg Minster. One sees very little by him. There is a flat, carelessly painted portrait in the Munich Pinacothek (Cabinet vii, No. 148) signed with his full name (I have not been to Blaubeuren). At Schleissheim there is a portrait (man in a red cap) signed HGB 1515, not much better; and an unimportant painting of a naked woman with a fiddle in her hand. In the Moritzkapelle in Nuremberg (which at present houses a royal collection) there is a hard, unimportant group consisting of Saints Rosalia, Ottilia, Anna, Margaret and Barbara on a gold background, which can hardly be by Baldung, but with his name in the catalogue, and further, No. 91, "Cleverness in the Abyss," more or less of a pendant to the woman in Schleissheim; and finally No. 124, an altogether unimportant Madonna. Finally in Prague, a beheading of St. Dorothy and Curtius's leap. In Dresden I noticed nothing. But then I was only three hours in the gallery; it was high time to be in Berlin....

19. I.e., Romanesque.

And this same man, whose easel paintings are so insignificant, created the greatest thing that German painting has produced! For as long as the connoisseurs have nothing else to show me, that is how I shall look upon your triptych. In his one great work, Baldung achieved the highest art, superior to Dürer and Holbein, not to mention the magnificent, cold van Eycks, and at the same time he knows quite as much about drawing as the two first named, and shows a delicacy of feeling, by comparison with which Dürer is a lout. . . .

I now feel courageously free, and I shall never forget that I owe it largely to you; I shall try to honour the trust you put in me and to please you. Your undeserved friendship will sustain me in times of trouble, and encourage and spur me on at other times. Here I lack nothing but a teacher like you to spur and curb me by turns. Although I had no recommendation to Droysen, I was very well received, and visit him and ask his advice frequently, but his influence passes wholly through the medium of the understanding, and what I lack entirely here is a fatherly friend. What a letter from your hand would mean, in these circumstances, you can easily guess.

To Theodor Meyer★

Berlin, 11 March 1840

. . . I believe that home-sickness, or at any rate "away-sickness," is on the increase. Berlin *qua* Berlin is a preposterous abode, and I take as little part in it as a Polish Jew at the Leipzig Fair takes part in the life of Leipzig. The professors one has to do with are not Berliners at all, and neither are my acquaintances. What I long for, you see, is to stand for just a moment on the Hauenstein and watch the sunset on the Alps! Or perhaps to wander about on the Gotthard, somewhere below Amsteg, or better still on the other side, near Bellinzona, or Lugano—*et cetera,* just for one evening, and then, for all I care, back into the sand-pit of the Holy Roman Empire of the German Nation, the noble Mark of Brandenburg, and behind my books again.

I have no particular longing for Basle itself—but Switzerland, and the mountains! During the Whitsun holidays I am going to see Chorin with Professor Kugler, a glorious ruined Abbey nine hours away from here, and then, in the autumn holidays if possible, I go to the North Sea for the bathing. Why don't you come here too, if only for the sake of mortification? Tell Schreiber, when you get the chance, that my longing to see him and his Minster is beyond belief, and also that I have met Prof. Kugler, the historian of art, and sometimes accompany him on his daily walks: also that Kugler has at last found a hitherto untried method of dating Byzantine buildings, and armed with it I shall travel observantly through the Harz, Rheinland, Mosel and Main on the way home. Ask him if he got my letter of 16th January (of course in such a way that he should not think I was fishing for an answer). Tell him, too, that the whim to confine myself to Asia Minor has passed by. . . .

Camuph lives very quietly here on fixed principles. Manzer slogs away all day long; he has done quite extraordinarily well here. The best thing about Berlin is that one feels quite free and easy; nobody knows one, except the few to whom one is specially recommended. And even they do not bother one. I have made one very lucky shot here, in that I have made friends with Kugler, although not recommended to him. The good man has to go for a daily walk on account of superfluous fat, and allows me to go and fetch him whenever I like. I have done so frequently, and then we toddle along for a couple of hours through the most beautiful writing sand; it looks pale yellow and is quite lovely. I wisely let the fat gentleman go first over the frozen bogs; if they carry him, they'll carry me. I simply loath the wind-mills on the *soi-disant* hills round Berlin. . . . From time to time there is a charming light effect, and then the pine forests are grandiose. And that is all.

To Friedrich von Tschudi

Berlin, 16 March 1840

You say in your letter that the step you took was much more certain than mine because you took it quite independently. This has proved — more or less — true; left to myself I have latterly tended to lose sight of the point which I had made the corner stone of my life, led astray by the exceptionally distracting character of my work; there has been a gentle ebb, I will not say reaction; Zwicki will probably not always want to drive me along, so I am afraid you will find a lot that needs looking to. O what an inconstant man! you must be thinking, who needs an external impulse to drive him to renew his spiritual life; my path, however, is through dependence *to* independence.

One habit I have not lost, however: the philosophy of history is daily, if only incidentally, in my thoughts. Unfortunately the lectures on it for the coming term are all by secondary lecturers, and what is more they are almost all post-Hegelians, whom I do not understand. Droysen was most stimulating on the subject; but having heard him on Ancient History, I now unfortunately have to look on while he packs his traps and moves on to Kiel. The loss is all the more disastrous as he had received me very well, and I was able to visit him whenever I chose. There can be little doubt about his importance, and in ten years' time he will be numbered among the great. My poetry, for which you prophesied fair weather, is in great danger of being sent packing now that I have found the height of poetry in history itself. There was a time when I looked upon the play of fantasy as the highest requirement of poetry; but since I must esteem the development of spiritual states, or, quite simply, inner states as such, higher still, I now find my satisfaction in history itself, which exhibits this development in two distinct phases running parallel, crossing and intermingling, and indeed identical: I refer to the development of the individual and the development of the whole; add to that the brilliant *outward* events of history — the gorgeous motley dress of the world's progress, and I find myself back at the old, and much misunderstood saying that the Lord is the supreme poet. You may reply that poetry is not just the development of inner states, but their *beautiful* development, according to laws of harmony which are ideally performed in man's poetical mind; that I allow, thus granting poetry a sufficiently wide field; but to me it is far from having the attraction which it possessed while I still ignored the incomparably greater Guidance of the world's progress. As you see, I am using a dreadfully inadequate philosophical language (of course it cannot but correspond to my way of thinking)—and that is why I need philosophical friends more than ever.

To Louise Burckhardt

Berlin, Thursday, 16 July 1840

A thousand heartfelt thanks, particularly for being so gentle and kind in telling me confidentially and at once about Maria's engagement[20] before I learnt of it from Father's letter. In return, I think I may confidently say that your expectations of the way I am taking the whole matter will not be disappointed.

I am indeed—why should I deny it?—deeply affected by what has happened. I had already built my castle in the air—and it all collapses so unmercifully. There are still sad times ahead of me, for the greater the good, the more bitter resignation becomes. One thing has, however, given me strength and support, even in the first moment of sighs and bitter tears, and that is the realization that she is destined for one whom I can recognize without loss of respect as a better man than I am, and not *for a certain man* who did not respect the reputation of two other girls, altogether conscientiously. Though I am promising to be resigned to my fate in the first moments of grief, I hope I shall be able to meet Hufeland

20. Maria Oser, a cousin of Burckhardt's, the daughter of his father's sister.

without constraint (or at least give that appearance), for during the few moments when I first met him, he won my entire respect, and *he will make Maria happier than I, a man of strong passions, could ever have done.*

Dear Louise, listen to what I have to say in all sincerity. It is most likely that we shall live together one day. We must see to it that sincere friendship and the blessings of a profound culture sweeten our lives. Man can mean so much to himself, and the more he means to himself, the more he is to others. Every day in the course of my work I am discovering new sources of greatness and beauty; poetry must sanctify my sorrow and be my companion through life. Our travels—perhaps by then you will have been to Moscow[21]—will have left a great treasure of things seen, and we shall be happy. The prospects for my return are, taken all in all, quite good, and at any rate I shall not find it difficult to earn my living with a modicum of hard work, so that I can go on studying at the same time. So let us build a new home out of shattered dreams and wreckage of all sorts, like the Roman vine-grower building his *vigna* out of old marble friezes and broken columns! Perhaps you may even be surprised from time to time by my carefree view of life, but believe me, my faith in an Eternal Providence stands as firm as a rock. Providence is no mere blind fate, but a personal God. This belief will never again desert me, however my view of Religions and Confessions may be modified. And it is to Providence that I shall confide my worries from now on.

But I do not want to talk beyond my means. For I have often had to control myself while writing, and this page is written under the influence of saddening thoughts. But I promise I will make every effort to be a man and not give in to idle complaining. I shall try to meet Hufeland cheerfully, as I am making a sacrifice for his sake. As a pendant to the sentence opposite, I should like to say again that man means little or nothing to himself if he is nothing to others. Let us, dear Louise, live for others, in the first place for each other, and then resignation will come easily. The sum of Christ's teaching is surely the law of love and sacrifice for others.

21. Burckhardt's step-mother had been a governess in Moscow.

I see before me an indefinite period of teaching; may my guiding principle always remain the same! I still, thank God, have good old Zwicki
here, who knew I was in love, to whom I shall pour out my heart. He
tells no tales and knows neither names nor circumstances.

If Father's permission arrives, as I hope, I shall be in the Harz mountains in five weeks' time, and what is more, in the company of two good
and sensible friends from Pommerania, whom I met at Frau von W.'s.[22] I
have given up all thought of Hamburg; it would cost too much as one
has to *go there by coach.* I cannot tell what the journey will bring forth — is
it profanation or is it permissible to hope for *distraction?* My work is going
fairly well, and I am full of hope. In fact I have even made one or two
discoveries in the history of art. Kugler is still the same wonderful, lovable man; (his wife is expecting a child today or tomorrow). On top of
everything I have got to write in Frau von W.'s album tomorrow. . . .
What? I don't yet know. The custom is to write something in sonnet
form. And then think of my mood! Dear Louise, there is one cure for all
troubles and worries, the consciousness of the sympathy of others. I
know that you sympathize with my fate; and I promise to be faithful to
you all my life.

To Heinrich Schreiber

Berlin, 11 August '40

. . . Now here are my plans. I leave Friday next for the Harz mountains
and from there shall visit Hildesheim, which is said to be very rich in
historic things and unexplored works of art. Once there I shall try out the
work I did on the history of architecture last winter, and see how things

22. Frau von Winterfeld, the wife of Karl August von Winterfeld. It was in their
house that Burckhardt heard a lot of music and first met many of his friends and
acquaintances in Berlin. Among others he mentions Ranke, the sculptor Tieck (a
brother of the poet), and President von Kleist.

go. I shall spend next summer in Bonn, for Wolter's sake,[23] and because it is near Cologne the Holy. During the holidays I go to Belgium, etc. What do you say to all that?

Next winter I shall attend Ranke on the Middle Ages, that is all I know for the moment; I joined his history class this term. Although nothing concrete came of it, one certainly gained a great deal from it. I am only now beginning to suspect what historical method means. Wilken is no longer lecturing; I see him from time to time, looking like death. What a shame they let Droysen go to Kiel. The result is that the leading University in Europe, as Berlin likes to call itself, has no one to lecture on Ancient History. I never got as far as Raumer's lectures, who is anyway said to be boring to the point of extinction, because Ranke and he, in defiance of each other, choose to lecture at the same time.

You can have no idea, in Freiburg, of the envy and the vanity of the greatest of scholars here! Unfortunately Ranke, as everyone knows, though very pleasant to meet, is lacking in character, and you can see that in black and white in any review of his writings. He is very pleasant to us. Lachmann hits out in the commonest way in his lectures, calling people donkeys and asses. And then the doctors! They all hate one another like poison, and I should not care to lecture here for four thousand thalers a year. But one can learn a bit.

How I long for the Rhine! It is after all the bloodstream of Germany. You can form no conception of how miserable the Mark of Brandenburg is, but its historical work must be put correspondingly high. . . .

23. Ferdinand Wolter, at Bonn since 1819, lecturer in Roman Law and Canon Law.

To Louise Burckhardt

Berlin, 15 August '40

My sincere thanks for your letter which reached me just in time, as I am leaving early tomorrow. During the last four weeks a lot of pleasant things have been happening to me; it has been about the most agreeable period of my stay here. Hufeland has been here a week; he came to find me at once, on Sunday, and left me a message, as I was not in, to say he would expect me at home in the afternoon, or on the following morning. Of course I went to him at once, as soon as I found his card on my table. He is one of the most lovable people one can imagine, and we were both very pleased.

If only Aunt Oser had lived a little longer, how delighted she would have been. And what do they say, in Basle, to *three* sisters getting engaged in *four* weeks? That's news for the Reading Club!

Tell Father I am very pleased with the list of lectures published for next winter; my principal course will be Ranke on the Middle Ages. If only all the Professors here were not arch-enemies! But what is the use of complaining when Ranke and Raumer always lecture at the same time (12 to 1) out of sheer spite? They have done it for four years and are sure to do so for the remainder of their lives, at any rate until one of them has got the Ministerial rank they have been working for so long. If only people would recall the miserable example of Johannes von Müller. Raumer's prospects are as good as done for; Ranke, on the other hand, as the personal friend of the King, may certainly hope for advancement. It is really a pity that for all his colossal learning, his penetrating mind, his very great social gifts (he was also very civil to me) he should be so utterly bereft of character. I must tell you a very good and *perfectly true* anecdote on this score. Ranke was once alone with Bettina;[24] their con-

24. See Introd., p. xxxv.

versation drifted on to the subjugation of Poland; Bettina was naturally full of indignation against Russia, and Ranke fell in with her ideas, agreeing entirely with her. A few days later he was again *chez* Bettina at a big reception; an important Russian diplomat got into conversation with him, in the course of which Ranke described the behaviour of the Poles as revolutionary and execrable. At that moment Bettina looked at him from behind, rolled her eyes heavenwards, and said nothing but *Pfui!* Ranke left the house as soon as possible and has not set foot there since.

On another occasion Varnhagen's[25] election to the Academy of Sciences was in question. Ranke, who cannot abide him, but would have liked to win him over, made an enthusiastic speech in V.'s favour. And then the voting followed, but *not one* vote was cast *for* Varnhagen. Glances were exchanged, and everyone drew their own conclusions. And yet one cannot really say that Ranke's convictions, feeble as they are, influence his presentation of history, though they have become a byword all over Berlin. No one has ever heard anything frivolous pass his lips; he often makes jokes, and good ones what is more, but when he speaks of great things the seriousness with which he treats history becomes clearly, almost frighteningly evident in his expression. I remember quite clearly how he began his lectures on German History: "Gentlemen, nations are God's thoughts!"

To Louise Burckhardt

Frankfurt, 5 April 1841

Excuse (a) the style;
      (b) the handwriting.

I know you have patience enough to read a disorderly account of my journey, and love enough to share my happiness; and when I think of all

25. Varnhagen von Ense, 1785–1858, historian and biographer.

that Germany has given me during the last ten days, serious as well as enjoyable, I feel quite beside myself.

On Friday, 26th March, I left Berlin. My German friends accompanied me to the Post, where I found good old Max. I was really very sorry to leave Berlin, which a year and a half ago, on my entry into the city, I had looked forward to leaving with pleasure. Through Siegfried Nagel, a cousin of Max's, I had latterly made friends with a delightful Club of Westphalians, which was all the more pleasing to me, as my few closer acquaintances had all left last summer. Since New Year's Eve we were all on terms of "du" and there can seldom have been such a well-suited company. Nagel is one of the finest characters I know; in addition to other gifts, he also has a fine tenor voice, and so we made up a quartet which could hardly be equalled in any other University. In short, it was a heavenly life—and I hope it won't be any worse next winter; I shall find almost the whole crowd there again. I can *thankfully* say that I decided to ask Father for another half year in Berlin *before* making these acquaintances; and I now feel much happier when I think of it.

Eduard Schauenburg was one of the principal members, in fact the moving spirit of the Club; on my departure he gave me a letter to his elder brother in Leipzig and begged me earnestly to deliver it personally. You see I am casting my net wider.

I expected little of the journey till I got to the Rhine; ten or fourteen gloomy days lay before me, so I was naturally very depressed at going away, particularly as I had left Kugler unwell. As the coach rolled through the Potsdamer Thor at nine o'clock at night, I made a fervent prayer for my happy return. And I fell asleep with historical and poetical plans waltzing round my head. Next morning in Wittenberg I went to look at the Market Square with its statue of Luther; but my departure still weighed too heavily on me for me to be able to pull myself together and do any hard thinking. In the evening I spent a quarter of an hour in Halle and then went on to Leipzig at once, by the next train. On the way I counted the days of my journey on my fingers. Early tomorrow, I said to myself, you go and look up Theophil, then deliver Schauenburg's letter and then on to Naumburg in the afternoon. But who could have reckoned it all out! As Leipzig appeared on the horizon, with its parks and church towers, I began to suspect that I had miscalculated. I took a room at the hotel "zum Deutschen Hause," admired the formal squares and promenades, and went off to the theatre where Emil Devrient was giving *Egmont*. It was wonderful.

Next morning I learnt that Theophil was in Halle, and then looked at the address on my letter. The receiver, Hermann Schauenburg, did not at first sight seem to be exactly my man. A fine figure of a man, an interesting face, friendly blue eyes, a fair moustache; a very earnest expression. I was polite and reserved. I already knew that he was the author of some fine poems, and those who write good poems are not always outwardly the most pleasing. But he took me by the arm, led me down the beautiful promenades, and treated me as a friend. I soon found that he had strong nationalist convictions and a very serious view of life and poetry. I had to promise to remain on for today, and stay in his rooms. He persuaded me to dine with him and his friends at midday, and I spent the whole afternoon with him. Little by little our conversation involuntarily took a political turn, however much we both of us would have liked to avoid that tender spot. (Dear Louise, I hope I'm not boring you?) He was ultra-liberal, I conservative. In the Küchengarten, in front of Gellert's and Poniatowski's memorial, among the crowds in the Grimma'sche Strasse, or in the peace and quiet of the parks where the bullets of the battle of Leipzig are still to be seen in the trees—everywhere in fact, we talked of nothing but German Princes and Constitutions. Finally, in the evening, in his room, he said: "We have talked so much about it, let us have it out; nothing can disturb our mutual respect any longer." At that moment, certainly one of the finest in my life, the glorious future of Germany came clearly before my eyes; I saw the coming constitutional struggles of Prussia before me and thought to myself: *Now* is the time to offer your contribution and enlighten one of the best of fellows on his wild, confused pursuit of freedom—and so I was able to start afresh from a new and higher point of view; I had the courage to be conservative and not to give in. (The easiest thing of all is to be liberal.) We were deeply moved and spoke with feeling, and I do not recollect ever having been so eloquent. He fell on my neck and kissed me: I was the first person he had ever heard talking in a conservative vein from conviction. And I made a silent vow *never* to be ashamed of my convictions. He admitted that in the course of my studies I had thought out these questions far more thoroughly than he had done, but from youth up, as the result of some obscure impulse, he had been enthusiastic in his love of freedom, and would never cease to be so. I had done all that could be done; he promised never to scorn the Royalists and Conservatives thoughtlessly in future. The rest of the evening flowed on peacefully, and it was obvious that I would have to stay over Monday. He read me some of his poems unaffectedly; one or two he laid before me and told me to read them to myself—you can guess what they contained and which chords in me they touched. They are among the most beautiful sonnets ever written in the German tongue.

Dear Louise, what can I tell you about Germany? I am like Saul, the son of Kis, who went out to look for lost asses, and found a King's crown. I often want to kneel down before the sacred soil of Germany and thank God that my mother-tongue is German! I have Germany to thank for *everything!* My best teachers have been German, and I was nourished at the breast of German culture and learning; and I shall always draw my best powers from this land. What a people! What a wonderful youth! What a land—a paradise! . . .

To Eduard Schauenburg*

Sancta Colonia, 15 April 1841

The devil take solitary artistic tours; I for one shall undertake no more. I am not bored, God forbid! But melancholy (alias, sad-stupid) to excess. Regarding my journey up to and including Leipzig, ask your *fratello;* and for a long stretch of my journey, Leipzig was the one bright spot. At times I raised my hands to heaven and sighed, O dear heavens, send me down just one of our wonderful set, on a cloud! but *durae coeli aures*—till Mainz I remained alone or in the ennobling company of cattle dealers, commercial travellers on their way to the fair, old maids, boors and others, mostly awful philistines. And yet the journey meant a very great deal to me; it was often made delightful by a vivid recollection of happy days in Berlin and Leipzig, and by the prospects of a smiling future in the Rhineland, and at times I forgot everything else. I shall never forget the morning when I first fully realized that I was again near the valley of the Rhine: between Fulda and Gelnhausen I went on a little ahead of the waiting omnibus, with two old ladies; it was dark and fairly cold, until we turned a corner and suddenly saw vineyards and a large patch of blue sky before us, while a lovely warm breeze blew up to us. "You come from the Rhine!" I cried. In Frankfurt I completely forgot to see Dannecker's Ariadne; and to think that that happened to *me* of all people! Imagine my irritation when I was reminded of it on the steamer! I remained Wednesday and Maundy Thursday in Mainz; but Good Friday I could bear it no longer; it was lovely weather, and after the Bishop of Mainz had given me his blessing in the morning (as a genuine and proper member of a crowd of people gathered in the Cathedral), I left for Bingen. I spent the whole afternoon wandering round that charming little place sketching, in a mood of recollection; I went on to Rüdesheim, drank Nectar (or as you maintain Ambrosia, although it comes from βιβρώσκειν, to eat) and then went on through the Niederwald; there the view was as poetic and as picturesque as anything I have ever seen. Then back via Assmannshausen and Rheinstein under a superb stormy sky, straight to church, where Our Lord's Body was illuminated and pretty girls were singing. A full, beautiful and sadly peaceful day.

Saturday I went to Bacharach, sketched there for a couple of hours, and went to the Pfalz in the afternoon in brilliant sunshine and showers, and past the golden Loreley towards S. Goar. There, and in the neighbourhood, I spent the whole afternoon, in S. Goarshausen, Petersberg,

Rheinfels, etc., and in the evening took a skiff and went once more up to
the Loreley; I took the oar out of the boatman's hand and sailed gently
forward against the stream; O if only you godless people had been there!
Thus alone, one can only make a mental note of such wonderful things,
as though they were cold experiences — just like the Beefsteaks.

I went to Coblenz on Easter Sunday in cold stormy weather. Round
about Stolzenfels and Lahnstein thick clouds were driving past; it was
lovely to see. On purpose I only looked up August Focke in the evening,
towards five o'clock. Two cousins who lived with him, though very nice
fellows, rather cramped our style, but in the evening he came with me to
"The Giant," where we ate, drank and enjoyed ourselves. The happiest
Easter Day in my life, God forgive me, although I did not go to Com-
munion. On Monday we dawdled about the whole day long in the Mo-
selle valley, and never got further than Kobern and back. It was wonderful. Tuesday too we spent, I hardly know how. Drinking! Yesterday,
Wednesday, I could rest no longer; I had to promise to be back in Coblenz
by Monday next at the latest, and in ideally beautiful weather went on
down the Rhine.

O God, how beautiful the German countryside is! Andernach! Sieben-
gebirge! And then Bonn! Was I to get out? No, there was still no one
there for me to talk to. So I saw the place from the steamer, looked out
for my rooms in the Judengasse, enjoyed the wonderful view to the very
depths of my soul, and sailed on quietly down the Rhine. First of all
St. Martin's appeared above the horizon, then above the trees rose the
Cathedral: the city grew and spread out before me, quite glorious! I despatched the business of arrival as quickly as possible, and raced, almost
off my head, to the Cathedral. The inside of the Choir was cluttered up
with scaffolding, but not to such an extent, thank God, that one could not
get a proper view of the whole.

Dearest friend, what can I say? I am entirely possessed by one feeling:
you are not worthy to tread this ground, you are in a holy land! And the
debt I owe to Germany lies more heavily than ever on my soul. . . .

You can have no idea of the extraordinary atmosphere here, at the present time. The day before yesterday, at a solemn session of the City Council, it was decided *in Gottes Namen* to carry on with the building of the Cathedral in spite of all the difficulties; the town is full of it; even the builder's men are seized with enthusiasm for the idea. I myself am beginning to believe, since yesterday, if not in the completion, at any rate, in a very considerable advance in the building.

It really is a wonderful feeling to be working for the completion of an edifice such as this. I knew, of course, though it has now struck me with the full force of a profound impression, that this church is not just one among many; it is the inexplicable revelation of an incomparable, heaven-sent genius.

Take the "enthusiasm" into the bargain, my dear fellow; this time "I can't do otherwise."

To Louise Burckhardt

Braunschweig, 25 September 1841

I have kept you waiting for a letter and fed you with hopes of one for a long time now; and it is you of all people to whom I owe one.

Our ways in life are leading in different directions. Fortune is beckoning you to a happy, cheerful life;[26] what is to happen to me, God alone knows. But we shall ever be close to one another spiritually, and see one another as much as circumstances permit. I think of you and your destiny daily, at the best moments of the day; you can count upon my unwavering affection. And now let me tell you how my affairs stand.

The sight of Germany, after having been away for two short weeks,[27] moved me more deeply than ever. It was a lovely Sunday morning, a few days ago, when I crossed the frontier not far from Henry-chapelle and

26. Louise was engaged to Jakob Oeri.
27. In Belgium, preparing his guide-book mentioned below.

Jacob Burckhardt in 1843
A drawing attributed to Franz Kugler

A view of Cologne, 1843

saw the sun rise over the tomb of Charlemagne, above the Minster of Aix-la-Chapelle. Towards midday I saw the Cathedral of Cologne once again, shimmering in the sun, surrounded by its crown of churches, and the majestic Rhine. For one whole lovely afternoon I walked round the town, which had come to mean so much more to me than I had ever expected. Another visit to the Cathedral, bathed in the morning sun, brought my happiness and delights to an end; I could only cry like a child. I spent all next evening with my revered Madame Matthieux; she was alone with her mother, as Dr. Kinkel was away. I am repeatedly struck by the thought of my good fortune in Germany; who could have foreseen that the little circle centred round Mme Matthieux, the object of so many attacks, should have idealized my entire stay in Bonn. What delightful evening excursions we made on our walks in the lovely surroundings of Bonn! Our objective was usually the terrace of a small inn in Küding-hoven, with a wonderful view towards Drachenfels and Rolandseck, where we sang and recited; Kinkel was our hero and Mme Matthieux a prophetess; and we three were in such an ecstasy of happiness that we said we would remind one another of it in years to come. The evening before my departure for Belgium I was honoured with a trip up the Rhine past the most beautiful, motionless beech trees; the boat rang with our songs and laughter. That last evening with Mme Matthieux was one of the loveliest I remember in Bonn; at the close she said: "I have given Herr Focke a letter of introduction for you and him to Frau Bettina!" That was the coping stone and crown of all her kindness to me.

In Coblenz I stayed two days with Focke, and then travelled with him here via Frankfurt. On the way all the papers were full of unpleasant news from Switzerland. Schaffhausen wants to break away; the question of the religious orders gets more and more involved and awful; in short, the unmistakable signs of inner decay are beginning to show, because people are no longer prepared to recognize the *law*, which is the one and only safeguard for Switzerland. Am I for that reason giving up my country? Certainly not; I mean to devote myself to *its* history, but first and last I shall say to my countrymen: remember that you are Germans! Only a definite — though not political — *Anschluss* with Germany can save Switzerland. I am not unfaithful, dear Louise, when I say this, for only someone who tries to further the interests of German culture can be of any use in Switzerland; there is only *one* remedy against the threatening decline of a people, and that is: to renew its links with its origins.

I express myself badly and write in great haste. Whenever will the time come when, infinitely enriched by all that we have thought and experienced, we shall once again be able to talk to each other? It is on you, my dear sister, that I count.

J.

PS. Greetings right and left. By 27th or 30th I shall be in Berlin.

To   Louise Burckhardt

Berlin, 29 January 1842

First of all, my sincerest wishes for the lovely new year heaven has prepared for you. In spite of all my work, it is going to be a lovely summer for both of us. Perhaps I shall be able to unroll before your eyes a picture of Germany, great and unforgettable, and if not, at any rate there are endless things to talk about and recount.

A week ago yesterday, at half past ten in the morning, Focke and I had ourselves announced at Bettina's. We were shown into a gorgeous room. Not many oil paintings on the walls, but good ones, and among them a fine old German picture. At last the door of the adjoining room opened, Bettina came in. A motherly little woman of fifty-four, short, with a fine bearing, decidedly gipsy traits in her countenance and a wonderfully interesting head, which is quite *exceptional* among women; beautiful, real chestnut brown hair, the most wonderful brown eyes that I have ever seen. She wore a dark violet silk dress, and over it a pale sea-green shawl which she continually draped in the most delicate folds; it must have been of the finest material, for when she drew it tight over her hand one saw the whole of its—still—beautiful shape. "O, you have a letter! Give it me, or better still come into my room over here." We went into a very simple study. On the wall above the sofa a copy of Io after Correggio, on the left-hand wall Achim von Arnim, her late husband; on the right-hand wall Sophie de la Roche, her grandmother, in a cap, and on a console a plaster cast of a magnificent head of Jove, etc. Finally, on a *trumeau* between the two windows, under the looking-glass, a Goethe monument in miniature as she had planned it—she has made several of them. Goethe sitting on a throne, his head thrown back splendidly, looking into the distance, contemplating poetry. Round the throne in relief are his principal creations, Mignon, Leonore, etc. His right hand is resting on one arm of the throne, in his left hand he holds a lyre; in front of him, Psyche leans on his knee plucking at the cords of the lyre, and listening to the tones with a sweet smile.

Bettina sat down on the sofa, with us on chairs on either side. She took up a bundle of quills, playing with them, while she read aloud the letter we had brought her from Mme Matthieux. Think of it! Our recommendations read aloud to us! Though it didn't matter at all. "Now, let's see what more she says: 'Why haven't you sent me your Günderode?' Of course! Have you read Günderode, gentlemen?" We answered truthfully: "O yes, several times." "Well, wasn't she a wonderful girl? Didn't you fall in love with her?" She turned to me and, while I got red to the tips of my ears, said: "Yes, I can see it from your look, you fell in love with Günderode."

(*Par parenthèse:* Have you read Günderode? It's one of the most wonderful books; get it from the Reading Club. She was Bettina's greatest friend, a great character, who went to pieces over an unhappy love affair—said to have been Professor Schlosser [28] in Heidelberg—and ended

28. Burckhardt's guess was wrong, the historian in question was Creuzer of Heidelberg, a dry old stick according to Bettina's brother Clemens Brentano.

her life by throwing herself in the Rhine.) So I was in her good books. There is something very moving about seeing before one a woman who has been through such an experience and dared to give her correspondence with the unfortunate girl to an unfeeling public, together with a dedication *"to the Students."* Bettina went on: "What have you got in that roll of paper in your hand?" I handed it to her explaining that they were Mme Matthieux's latest songs for Fräulein Maximiliane. She at once had her eldest daughter called, a pale and interesting girl of about nineteen, and closely following her came her two other daughters with a lovely greyhound. Now Bettina, you know, wanted to bring up her children entirely by herself and in her own way, i.e., without any thought of convention, but her relations took them for a couple of years to Frankfort with them. And so they have the *"ton"* of society combined in an indescribable manner with their mother's fine *laisser-aller.* We went at once to the piano and I sang three or four songs, accompanied by Fräulein Max (as she is called). Bettina thought I had a good bass voice. The result was that we are both to go again very soon, and spend a whole evening singing. We wanted to pay our respects and leave, but one of the girls said very naïvely, "Mother, the gentlemen made a sign to one another that they wanted to leave," and so we had to stay. Frau von Savigny,[29] Bettina's sister, joined us, and we went to and fro in the rooms, and all at once I found myself alone with Bettina in her study. Our conversation lasted a whole half-hour, about Youth, the students, Germany's future. A great woman; she takes up every subject from the highest and grandest standpoint, although she may be something of a liberal. "What can become of you," she said, "as long as the older generation won't allow you to become anything?" You can form some idea of her *franchise* from the following: She spoke of a young man who has been arrested here in a coffee-house because he had said in front of one or two witnesses: *"Que S.M. n'avait pas été à jeun lorsqu'elle donna telle et telle ordonnance."* "That indeed must have damaged his reputation," I said. "You know," Bettina

29. The wife of Friedrich von Savigny, a friend of Clemens Brentano's.

said, giving me a sharp look, "I could really hate you bitterly for that; it didn't harm him; it must be useful to him!" I hastened to observe that I was thinking of the vulgar public. Finally, after an audience of two hours we paid our respects and after shaking hands were allowed to take our leave, and were given permission to call again.

A few days ago Liszt gave a concert here for the students, at reduced prices (9 batzen), whereas the normal concert costs one or two thalers. I decided to go, although I normally regard *virtuosi* as the corrupters of art. But for once it really was something out of the ordinary, and it would be quite impossible to form any idea of it without having heard him; the Parisians are, in fact, not far wrong in picturing Liszt with twenty fingers. He played his most famous pieces. And now that I have heard Rubini and Liszt, anyone can try to outbid me; I can deal with any lion-hunter.

O what a mass of things there is going to be to talk about when I get home. In the meanwhile you have plenty to serve up if anyone asks after me. All the same, I should have liked to have filled my letter with something better, but who in the world can so control his moods that he can always write as he wishes?

Adieu, dear Louise, and continue to love your

FAITHFUL JACOB

To Heinrich Schreiber

Berlin, 4 March 1842

. . . As to my future, I only know that I shall be able to get along decently in Basle with a couple of hours' teaching every day. And for the time being I fill in the rest of the day with all sorts of historical plans; secretly, I am thinking of a history of the Counter-Reformation in Switzerland. All my work has always been devoted to medieval Germany and modern times; and naturally enough—it was inevitable that I should have to feel my way.

Ranke is on close terms with hardly anybody here in Berlin; still, I have succeeded in gaining his goodwill. One day I shall be able to tell you quite a lot about that odd fish.

For the last two years I have found a real friend in Prof. Kugler, full of goodness, patience and *esprit;* I have learnt the history of art from him, and you will find his name at the beginning of a *Guide to the Artistic Treasures of Belgium,* which I wrote on a trip last autumn, and of which my father will send you a printed copy very soon.

I am quite content here. Frau Bettina v. Arnim consoles me for many of the ugly sides of Berlin, and I often visit her. My German friends are those I count on most. At times, however, I feel very sad when I think how soon I shall have to say farewell to this wonderful country.

This winter, and the winter before, I finished some things for Ranke's Seminar, which I should like to show you. One is on Charles Martel, the other, inspired by last summer, on the wicked Archbishop Conrad of Cologne, the leader of the German Interregnum. The latter fills 254 pages. Ranke spoke of having it printed; but one never knows where one is with that Satiricus.

To Gottfried Kinkel★

Berlin, 21 March 1842

Since yesterday something that looks like spring has announced its arrival, so I take courage and at long last answer your letter. To be sure, I can give you no news, for in Berlin, as everyone knows, nothing ever happens. There could be no more miserable business under the sun than to be a correspondent here and under the necessity of writing articles. Before anything else, and before I forget it, I must give you the date of my departure from Berlin; it will take place *circa* 10th June 1842, so that it is quite possible I shall spend the 29th June with you. I shall begin with an eight-day visit to Dresden.

My *Guide* (to the art of Belgium) is even now making its rounds of the publishers, and will probably return very soon unprinted and unpublished. Material for a *Weltschmerz* poem: your *Otto Schütz* and my *Guide*, lying next to one another on the same desk! My *Guide* does not really matter, but it would be sad about your *Schütz;* that's the difference. I do not mean to compromise my *Hochstaden* by circulating it, although I always had the public in mind, and not little Ranke. Still, he was really quite pleased and said I ought to have it printed, but smiled maliciously as he said so, and I was puzzled as to what he meant.

There is little to tell you of *poeticis.* I have latterly been in a thoroughly good mood for poetry, but distractions and work brought it all to nothing. I have written a boisterous story for my friend Ed. Schauenburg, "Three Poor Devils," that takes place in Rüdesheim and fills *circa* two galleys; but I can only show it to my closest friends as it is altogether too boisterous. Perhaps I will bring you the sketch to Bonn.

Then a short while back I began work on a tragedy, *Johann Parricida,* which I thought of sending into the *concours*—since I always sell the skin before shooting the bear (or is it a donkey this time?); but it had too many failings and I have dropped the plan.

A libretto, about which I think I have already written to you, progresses slowly and seems to me *a priori* to have misfired. It's the saga of the Swan Knight. . . . A whole series of historical undertakings are occupying my thoughts; they would suffice to fill a man's life for eighty years, and I hope I won't live that long. One vow I have made; to try to write a readable style my whole life long, and always to aim at what is interesting rather than at dry, factual completeness. It is really a shame; the work of most German historians is only read by scholars, and that is why the moment he appeared Ranke found a huge hungry public. The French have been much shrewder, and Ranke learned a lot from them, only he won't admit it. People are always talking about the art of writing history, and many of them think they have done enough when they replace Schlosser's labyrinthine sentences by the dry narration of facts. But no, my dear chap, it's a matter of sifting the facts, of selecting what can interest *man;* if you can achieve something in that direction, even the book-worm will have to thank you. I have fallen on a lucky period for studying history; the public is taking to history more than ever before and would never have turned away from it if our donkeys of historians had not gone mad over their own aims and ends—the greatest of them are the worst offenders.

To　Gottfried Kinkel

Berlin, 13 June 1842

. . . You ask for my views on present-day political philosophy and ethics. This is what I think about it.*

* *N.B.* I hammered this out myself.

Practically all European peoples have had what is called the historical ground pulled from under their feet, Prussia into the bargain. The complete negation in matters of State, Church, Art and Life, that occurred at the end of last century, precipitated (among the better ones: developed) such an enormous mass of objective knowledge into even moderately active minds that a restoration of the old status, in which the people were really still minors, is quite unthinkable. Just as nowadays Art had lost its naïvety, and the styles of every age are all objectively present, *one beside the other,* so too with the State; a personal interest in the particularities of his State has had to give place, in the individual, to a conscious idealism that involves free choice. Restorations, however well meant, and however much they seem to offer the only way out, cannot obscure the fact that the nineteenth century began with a *tabula rasa* in relation to everything. I neither praise nor find fault with it, it is simply a fact, and the Princes would do well to face up squarely to the difference between their former and their present position. The frightening accentuation of the rights of the individual consists in this: *cogito* (whether correctly or falsely doesn't matter) *ergo regno*. I still anticipate frightful crises, but mankind will survive them, and Germany will then perhaps attain its golden age. But what, in the meanwhile, is the individual to do? If he is unprejudiced and intelligent the prevailing spiritual currents will help him to form a philosophical postulate, and according to that he must live. There is one thing no revolution can rob him of: his inner truth. One will have to be still more frank, and still more honest than in the past, and perhaps love will found a new Reich on the ruins of the old States. As far as my unimportant self is concerned, I should never think of being an agitator or a revolutionary; a revolution is only lawful when it erupts unconsciously and unsummoned out of the ground. So I shall dedicate myself with all my strength to the advancement of the German spirit, and do what I think right. . . .

PS. Forgive the grubby paper; and may Frau Directrix[30] too forgive me; my writing-paper is at an end. *Schelling,* so it is said, has miscarried with his *philosophia secunda.* You will be sure to find the most comprehensive review of his doctrine in the *Deutschen Jahrbüchern.* I attended his lectures a couple of times as an outsider during the most turgid of dogmatic discussions,[31] and explained it all to myself as follows: Schelling is a gnostic in the proper sense of the word, like Basilides. Hence all that is sinister, monstrous, formless in this part of his doctrine. I thought that at any moment some monstrous Asiatic God on twelve legs would come waddling in and with twelve arms take six hats off six heads. Little by little even the Berlin students will not be able to put up with his frightful, half-nonsensical, intuitional, contemplational form of expression. It is awful to have to listen to long historical explanations and discussions of the

30. Kinkel's wife.
31. Kierkegaard attended the same lectures and thought as poorly of them as Burckhardt.

destiny of Messias, epically drawn out, complicated and entirely formless. Anyone who can love Schelling's Christ must have a large heart. *En attendant,* the great world here is interested in Schelling from an orthodox, pietistic, aristocratic standpoint; interested in the way this unfortunate city has of always having sympathies or antipathies without knowing why, simply at a word dropped by a Minister. Such disgusting servility in deed is unknown in Vienna and Munich, that is my opinion. Vale.

To Willibald Beyschlag*

Berlin, 14 June 1842

In my letter to Frau Directrix, you will find how and why you will most probably discover me still here in October. In the said winter we shall both be here, and can write poetic letters and Tenzonen to our beloved M.K.[32] Isn't Sefren[33] coming to Berlin at all? I count on you and him to provide me with society this winter. And anyone who wants to know Berlin does well to come here for the first time in late autumn.

I am an exile and shall always look upon myself as one in Berlin, as long as the town and its surroundings continue to jar on me with their shrill discordant notes.

O for just one sight of a crooked, narrow old street in a Rhenish town, where the rocks and the blue mountains look down from above; for I suffer great distress in this sandy desert! You may laugh at me, for always lamenting in this tone; but in time you too will know what it means to moan and groan! In any case I advise you, dear Willibald, to leave a door ajar for the summer of 1843, so that in case of an all too violent antipathy for Berlin, you can pack your traps at a moment's notice and go and settle

32. The Maikäfer Club.
33. Karl Fresenius, another member of the Club.

elsewhere for the summer. I am nailed down here, and my advice is thus contrary to my personal advantage.

I say nothing here about Italy; the Rhine would satisfy all my longings. After all, you must long ago have recognized the one-sided bent of my nature towards contemplation. My whole life long I have never yet thought philosophically, and never had any thought at all that was not connected with something external. I can do nothing unless I start out from contemplation. And of course I include in contemplation spiritual contemplation, e.g., historical contemplation issues from the impression we receive from sources. What I build up historically is not the result of criticism and Speculation, but on the contrary, of imagination, which fills up the lacunae of contemplation. History, to me, is always poetry for the greater part; a series of the most beautiful artistic compositions. Accordingly I simply don't believe in an *a priori* standpoint; that is a matter for the World Spirit, not for the man of history.

And so my poetry will always lack real depth, though not warmth and enthusiasm. My historical work will perhaps become readable in time, agreeable even, but where there is no inner *picture* to be set down on paper it is bound to be insolvent. I owe you this hint, so that you should judge my Archbishop fairly. My entire historical work, like my passion for travel, my mania for natural scenery and my interest in art, springs from an enormous thirst for contemplation. But enough about my own person.

If you write to Sefren, tell him he will shortly get a letter from me. Though he has become a philosopher, he will continue to understand me.

Your songs prove a long, silent love of poetry. You must have written poetry for a long time; why did we never hear anything about it in Bonn?

To   Karl Fresenius*

Berlin, 19 June 1842

. . . Although you are a philosopher, you must allow me the truth of the following: A man like me, who is altogether incapable of speculation, and who does not apply himself to abstract thought for a single minute in the whole year, does best to try and clarify the most important questions of his life and studies in the way that comes naturally to him. My surrogate is *contemplation*, daily clearer and directed more and more upon essentials. I cling by nature to the concrete, to visible nature, and to history. But as a result of drawing ceaseless analogies between *facta* (which comes naturally to me) I have succeeded in abstracting much that is universal. Above this manifold universal there hovers, I know, a still higher universal, and perhaps I shall be able to mount that step too one day. You would not believe how, little by little, as a result of this possibly one-sided effort, the *facta* of history, works of art, the monuments of all ages gradually acquire significance as witnesses to a past stage in the development of the spirit. Believe me, when I see the present lying quite clearly in the past, I feel moved by a shudder of profound respect. The highest conception of the history of mankind: the development of the spirit to freedom, has become my leading conviction, and consequently my studies cannot be untrue to me, cannot let me down, and must remain my good genius all through my life.

Another man's speculations could never satisfy me, and still less help me, even if I were able to adopt them. I shall be influenced by them as by the spirit prevailing in the air of the nineteenth century; I shall even perhaps be unconsciously led by certain tendencies in modern philosophy. Leave me to experience and feel history on this lower level instead of understanding it from the standpoint of first principles. There will always be odd fish like me about. The unending riches that stream in upon me through the lower medium of immediate feeling are already making me happy beyond measure and will surely enable me to achieve something, though not necessarily in scientific form, and then perhaps even the philosopher will be able to make use of it.

You may reply that speculation is part of my endeavour, its second, more important half. One day perhaps it will take me by the arm, when I grow dissatisfied with what has satisfied me hitherto and begin to sigh for the brightest stars in heaven. I shall always enjoy talking to you about these things because you like me and don't run away at once, proudly turning up your philosophical nose the moment anyone does not express himself in good Hegelian. You see, I respect Speculation as in every epoch one of the highest expressions of the spirit; only instead of Speculation itself, I am looking for its correlative in history. A little while ago I applied myself to a short survey of the philosophy of history during the last six centuries, and mean to do the same for antiquity; and only then (in any case this summer, as ever is) shall I take up Hegel's philosophy of history; I want to see if I can understand something of it and whether it makes sense. Only it's a pity that, in spite of being quite unconstrained, my mind is not formed on a larger, freer scale.

To me history is poetry on the grandest scale; don't misunderstand me, I do not regard it romantically or fantastically, all of which is quite worthless, but as a wonderful process of chrysalis-like transformations, of ever new disclosures and revelations of the spirit. This is where I stand on the shore of the world—stretching out my arms towards the *fons et origo* of all things, and that is why history to me is sheer poetry, that can be mastered through contemplation. You philosophers go further, your system penetrates into the depths of the secrets of the world, and to you history is a source of knowledge, a science, because you see, or think you see, the *primum agens* where I only see mystery and poetry. I should like to be able to say it more clearly; but perhaps you see what I mean. In your letter you asked very sympathetically about the melancholy sadness that comes out in my letters. I was certainly not depressed by anything external; that kind of thing rarely upsets me. But think of me as an artist, learning and aspiring—for I too live on images and contemplation—and then think of the melancholy that from time to time comes over artists, simply because they cannot give form to what has awakened within them—then you will be able to explain to yourself why it is that I too am sometimes sad, however cheerful I may otherwise be in heart and mind.

To Heinrich Schreiber

Berlin, 1 July 1842

For almost two months now I have been tutor in the house of Count Perponcher, the former Dutch Ambassador, with a salary of 50 louis-d'or, free meals and lodging. I am entirely free until eleven o'clock in the morning and after nine in the evening, and between times I can snatch two or three of the best hours of the day. Yet I am not sure you would not have counselled me against taking the step. My patroness, Frau Bettina, did not at all want me to be here; she was afraid I should be untrue to my liberal principles. As though an historian could change his principles from one day to another!

You will probably already have received my "Belgian Art" from my father. Only two words in defence of my undertaking. I found the purely objective, impersonal standpoint of the usual guide-book inadequate, and so was not afraid for once, by way of trial, to let the fullest subjectivity have its way.

In two years' time I want to go for a few months to Paris and then, if possible, for a year to Italy, and make use of Libraries and Museums all over the place, so that I shall be in a position to write:

1.   a history of art from Constantine to the Ottos or the Hohenstaufen, and
2.   a history of the Counter-Reformation in Switzerland.

What do you say to all that?

To Gottfried Kinkel

Dresden, 19 September 1842

Just a few words to you too, dearest friend, while Geibel,[34] whom I happily met here, makes his farewell visits. With the greatest difficulty, I extracted six days' leave from the Countess for a visit to Dresden, thinking to live quietly there, entirely by myself; in fact, I shortly met Geibel on the street, and the result was that he moved over to me, and goes with me to Berlin tomorrow.

I have been meaning to write to you for a long time! What a long vigil, waiting for a propitious moment!

First of all, thank you for the Songs, which reduced me to complete despair. All the time I was in Berlin, fit to collapse, every street and alley in Bonn was full of high spirits. But just wait, I shall be with you again; you shall not have everything your own way.

I got your parcel at a really odious moment, and it strengthened me in my defiance. As the Countess still hasn't stopped nagging at me, I shall, whatever happens, give up my post this winter, and if possible stop a month in Bonn on my way to Paris, somewhere about May, that was so heavenly last year.

I hardly dare think what Berlin is going to look like tomorrow evening. I should never have imagined Dresden so rich in wonderful things. The most wonderful material for short stories leaps out at one from every nook and cranny among the Palaces and Gardens, and the Strong Augustus and his Rococo is a theme ready to one's hand. Napoleon and his train of Kings in the year 1811 haunt every corner of the place.

34. The poet.

To Gottfried Kinkel

Berlin, 25 November 1842

Out of sheer excitement over your letter I never got as far as writing all day yesterday; your picture was uninterruptedly before my eyes; I would risk everything for you and try to merit your unmerited love. I have the feeling that we are not always to be separated, and that I shall some day or other be able to offer you something. As long as I was in Bonn, I could not say how I loved you; but now I can be freer in my relations towards you, I am inwardly more complete, and come to you as I am, loving and needing love. Don't forsake me! I shall do what I can to reward you for it.

You have summoned me to be best man at your wedding, but I can't promise to be there. On the 1st November next I must be in Basle to lecture, God knows what about! And then too my family are asking after me and are upset because I have set aside two months for Paris. The real thing is that my sister may be getting married at about the same time, which may well alter or postpone my Paris plans to such a degree that I should have to go there from Basle in the summer. But all that is far off. To let my heart speak frankly, I would sooner be at your wedding, as my sister and her fiancé are in fortunate circumstances, and have friends enough; my presence there would be a purely ceremonial service, which someone else could fulfil as well; but for you, it would be a service of love, the first that I should have been able to perform for you. It is not at her wedding that I want to support my sister, but afterwards, when she is alone, longing for the brother for whom she has suffered and prayed so much, and who occupied a large place in her heart because he understood her!

Finally, I am not sure that I can fulfil the functions of best man. I don't dance! You had better mention that. I should not in any case be able to stay on for the Founder's Day; I thought of arriving about the middle of April, and leaving about the middle of May. Brussels alone will take me eight days. As far as depends upon me, then, I accept; but I cannot answer for what may happen. In this way, I should be in Paris by the middle of June, which is soon enough.

I am altogether delighted that you have succeeded in getting Habicht to take my "Archbishop"; I accept all your propositions, and in case Habicht should become intractable, you have full powers, should it be necessary, to leave out part of it. The enclosed official note contains your authority to act for me, as far as the publisher is concerned. Even if I were never to see a heller, it doesn't matter as long as 'tis printed.

You will probably be astonished and ask: Why this change of mind? In the first place you gave me courage; secondly, I accept what you did behind my back as a pointer from God; thirdly, the fear of having to run all over the place played no small part in my hesitation; fourthly, I now need not copy it out again for the green baize table in Basle, or even latinize it, and can satisfy the examiners with a printed copy and a miserable bit of "Charles Martel" which is already part of it in Latin; fifthly, in a fortnight's time I shall be sending you the *exposé* of the Constitution of Cologne, rewritten, but not augmented, beginning with the words (early on in Cap. V): "It cannot be denied that the Archbishop . . . ," etc.

To Gottfried Kinkel

Berlin, 3 March 1843

I leave here *circa* the 20th March, going first, perhaps, through the Harz, but in any case via Naumburg and Jena. Then through the Schwarzathal (even if there is snow) to Coburg and Bamberg, for which I have a strong inclination of long standing. Then (perhaps as far as Nuremberg) to Würzburg, from whence I shall go through Odenwald to Heidelberg, Weinheim, Speyer. Then through Worms, Oppenheim, Nierstein, Bodenheim, Laubenheim to Mainz and Frankfort, where I must remain *circa* four days for the sake of the second-hand bookshops. Then slowly and determinedly down the Rhine. From Coblenz I shall visit Limburg. Thus

I shall arrive in Bonn between 20th and 25th and stay on for your wedding. That gives me a full month's rest, though with the following *servitude* hanging over it: two to three visits to Cologne, a tour in the Ahr, and a visit to Siegen to see Schauenburg, who is there for the moment, teaching in the Gymnasium.

Immediately after your wedding I go down the Rhine to Cleves, to Siegfried Nagel, and from there to Holland, Belgium and Paris, where I hope to arrive about the 20th June.

On the way I hope to sketch, compose, and see a lot. (Under the last rubric I subsume pottering about, coffee-housing, etc.) I am sending a small trunk in advance to Bonn and travel with a knapsack and a nightgown. I shall pay special attention this time to Saxon and Franconian Byzantine, and to the Main wines, of which up till now I only know Bocksbeutel.

The eighth sheet of Conrad is already corrected. I expect the ninth today. Altogether there will be eleven, which I hope to be able to correct here.

And now God preserve you, dear friend. I shall write to you again about the middle of this month, and, God willing, send you a sign of life on my travels, to Bonn, so that you should not think I have got lost.

To Gottfried Kinkel

Berlin, 16 March 1843

The Petition of the Estates of the Grand Duchy of Posnania and the Royal Responsum thereto appeared in the papers here yesterday. It throws a terrible, glaring shaft of light into the abyss towards which we are hurrying. One can see that His Majesty thinks he is in the right, and in fact the law of the realm is safeguarded completely in the reply. But its approval is no longer safeguarded, and public opinion and the wishes of the nation still less so. Woe to the adviser who led the King to this step;

the King himself will one day curse him, when it's too late. They dare to call a decision, passed through the Estates by a majority, a party measure!—and threaten not to summon the Estates again. And so in a word Prussia is in the same state as Hanover. Not to mention the really ugly mood in which the Estates again refused—what sort of advice can have been given to the King, if he thinks that his arguments against the freedom of the press make any impression on the public! I think I see more clearly in these matters than hitherto, and it seems to me that quite early on the King was confirmed by his teachers in the old notion of the State (i.e., Absolutism in juridical form), and cannot get beyond certain deductions therefrom—which is no doubt what would happen to us in his position. Moreover, he is much more dependent on his entourage than one imagines, and this involves him more and more in a certain way of seeing things which is bound to lead to a break sooner or later. I am really saddened at the thought of these things; it is just as though the Palace in Berlin lay under a magic spell, as though the King himself longed for freedom, peace and understanding, without being able to attain them; for, through the enchanted windows of the Palace, the whole countryside looks flourishing, rich and peaceful, and the groans and complaints that sound in the distance are declared by the Minister to be the party voices of one or two ill-disposed individuals standing sullenly in the background like oaks and pine trees.

Addio, dear friend; in five weeks' time I shall be with you.

To Gottfried Kinkel

Paris, 16 June 1843

I arrived here on the 8th and have been enjoying Paris for eight days; mornings in the Louvre and the churches; evenings on the boulevards and at the theatre. But so that you should see how dependable I am, let me tell you that on the first of this month I sent a review of your Poems

Pont des Arches, Liége, 1843

Bei Ponte rotto

Ponte Rotto, Rome, 1847

to the *Kölner Zeitung,* from Rotterdam, and it must have arrived as I paid the stamp on it; though the rascals haven't printed it yet.

I saw Hugo's *Bourgraves.* The intentions are here and there very grandiose, but in the end it is weighed down by nonsense. Beauvallet, in his best moments, reminds me of what I have heard tell of Ludwig Devrient. But the Alexandrine is an unbearable line, even at the Théâtre Français. At the Odéon I heard an exquisite little thing by Molière. Then came Racine's *Andromaque,* and I fled after the First Act. What do you say to the little play I saw at the Théâtre du Palais Royal—*La fille de Figaro*—a female Figaro, i.e., everybody's friend, who arranges things and protects two lovers through all kinds of intrigues? Beaumarchais' Figaro is a rascal and does what he does for money, while *La fille de Figaro* (who has nothing to do with Figaro) does everything out of kindness of heart. It is very strange that on the French stage one very rarely comes across a great talent, but an average good French actor is always average *good,* while an average good German actor is, as a rule, average *bad.* That is why even some hole-in-the-corner theatre in Paris is *always an ensemble,* and the audience can enjoy it. But no one can conceal the fact that French drama, that is tragedy, is in a parlous way.

To Willibald Beyschlag

Paris, 19 June 1843

Shall I confess to you or not, that one can be homesick for Berlin in Paris? That is, not for Berlin itself, not for what it contains, but for you all. You can have no idea how solitary one's life here can be, in the midst of the colossal noise and the everlasting show. But just wait, and I shall make some acquaintances! Of course I shall not, I know, experience another winter like the one in Berlin in 1842–43. Yesterday it was terribly hot and close in Paris; and as it was Sunday, the streets were crowded with people, so I went out to Saint-Denis to restore myself with an historical, elegiac cure of the very first order. It was three o'clock as I walked into the beautiful cool old abbey church, to which all the memories of France for centuries are linked. A mass of people crowded towards the crypt of the kings, while the organ thundered out its chords. The tombs are of course empty, but the bones all lie in the great central crypt which Napoleon had prepared for himself. One is driven through in under a quarter of an hour, from Clovis and Charles Martel to Louis XI and the remains of Marie Antoinette. On one wall one can see the barbaric mosaic portrait of Frédégonde taken from her tomb. And when one climbs up into the church again a Napoleon and a Louis-Philippe in huge stained-glass portraits shine down at one. Briefly, it's enough to send one mad. Above the High Altar waves the oriflamme of Philip Augustus, the one he took with him to Palestine. Now I know: next time I want a cure, I shall go out to Saint-Denis one morning and spend a couple of francs and have myself shut up in the crypt.

As for Paris itself, it is far from making the historical impression which one expects of it. In spite of the foolish love which French art and Paris society show for the Middle Ages and the Renaissance, everyone is anxiously on the look-out for what is most modern, and a hundred life-size advertisements cry down every memory of the past at all the classical spots in the town. One only gets a mythical notion of the first Revolution; on the whole, Paris is far more absorbed in an anxious care for the future than in recollections of its past, although the individual memorials are legion. I do not think it can be very long before there is another explosion. In the meantime everyone is living from day to day, that is the predominating impression.

To be day after day without company, taking in this, that, and the other thing, quite confuses one; more than once I walked till I was silly. There is no doubt about it, Paris is beautiful; when I compare the view from the Berlin Marienturm, over the dreary rows of houses, and the still more dreary heaths and steppes with the magnificent view from the Arc de Triomphe at the Étoile, I realize that only you and my Bonn friends are lacking for it to be a heavenly *amusement*.

And now, above all, one thing more. I long for news of Hermann. Couldn't the fellow come to Paris, if he is ever exiled? Then for his sake I shall move into the Quartier Latin, and remain there till the end of November for love of him . . . and economize as best I can. The business with Bettina was, I fear, a false step;[35] she cannot do nearly as much as one imagines. . . .

To   Albrecht Wolters*

Paris, 20 July 1843

À *propos* of Versailles. One Sunday nearly three weeks ago, the Great Fountains, as they are called, were playing. As I stood there looking at a pair of gods belching forth water, opposite me, behind a halo of shimmering water spray I saw—little Ranke. I went up to him—I would far sooner have ignored his presence, but it was possible he had already seen me. He gave me a very superior, diplomatic smile; in that moment he was shrouded in a little stale air from the court of Versailles of long ago. I tried to pump him about what he was doing in Paris, and maliciously gave him to suppose that I was thinking of diplomatic missions. He smiled doubly as delicately as before and fell into the trap, answering: "I have found some very choice things in the archives!" I knew quite well that his diplomatic missions were of no importance, but he is flattered if one appears to believe in them. A couple of days later one of my companions was with a well-known German, and told him about our meeting with Professor Ranke. "Ach! little Ranke," he said, "is quite simply a swine! Do you know," he went on, "not long ago I met him at a soirée

35. Bettina had tried to help Schauenburg in his difficulties with the authorities.

at Thiers, and the latter began talking insultingly about the late King of Prussia and Queen Louise, obviously in order to provoke Ranke to contradiction . . . but *Ranke remained quite silent."* Ranke did not know the German and thought he was unobserved.

I shall have to sweat hard this winter in Basle, prepare lectures, write books, give lessons, etc. And when I have carried on like that for a couple of years then, God willing, quieter times will follow, and a more or less secure, if poor, job. Journalism appeals to me less and less; I do not think I am really fitted for it, and fear the inevitable distractions that go with it. However, something will come of it all. For the moment I am going a great deal to the theatre, sometimes even to two in an evening, to the galleries, and daily to the Bibliothèque Royale, where one is treated most liberally, can get out even the rarest books, and copy as much as one likes in ink. If I did not know Paris I should be lacking in a great deal that is essential to my calling. I can hardly say that I respect it, for the masses are just as unstable as the masses in Berlin, and the town makes no real historical or moral impression, though it is unbelievably rich in individual things.

To Gottfried Kinkel

Paris, 20 August 1843

In Basle I shall live a life of polite reserve; there is no one I can altogether confide in; and there is no one with whom one can have an unreserved companionship of mind. The few Lecturers are respectable young gentlemen of the town, with whom it would never occur to me to try to get on easy terms; for you have simply no idea of the futility and ubiquity of the purse-proud in Basle, however wide your experience. One or two of the University staff are well disposed towards me, but you know well enough what a gulf divides the teaching staff and the Lecturers, and then I have to treat Wackernagel, who has turned pietist, so Hoffmann von

Fallersleben tells me, like a child. Really there is nobody left but my old friend Picchioni,[36] at one time a Carbonari and an engineer in Lombardy; a splendid, really remarkable personality, courageous and young at sixty, in spite of all his misfortunes. He is not, of course, a scholar, but has lived through our century with his senses alive and can tell a long story on the score of human folly. He is Professor Extraordinary and is on good terms with everyone.

A German whose youthful illusions are shipwrecked very easily becomes sullen and unbearable; Latins, in such cases, become thoroughly likeable; I have been able to observe the fact freely here; the young Frenchmen who take any part in the decadent politics and the social confusion of France are excitable, rude, ill-humoured, whereas there is nothing more agreeable than an elderly Frenchman who has been deceived and disappointed by Convention, Directoire, Consulate, Empire, Restoration and the July Revolution. Then begins that charming, affectionate *Allerweltshumor* which even carries the youth along with it.

I am very curious about Schnaase.[37] Kugler is as happy as a child that the work is dedicated to him. O what a lovely letter I got from Kugler! He offers me his friendship! And that privilege is granted to very few students arriving from abroad. He has always spared me, and yet always told me the truth (e.g., about my poems), and now quite freely gives me a mark of his friendship that means a very great deal from so reserved a man, and one to all appearances cold. And what have I been able to do for him up to now?

O Lord, my poetry has quite dried up! The perpetual excitement that one feels in Paris consumes the little bit of recollectedness that one can save up each day. So how am I to answer your beautiful *Maikäfer* letter? Quite alone as I am, one has no humour left, heaven knows, and I don't call laughing out loud in the middle of the street at the hundred million

36. Burckhardt dedicated the *Renaissance* to Picchioni, who had been one of his teachers in Basle.
37. The young historian of art, Karl Schnaase.

follies of the Parisians, humour; and though the ground sometimes quakes beneath my feet, for example in Notre-Dame or in the Tuilleries, I am not inspired.

The Spanish affair is shocking, and proves how infernal pious old Guizot's policy is and always will be. You ought to see the anger of the French at the futility of their foreign policy! The Ministry, so they say, ought to risk a brilliant demonstration for the sake of French prestige. Only never, my dear fellow, believe in the loyalty of France's foreign policy, for they always think they are in the right as against foreign powers, however disgustingly they may behave. For the French still believe they have rights over Europe, and other countries, and look upon the infamies of their Ministry towards foreign countries as a necessary *"réparation d'honneur"* for 1815. The idea that the Rhineland belongs to France, by human and divine right, is still *quite general;* I always reply to it with contemptuous politeness, as every argument that I have ever put forward breaks down before the narrow-mindedness of the people here. The French carry pride beyond the furthest limits of national pride, and I am beginning to believe that the nation is suffering from some feverish madness that can only be explained by the terrible excitements of the last fifty years. I am convinced it has left an incurable, gnawing injury in the heart of this generous people, with all its great potentialities. One cannot burn and lay waste Europe with impunity. You ought to see the lowering of political life that accompanies their anger! People still get excited, but they are worn out, and the Government can do as it likes. The sessions of the Chambers are treated with open contempt, even by the Left; all trust in the Republican forms of the July dynasty and in the Constitution has vanished. I have heard the following loudly applauded at the theatre: (1) a bitter, very lively and excellent satire on the Republic of 1799; (2) an unspeakable and thoroughly aristocratic contempt for the *Épiciers* and the *Épiciers'* wives at court at the present time, who take a "left" line; (3) innumerable little innuendoes dragged into almost every play about the meaninglessness of constitutional forms. That is how things stand.

After all that, you may well ask: What *is* the rascal doing in Paris?

Answer: he spends three hours of every working day at the Bibliothèque Royale making excerpts from all sorts of things; for the last six weeks he has had out Italian manuscripts on Switzerland (his and other rascals' country); since the end of June, however, he has begun to study the history of the Burgundian invasion of Switzerland in the year 1444. For next year there is to be a great celebration at Basle; it will be exactly four hundred years since the Armagnacs gave battle near Sankt Jacob in the neighbourhood of Basle. Johannes von Müller is the last man to have told the story from original sources, somewhat bombastically indeed, and inadequately. So the fellow is now going through sources and manuscripts in Paris and finds that everything happened quite differently from what old Müller says; and he is preparing an occasional work on the subject for the celebration. But it cannot be handled without gloves, lest offended national pride should be roused to anger and poorly repay the rascal, particularly on the occasion of his *début* in Switzerland.

To Johanna Kinkel

Paris, 21 August 1843

Music here has reached a point where one can only say, Heaven protect us! Recently I heard *La Dame Blanche,* which really cannot be said to have much style about it—it sounded quite old-fashioned, as though from another world. All the *best* things in the latest Paris operas are stolen from the Italians. There is neither rhyme nor reason in the rest; harmony and phrasing are usually cut about and abbreviated in a most intolerable way—and provided everything is *new,* little else matters. Bellini and Donizetti, who are inwardly so impotent, at least have the sense not to try to be piquant, while Balfe, Isouard, Halévy and company, having glanced at Meyerbeer's superb instrumentation, bring out their worthless motifs with the most pretentious artistry. You ought to hear one of the arias out of *Puits d'Amour* (by Balfe) accompanied by an oboe and two harps! *Tant de bruit* (and it's nothing more) *pour une omelette*. It is generally admitted that the future of French music depends, for the time being, on Meyerbeer's next opera. I can imagine your thinking: that's a lot of hope!

To Gottfried Kinkel

Basle, 26 November 1843

Dear friend, if only I could live near you! But for the moment I am hardly living at all, i.e., I am slogging away. If my former companions were to guess that I was so polite and reserved with them because they are all of them too boring and philistine for words, I should be attacked and slandered uninterruptedly. So nothing must be noticed. How true! Germany spoilt me by offering me the best company possible, and I naturally feel lost here — but I am quite prepared for that, and have memories enough to compensate for everything.

There is a simulacrum of an opposition here, all philistines, but of a somewhat different colour to the others; and among them some malicious ones, so that I don't want to get mixed up with them. Where politics are concerned, I am obliged to keep myself to myself, as I despise all parties: I know them all and belong to none. In the meanwhile I am slogging away at some lectures for next summer, on German History, beginning with all the "Alt Germania" nonsense. What I am to live on is not so clear; in the meanwhile Kugler has put me on to the new directors of the *Brockhaus Encyclopaedia* (ninth edition) for the articles on Art, which are very well paid. Letter E was revised and sent to the printer ten days ago. Kugler had revised A–D, but it was too much for him, as he has a lot of other things on hand, so he referred Brockhaus to me. If I could, little by little, become a correspondent for other things as well — for the *Leipziger Zeitung* for instance, I should have an untroubled existence. We shall see. . . .

I assume you got the money?

To   Eduard Schauenburg

Basle, 30 November 1843

I am arming myself to announce lectures for next summer on German History and the History of Art—for whether a lecturer at a university with only twenty-eight students gets to the point of lecturing is another matter. Please don't spread it abroad that there are so few students; it might prejudice the University still more. So you see what a fool I should be to plan my life (an expression I altogether abominate) on conditions ruling here. My entire prospects consist in: the highly problematical professorship at present occupied by a professor in the best years of his life, at 100 louis-d'or, which would moreover vanish if the University were to disappear, as seems imminently probable. Still, I can of course hope to earn some money with lectures for the general public.

To   Willibald Beyschlag

Basle, 14 January 1844

Yes, I fully believe that your feeling for the Church is genuine, faithful and true. I know that self-respecting people hold to the Church and that the Church point of view is still entirely justified and will undoubtedly remain so for a time. Little by little my studies have convinced me that the Protestant Church too, as the preserver of a common treasure, is a Church and not just a feeble external imitation of the Medieval Church. And I only respect you the more for coming to closer grips with it, in spite of the fact that you are not unaware of the contempt and scorn it has to endure, and although you know that the leading lights of the nation have fallen away from it. I have broken with the Church for ever, from quite personal motives, because I quite literally can't make sense of it. My moral life, *sit venia verbo,* marches forward without the help of the

Church, and retreats without the sting of ecclesiastical conscience. The Church has lost all power over me, as over so many others, and in a period of dissolution that is no more than is to be expected.

Yet this need no longer separate us, since the ground on which we meet and clasp hands is neutral ground, as far as the Church is concerned. Only take care, Balder, when it comes to practical life! Will you be spiritually free enough to recognize in others a spontaneous, personal and perhaps altogether undenominational religion, the witness to a period of disintegration, and to treat everyone accordingly?

I should not, for example, ask you, as a member of the Consistorial Council, to vote for the appointment of Bruno Bauer,[38] for people like him ought to be honest enough to keep their distance from *sancta theologia*. But what, for example, would be the position regarding the appointment of an honest history teacher with no ties whatsoever to any Church? Why should you, of all people, have to be in the thick of the coming *mêlée* between the Church and the intelligentsia? You certainly can't think that the present restoration of Church communities is merely a reaction against rationalism, and is, consequently, transitory; you believe things are moving towards a genuine restoration. If that were possible, it might perhaps win my approval.

I will, for once; say straight out what so many *viri doctissimi* think and dare not express: from our point of view Christianity has entered the realm of purely human periods of history; it has brought up the nations morally, and given them strength and independence to reconcile themselves from now on, not with God, but *inwardly,* with their own consciences. Time will tell in what forms of thought the Germanic and Latin peoples will possibly once again approach God personally. God has only to be personal again, and people will believe in His personality. I believe His last Incarnation lives in us all.

O, had I lived when Jesus of Nazareth walked the countryside of

38. Bruno Bauer, 1809–1882, an adherent of the young Hegelian school whose destructive criticism of the Gospels ended in violent polemics.

Judaea—I should have followed Him and should have allowed pride and arrogance to vanish in love of Him, and should no longer have thought of my own independence and worth—for if one were close to Him, what would it matter if one were lost as an individual? But though longing for Him, we are separated by eighteen centuries, and it is only when I am alone and in moments of melancholy longing, that a majestic image appears before my soul and consoles me, the image of the Greatest of Men. As God, Christ is a matter of indifference to me—what can one make of Him in the Trinity? As man He is the light of my soul, because He is the most *beautiful* figure in history. Call that religion who likes—I can do nothing with the concept. You, dear Balder, will regard it as the aftermath of an aesthetic Christianity with none too savoury a reputation. As far as I am concerned think what you like; I make no claim to call it religion.

30 January

And now about Kinkel. For a long time past I have made no secret of the fact that I prefer him as philosopher to theologian, and believe that since people are determined to prop up the old orthodoxy *à tout prix,* the freedom to teach will be more and more restricted. If you don't know whence the wind is blowing at present, read the shoulder-shrugging article on Schleiermacher and his school in the *Literarische Zeitung.* That is, unfortunately, the opinion at present prevailing in the Ministry. Moreover, I have no illusion on the point that from now on even the most liberally minded Kultusminister will be unable to tolerate *freedom of theological instruction* as I understand it; that is, as long as Church and State are not separated. With every breath of fresh air, learning *lays bare* the disintegration of the Church as an inner fact, and hastens it as an external one. *Summa:* until Church and State are separated, the most prudent thing a negative theologian can do is to change over to another faculty. The separation will, moreover, take a long time, and the real battle will only begin once that has happened. So much was clear to me when I gave up theology.

To Johanna Kinkel

Basle, 29 January 1844

No one grieves because I avoid going into society, no one was waiting for me, and if I am silent till my hair goes grey, not a soul will bother themselves about it. That is as it should be. I do not for a moment regard myself as a phoenix, and there are plenty of people here who are mentally superior to me. What a pity that the majority should be the victims of an odious philistinism! If I don't spoil my matter by being impatient, then little by little I can perhaps encourage a friendly attitude to the visual arts.

I know perfectly well, dear Directrix, that you are examining this letter from every angle to see if it does not conceal something about my love affairs! I can only tell you that so far there *is* no love affair, as with experience I have grown careful and do not want to tie myself here in any way. I do not want to cause *the girl* unnecessary sorrows. That sounds conceited, but in the circumstances is a very appropriate ultimatum. Time will tell. Basle will never be my heaven, not even with her. Away! Away! That is my watchword, and will probably remain so.

To Eduard Schauenburg

29 January 1844

This evening there is a soirée at Wackernagel's. The Liberals have done him great injustice, just as they cold-shoulder those who are nearest them and who understand anything about art. I am more and more convinced that the Liberalism of the years 1840–1843 was only the first sour blossom that encloses the fruit, and is bound to fall. The victory of the new Liberalism which is bound to follow will be all the more complete, and a general public opinion will be formed, more and more free from extravagant notions in every field, and then the final victory will occur. Only a Liberalism of that kind, sustained by the people, will be able to direct power and form the basis of a new covenant.

To Gottfried Kinkel

Basle, 21 April 1844

Two main points: (*a*) Send me a copy of your lithographs as soon as you can, together with the compendium of notes; if I can make use of it perhaps I shall take a whole batch for use in my lectures. (*b*) From 1st June I shall be editing the local "Conservative" *Basler Zeitung,* which gives one an honest living, as long as one can bear it. I accepted mainly in order to exterminate by slow degrees the odious sympathy that exists among the ruling clique here for absolutism of every kind (e.g., the Russian) and on the other hand to come out against our raucous Swiss Radicals, which last I find precisely as repellent as the former. In doing so I shall draw upon myself, like all the editors of the *Basler Zeitung* hitherto, a continual stream of the vulgarest kind of personal abuse; but there is one consolation that will render me completely cold-blooded, and that is: Let the fellows have their fill of insults — two Post Stations north of Basle no one takes the faintest interest in their screams. The editorial work will take me, even when I am thoroughly accustomed to it, a good half-day, and that six days a week. "What will happen to poetry in the meanwhile, the devil alone knows, but one's first duty is to earn one's keep."

To Gottfried Kinkel

Basle, 22 May 1844

This afternoon I am going "across the fields" to Dornach, where I have
to go and greet my debtors; for you must know that I have taken over
the administration of the ruins of my property; though it only brings in
about 170 Reichstaler a year in rent I lie in wait for it like a lynx. Then
too, I must bid good-day to the Franciscans in Dornach so as to invite
myself as a guest to the next Portiuncula feast. May God prosper your
public lectures! As it has to be so, give up theology; one no longer comes
across a single green twig among its branches; the ground has been
worked over far too much. . . .

23 May

Among other work I have added to my notes on the sources of the history of art in the early Middle Ages and found more than 150 important
and/or minor passages in the 6th volume of Pertz. Witigowos buildings
at Reichenau are the most complete; about 120 verses on the decoration
and arrangements of the Abbey in the tenth century. I go on collecting,
and I shall soon have about 1000 quotations; and that does not include
Anastasius. No one else does anything of the kind because the labour is
too great for the artist and the *viri doctissimi* regard the material as quite
unimportant. Little by little I shall be in a position to become an authority
on the centuries from Constantine to the Hohenstaufen. . . .

To Hermann Schauenburg*

Basle, 10 June 1844

I feel at times as though I were already standing in the evening light, as though nothing much were to come of me. It is not the ideals that have failed; they remain true, but fate directs me more and more along by-ways that lead me far afield. Not long since I reflected earnestly whether I ought not to give up writing poetry for ever, but found it simply did not work; when all else fails it is, after all, my one consolation. Music no longer affords me much satisfaction; my other endeavours have most of them turned to dust. O, if only I had you here! How we would comfort one another. One cannot really correspond about such things. I think that a man of my age can rarely have experienced such a vivid sense of the insignificance and frailty of human things, in so far as they relate merely to the individual. But my respect for the universal, for the spirit of nations and of the past, increases correspondingly. How I like your *Lieder,* with their *laisser-aller* sounding through here and there. Send me more! I am at the moment so distracted that subjective, lyrical poetry has quite departed from me. Pictures, *Tableaux*—that is what I want; and in the background, lying in wait for me, is an ever-increasing longing for the drama. I'm a fool, am I not?

To Gottfried Kinkel

Basle, 18 April 1845

I must write and tell you that I am still alive and have not smelt powder this month. Things have passed off fairly well; the mobile anarchy, the leaders of which had in mind to go from canton to canton making havoc of everything, has for the moment run its head against the door-post of Lucerne; only, of course, sooner or later it will begin all over again and may very well bring the present form of existence in Basle to a close. Conditions in Switzerland—so disgusting and barbarous—have spoilt everything for me, and I shall expatriate myself as soon as I can; God willing, in the summer of 1846. The word freedom sounds rich and beautiful, but no one should talk about it who has not seen and experienced slavery under the loud-mouthed masses, called "the people," seen it with his own eyes, and endured civil unrest. There is nothing more wretched under the sun, *experte crede Ruperto,* than a government from under whose nose any club of political intriguers can steal the executive power, and that is left to tremble before "Liberalism," enthusiasm, boors and village magnates. I know too much history to expect anything from the despotism of the masses but a future tyranny, which will mean the end of history. The time will come in Germany too, when reasonable progress (with the Constitution for aim) will dissociate itself from blind, intriguing agitation. Until then you are factually political children, and ought to thank God that there are Prussian garrisons in Cologne, Coblenz and other places, so that the first crowd of communized boors cannot fall on you in the middle of the night, and carry you off bag and baggage. Believe me, "the political people" to whom certain ones boastfully appeal do not yet exist, in Germany or Switzerland at least; instead, there are the masses, and among them a number of splendid still undeveloped characters, ripe to fall into the hand of the first swine who comes along, and to behave like beasts.

Sapienti sat.

You simply cannot conceive how utterly this sort of business devastates one's mind and puts one out of humour. One cannot even work, not to mention better things. The last four weeks have been a total loss, entirely taken up by the newspaper and running about. The reason I remain here for another year is that I want to earn a little money, and calculate my patience with this degrading *métier* of journalist at about fourteen months; then, I know, it *can't* last any longer. I think I told you both that I have, in the interval, been appointed *Ausserordentlicher Professor* at the University, without salary; once I stop writing for the newspaper, I shall not earn anything here, and so might just as well live elsewhere, as I shall have to live on my earnings. But there can be no doubt I should live better, and cheaper too, almost anywhere else; and then I shall want to find something to do.

To Gottfried Kinkel

Basle, 28 June 1845

As far as the Orthodox are concerned, I saw it all coming in the winter of 1842–43. There was a smell of the High Priest about Balder[39] and Wolters, even then. But what I cannot understand is that Balder should want to convert you to the Lord, and in 1845. My advice to you would be to drop theological discussions, where you won't come across a single green twig. If, as I must conclude, you let yourself in for answering their whims and fancies, after giving up theology, then, to say the least, it's a luxury. Added to which those people have taken a *decision* to *will* to believe (more or less as one has to *decide* to take an emetic) and then nothing one can say is any good. Have the gentlemen really forgotten their Church history so completely? Do they no longer know that every Faith, so long as it was entitled to the dominion of the world, came upon men as a *power*? How enormously vital and positive the religion of even the heretics was! That Christianity has its great ages behind it is as evident to me as the fact that twice two is four; in what way its eternal content is to be saved in new forms, history will teach us in due course. But I am really sorry for the present restorers, though when they lay claim to the arm of the State, I despise them. Once let them have their way, one would be as

39. Willibald Beyschlag.

badly off in a couple of years as with the Jesuits, simply because they are more honourable than the latter, i.e., inwardly still more blind.

I see from the papers, and from what Freiligrath told me, that Socialism is increasing rapidly in the Rhineland, and I am curious to know whether something of it has really reached down among the wide masses. I think it's an altogether bad business, quite specially because it is combined with political discontent, and even in the form in which it appears comes as the logical continuation of the latter. As far as I personally am concerned, I have sported my oak against every sort of participation, and for this reason: because in a matter where means, end and starting-point are beyond control, one is bound to compromise oneself. And then I am firmly convinced that but for the forceful repression of political yearnings, socialistic yearnings would now be well in the background.

To   Gottfried Kinkel

Basle, All Saints, 1845

This winter I am continuing my lectures on Painting for the general public. The pietists tried, indirectly, to stop me; they would have preferred a more edifying lecturer to this child of the world. So now they shall get it as "worldly" as possible. What I said at the end of my essay on Murillo will be developed for their special benefit and the hair on their heads will stand up like quills, so that what was said may be fulfilled when I take my leave: And he went out and left a great stink behind him!

To Gottfried Kinkel

Basle, 11 January 1846

At the end of March I go straight to Rome. I feel absolutely certain that I shall never get there if I don't do something about it now. Although as a bachelor, living very simply, I cannot manage on less than 100 louis-d'or, I have saved a decent sum of money which is to be chucked about in the happier beyond. What do you say to that? Even the poet must have some grub now and then, if he doesn't want to go to pieces.

As to the beautiful English girl, she was indeed an Angel, but cold as marble. The little thing cannot really even claim to have led me around by the nose; I knew from the beginning what I was about. Now I have something else, glowing and black-eyed, attending my lectures. As a matter of fact I am supposed to have made an impression here and there, which does my poor disdained heart good, like the smell of apple tart in the forenoon. I don't say: like apple tart itself, for it is all too clear to me that things never get beyond the stage when the treasure of life is carried past my nose—but to tie oneself to the gold bags of a father-in-law here—*pfui, Teufel!* (Pardon!) God forgive me, at the moment I prefer Italy, seen by the light of day, to even the most glowing, black-eyed. . . .

To H. Schauenburg

Basle, 28 February 1846

In four and a half weeks I leave for Rome, and have not answered you for as many months; but I would like a word from you for my journey, so it's now high time I wrote to you.

You weather-wise fellows vie with each other in getting deeper and deeper into this wretched age—I on the other hand have secretly fallen out with it entirely, and for that reason am escaping from it to the beautiful, lazy south, where history is dead, and I, who am so tired of the present, will be refreshed by the thrill of antiquity as by some wonderful and peaceful tomb. Yes, I want to get away from them all, from the radicals, the communists, the industrialists, the intellectuals, the pretentious, the reasoners, the abstract, the absolute, the philosophers, the sophists, the State fanatics, the idealists, the "ists" and "isms" of every kind—I shall only meet the Jesuits on the other side, and among "isms" only absolutism; and foreigners can usually avoid both. Beyond the mountains I must strike up new relations with life and poetry, if I am to become anything in the future; for I have quarrelled inwardly with the present state of things—quite quietly, without any special vexation; quite gradually, the drops have hollowed out the stone, until I finally realized: it can't go on. I shall probably remain a year in the south; you will get news from me, and what news! Perhaps the Lord will send me a merciful little fever, to put an end to a restless mind—all right, I have nothing against it; *vogue la galère!* even if it's Charon's barque. Mysterious fate often means well towards us.

But, my dear fellow, Freedom and the State have lost nothing in me. States are not built with men like me; though as long as I live I mean to be kind and sympathetic to my neighbour; I mean to be a good private individual, an affectionate friend, a good spirit; I have some talent in that direction and mean to develop it. I can do nothing more with society as a whole; my attitude towards it is willy-nilly ironical; the details are my affair. I now have enough education and method to enable me to find my way about politics should that be necessary, only I refuse to take any further part in them, at least in the confusion that reigns here at home. You can be cross for as long as you like; I will catch you again and draw you to my heart, believe me!

5 May

I think I can detect a look of silent reproach in your eyes, because I am off so light-heartedly in search of southern debauchery, in the form of art and antiquity, while in Poland everything is going to pieces and the messengers of the Socialist Day of Judgment are at the gates. Good heavens, I can't after all alter things, and before universal barbarism breaks in (and for the moment I can foresee nothing else) I want to debauch myself with a real eyeful of aristocratic culture, so that, when the social revolution has exhausted itself for a moment, I shall be able to take an active part in the inevitable restoration—"if the Lord wills, and we live," of course. Just wait and you will see the sort of spirits that are going to rise out of the ground during the next twenty years! Those that now hop about in front of the curtain, the communist poets and painters and their like, are mere *Bajazzi,* just preparing the public. You none of you know as yet what the people are, and how easily they turn into a barbarian horde. You don't know what a tyranny is going to be exercised on the spirit on the pretext that culture is the secret ally of capital, that must be destroyed. Those who hope to direct the movement with the help of their philosophy, and keep it on the right lines, seem to me completely idiotic. They are the Feuillants of the coming movement, and like the French Revolution it will develop like a natural phenomenon, involving everything that is hellish in human nature. I do not want to experience those times, unless I am obliged to do so; for I want to help to save things, as far as my humble station allows. For you I have no fears; I know well enough on which side events will find you. We may all perish; but at least I want to discover the interest for which I am to perish, namely, the old culture of Europe. It seems to me as though, when the time comes, we should meet in the same holy company. Shake yourself free from your illusions, Hermann! Out of the storm a new existence will arise, formed, that is, upon old and new foundations; that is your place and not in the forefront of irresponsible action. Our destiny is to help build anew when the crisis is past.

To Johanna Kinkel

9 March 1846

What a lot one has to hear about Fräulein G.! I think she has the characteristic of many young women of our time, who are all too exclusively *good daughters.* A grey-haired millionaire in his forties! And what is more, from Elberfeld, that horrible factory land! You know, dearest Directrix, that I really long to be in Italy, because there is so much begging there and so little industry. . . .

To Karl Fresenius

Rome, 21 April 1846
Address: Café del Greco

I have been here for about three weeks, taken part in the Carnival, walked the Eternal City from end to end, and have at last composed myself enough to write a coherent letter. Come to Rome! I say no more. . . .

My four-Scudi room is most beautifully situated with a view over half Rome; as I write, Saint Peter's (half an hour away as the crow flies) shines majestically towards me in the midday sun. Part of the pleasure of Rome is that it keeps one perpetually guessing and arranging the ruins of the ages that lie so mysteriously, layer upon layer. What I miss here is one perfect and beautiful building with towers and niches where my enraptured soul could pause — *Plump und zu bunt ist Rom,* says Platen with some truth, Rome is coarse and gaudy. But taken all in all it is still the queen of the world and makes a marvellous impression upon one, it rouses both memory and pleasure in a way no other city can rival. I know only Cologne that can compare with it; in Paris there are too few old monuments, and the recollection of modern horrors absorbs the older ones too much. I like the Romans, that is to say the common people, for the

middle class is wretched and as stupid as in Milan. The ordinary Roman
is not a pinched malicious creature, like the Milanese, he is more refined,
and more picturesque. He begs, of course, but does not attempt to black-
mail the foreigner with minor services. He simply leaves those who won't
give him anything, quite politely, and lets them go their way. And however big the crowd, one feels surrounded by decent people, particularly
in the poor, dilapidated quarters round the Capitol, and in the Roman
Sachsenhausen,[40] which in this country is called Trastevere. The city,
the poor quarters at least, seems to me incomparably poorer and more
tumble-down than the smallest village in Lombardy. People here have
armed themselves against work for centuries, as against their worst
enemy; there is not the smallest trace of industry; there are, for example,
no public shoe-cleaners at all; cabs and omnibuses hardly exist except in
the most elementary form; there is no such thing as a "Daily Advertiser";
and only one or two restaurants have modified their cooking to French
taste, etc. There is more tourist industry in the smallest Saxon village
than there is here, though there are 30,000 foreigners living here (mostly
for pleasure). That I regard as a blessing from God, for if one were be-
sieged by commissionaires and other such scoundrels in the same proportion as in Strasburg, it would be hell. The Roman waits until he is asked,
and a guttersnipe in rags is satisfied with a bajocco (a sou) for showing
one the way. That is one of the reasons that chains the foreigner to poor
Rome, with its complete lack of luxuries; leisure has made politeness
flourish like an art, which is most agreeable for the stranger. Come here,
say I. You can harvest such great and enduring gains in one month here
that your life will be worth a good deal more to you.

40. A suburb of Frankfort.

To   Gottfried Kinkel

Rome, 18 May 1846

Last Friday I had a sort of minor invitation to Berlin, not to the University but to the Academy of Art—as soon as it is reorganized—and a fee of 500 Reichstalers for my attendance. There is a shameful lack of proportion between your salary and mine, I know, but perhaps your affairs will soon mend; moreover, I don't get the 500 RT. at once, only after a certain lapse of time—briefly, it is at the discretion of the Minister, though Kugler has Eichhorn's letter in his hands, where the cash is mentioned. I shall have to be in Berlin in the autumn, and finish Italy in all haste beforehand. A fortnight in Naples, a fortnight in Florence, a fortnight in Venice! Naturally I shall travel via Bonn if you will put me up for a couple of days, and from there through Herford, for this time I *must* see Hermann.

To   Gottfried Kinkel

Basle, 12 September 1846

O how hard I found it to leave Italy this time! I know now that I shall never be quite happy away from Rome, and that all my endeavours from now on will be concentrated, foolishly enough, on the thought of returning there, even though it were as an Englishman's lackey. I could show you various spots in Rome, in the streets and in the gardens, where, for no special reason, the feeling suddenly came upon me that I was perfectly happy; it was a sudden inner joy, independent of pleasure. One of these spots is on the staircase of the Palazzo Farnese, on the first landing, so there was nothing special about the locality. Another place, where I once had the same feeling in the first days of May, is to the right of the Trevi Fountain. In Rome I felt the harmony of every faculty as I have never tasted it before, one or two lucky days in Bonn excepted. For of course I don't reckon times when one is in love under this rubric; times when one feels happy as a matter of course, though at the same time quite beside oneself, since there is nothing extraordinary in feeling happy in such circumstances. As I left Rome for the last time on 8th July, and the coach came to a halt at the Porta del Popolo for our passports, I got down once more and solemnly took three steps through the gate again, wishing thus to symbolize my return. It cost me a few tears on the Ponte Molle. Florence and Venice, with Rome in mind, were not at all to my taste; on the other hand I found a real echo of Rome in Ravenna, particularly when I visited the wonderful, lonely Basilica in Classe, that lies so beautifully and sadly on the edge of the great pine woods. What Mosaics one sees in Ravenna, dear Urmau! Next to those of Sts. Cosmas and Damian in Rome, they are the most beautiful, and all dated! I can only tell you that Galla Placidia is the least important, however lovely it may be. The Twelve Apostles in the Baptistry (in the Orthodox, not the Arian baptistry) are still of such extraordinary beauty that one hesitates to attribute them to the fifth century, although such wonderful things were created then—but more of all this aloud.

To Gottfried Kinkel

Berlin, 6 December 1846

I have often hesitated during the nine weeks I have been here: should I write to Bonn—or not? Ought I to drop a hint, or wait? Kugler wishes you well, but his influence may well be outweighed. I am careful not to enquire too closely, and have no desire to know what ought to remain a secret, because by doing so I might do you more harm than good. But one thing you simply *must* know—somebody, you will guess who, has drawn the Minister's attention to your blasted *Männerlied* at the end of the *Taschenbuch,* which has thrown K. into despair. A thing like that undoes a great deal that seemed to have been carefully built up. They are now trying to get you out of the mess; K. will say what he can in your favour to the Minister, and another friend will try and get *Otto Schütz* read before the Court. But keep that to yourself, don't go and compromise me with Kugler, and don't hope for too much. As for the rest, one of the things that I shall never understand is how a man of your age can have committed such a thoughtless act at a moment when perhaps your whole future hangs in the balance. You are no longer a theologian, no one in the world can require religious opinions from you, so why go and publish your views to the whole world, and on top of it all in *that* form? There is not much poetry, not much new in the way of thought in the *Männerlied,* and a good deal of ranting. And if I have been able to put away vapourings of that kind, so can you. You ought at least to consider those who are fond of you, and not alarm them unnecessarily.

7 December

Things are going pretty well for me; my history of painting is progressing. And as for my more distant future, the prospects seem to be good; the Minister is said to have spoken favourably of me. That's all right as far as I am concerned, and as for the rest, I count more upon publishers. In addition to what I am now doing, there is more work before me, of a tiring—but lucrative—kind, so that the likes of us can get along, and I don't ask for more. *"Längst ist der Brust ehrgeiziger Trieb entflohn,"* says Platen, ambition has long since left my breast; not that it was true of him, though it is of me. I shall probably never again be able to work to my own *Gusto,* i.e., at pure history, not at any rate until my best years are spent. However, the same sort of thing has happened to very different people.

I find Berlin as awful as usual, and my longing for Rome tortures me more and more every day. One day I shall smash all these well-meant plans to smithereens and bolt. I should feel quite happy doing so. People like me are far from wanting a life of ease and pleasure; they work readily enough, but *al suo modo*. Only I know that to abscond like that would sadden me, on Kugler's account, who is doing *everything* for this miserable "sujet," and shows him a deal of love and patience into the bargain.

Seriously, I feel genuine sympathy for Kugler's great plans. He himself is, of course, in a perfectly secure position, but the people here are sure to wreck everything he lives for, or at least spoil as much as their strength allows; for there is nothing more powerful at the present time than the conspiracy of small interests against thorough-going improvements. I am always telling him he sees things in far too youthful a way, but he usually laughs me out of it, and maintains that as things have gone badly for so long, why shouldn't they go well again for once. Geibel is in an elegiac mood and of course more interested in his personal poetic plans, which promise great things. He seems to like me because I follow harmlessly along, help him pass the time of day, and try to enter into his thoughts. I am altogether devoted to him; he is one of the finest fellows under the sun, and I reckon his one-sidednesses to his credit, because they are part of his worth. Where poetry is concerned, he lays me flat and utterly discourages me; I hardly feel I want to write a single line when I am near him. It's just as well; if I write no more poetry, I shall work all the better. . . .

9 December

. . . All my efforts are now concentrated upon saving enough to be able to go to the south once more, and *then* when once I am there, I shall not be got out so easily again. I hope to be able to get to the point of solemnly turning my behind on the wretched and meretricious life here, its literature and its politics. Say what you please, my dear Urmau, but admit that under present conditions in Germany no man can develop harmoniously. There are so many little worries and distractions nowadays that ruin the best men, while the worst profit by them. Nothing can help now but a thorough cleansing of the atmosphere on a grand scale, and that is coming; all that we do till then is a pastime, mere *odeurs* with which we conceal from ourselves the general corruption. Why not fly to simple and more beautiful conditions as long as they exist somewhere? I, at least, am determined to enjoy *my* sort of life once again before evil days come upon us.

10 December

In one respect, dear Urmau, you are certainly quite in the wrong: why this continual ranting about the Rhineland in the *Männerlied?* We Rhinelanders are by no means renowned among the Saxons, Swabians and Bavarians for being particularly energetic or excellent in character! Let your foible pass. The Rhine begins with the raw violence of the Swiss, then comes the common, crafty Alsatian, the boastful ranting Badenser, Rheinbayer and Rheinhessen, then the Frankfort Yid, then Coblenz with a population no one has ever taken seriously, and—at last, the Gau of Bonn and the Cologne Gau—well, I had better keep quiet. Geibel, too, is of my opinion—though no doubt he has his own special Hanseatic pride. But *this,* I do agree, is true; we are all, *tutti quanti,* worth ten thousand times more than the Berliner. . . . Now give my regards to the gracious Directrix! And now for 1847: after so many years of worry, I wish you a good, assured position! I wish strength to Mibes, and health, and everything good for the two little ones! . . . Politics are dead as far as I am concerned; I do what I do as man, and as man I love you, even though you commit ten times as many follies as the *Männerlied.* . . .

To Hermann Schauenburg

Berlin, 27 February 1847

I see it is high time that I wrote to you, or you will imagine I am going to visit you in the spring, and accompany you to the Rhine. I cannot, my dear Hermann; it is out of the question. I shall thank the Lord if, with a supreme effort, I am able to finish my work by the autumn. And you? How can you make yourself free when you are already involved in God knows how many ties? In your last letter I detect a certain premonition of a change in your destiny. Save your money for your honeymoon!

Moreover, I am quite certain that the most sensible thing you can possibly do is to marry. I should do the same. Once one has left twenty-seven or twenty-eight behind, everything around one seems damnably empty and gloomy; I should never have believed it. To be sure, I am in good hands, but they no longer make up for the friends of my youth and others, and if my temperament were to change, I might become melancholy to the very depths of my soul. But one thing comforts me: if you remain single you do not fall so easily into the clutches of this miserable world; at any moment you can give it a kick and steer out into the sea of freedom. Little by little, Hermann, I am becoming more daring and more determined, and in the end you will have the fun of seeing a man who was born more fearful than any of you playing quite impudently with life. It's not worth incommoding oneself overmuch for such a trifle. Whether or not you manage in the end, after unspeakable drudgery and toil, to achieve something in your profession, really means very little. How much better to be loved by one's beloved, and to have followed one's fancy. But my "fancy" is beauty, and it stirs me profoundly in all its forms more and more. I can do nothing about it. Italy opened my eyes, and since then my whole being is consumed by a great longing for the golden age, for the harmony of things, and the *soi-disant* "battles" of the present seem to me pretty comic. I ask you! Egoism here, egoism there, self-importance, boasting and sentimentality on both sides, all of it written down and reduced to the level of newspapers, and a leaden cover soldered down on the whole age. And there commend me Switzerland, where from time to time people hit out at one another, so that the air at least gets ventilated. Heaven help us, it always makes me think of Harmonia's commode, in Heine's *Wintermärchen*.[41]

The *Kölnische Zeitung* and other *carrés de papier*, as Alphons Karr calls them, deduce that politics are at last entering a great new phase, and have become "the people's politics," etc., but I can only assure you as a sober historian that there has never been such a common, unattractive period in the history of the world as that since 1830. I feel justified in turning where my soul finds nourishment. Geibel was saying recently that "it is not what the age demands that is beautiful, but beauty is eternally what the age requires." And with that saying I conclude for this evening as it is getting late.

To H. Schauenburg

Berlin, 22 March '47.

Some day we must really talk things over. If I were any use in the affairs of this world, and if I were not in perpetual need of beauty in nature and art, I should say: let's go to America together! But I simply could not live there; I need an historical terrain, and what is more a beautiful one, otherwise I should die, which at bottom would not be the worst thing that could happen. . . .

I have got to finish my work by the 9th September and am working like a nigger, saving like a Harpax, disdain elegance for the sake of my future freedom, all so as to satisfy my soul's thirst for beauty before I leave this world.

I think, Hermann, that the same thing is true of both of us. We have

---

41. See *Deutschland: ein Wintermärchen*, Caput xxvi, where Harmonia shows Heine Charlemagne's commode in which he sees revealed the future of Germany.

known thousands who as young men at the University were volcanoes of originality and poetry, and promised to remain so, and now are either servile or liberal philistines. We, on the contrary, are steadily becoming strangers to the world and its ways, and live a private life which (silently for the moment) runs clean contrary to present trends.

Doesn't it sometimes seem to you as though one fine day on a lonely path you would meet a dwarf who would open a secret door in the moss and stones of the forest and lead you into a new world? There are moments when I believe in some future miracle that would reconcile me to the things around me, in a talisman that would bring me peace and satisfaction in these miserable times. And yet—(for me)—it's impossible. The people who can bear things here below are those who either (1) through Christian love or (2) through ambition, are joined to the world. And those two things I do not possess; though a man who possesses one of the two, and is a strong character, can overcome the world.

Do drop your hostility to the Middle Ages! What weighs upon us somewhat, are the apes of the Middle Ages, not the real, genuine age of Dante and his consorts, who were, *au contraire,* wonderful people. Classical antiquity, if it were imposed *par ordre de Mufti,* would not be much less irksome. I have in my hands the historical proofs of how wonderfully people enjoyed themselves in the Middle Ages, when life was more colourful and rich than can possibly be imagined. But that is by the way. Only don't let yourself be imposed upon any longer by the Liberals in historical matters; at bottom they are still only jabbering away in the wake of the Encyclopaedists. "But look ye, I am going to tell you something, the culture we have now, etc."—is not worth a fig, and the only result is that everyone is made on one last. It is a long story, Hermann, the spread of culture and the decrease of originality and individuality, of will and of capacity; and the world will suffocate and decay one day in the very dung of its own philistinism. I've said it!

To H. Schauenburg

Basle, 23 August 1848

Life's beginning to be damnably lonely. What do the phantoms that I live with daily want of me? You at least have taken part and tried things out; I just spin away at my thoughts by myself. It is a very curious feeling to have done with the world, and to ask for nothing more but a place in the sun, in which to hatch out plans that no one bothers about in the end. And yet it is not just egoistic epicureanism that makes me act in this way; every nature, after all, has its particular needs.

I knew from the first that events would carry you along with them. You wanted to achieve something and had, therefore, to busy yourself with our confused and crumbling world; I want to contemplate, and seek harmony. I have entered the cool grove of the gods (*gelidum nemus*) with an outrageous, daily hunger, and piously remain there. You may say that I might easily become petrified there, like some antique—but all the same it has its good points.

Now that is all that I have to tell about myself. Day follows day; I have no real relations with anybody; I am more solitary than ever before in my life, and as for the rest, am looked upon as friendly, and enjoy a certain respect.

No one can grumble at your all wanting to go to America. I am, moreover, of the unauthoritative opinion that politics has only played a small part in that decision, and that you would certainly have stayed if Europe were not spoilt for you in other respects. But I simply cannot tell you how strongly I sense the general disorganization of private life in Germany. Everything is out of joint, and barriers have lost all their power. You are among the sensible ones. But I shall have to go through a lot more with Kinkel and others. Believe me, Kinkel is bound to fall between two stools in the most disgraceful way. He is utterly lacking in the prudence, thoughtfulness and inner balance which, as everyone knows, even a Republican needs. It is bound to end badly. . . .

Let us say farewell, and part as dusk falls. Let me have news of you wherever you may be, if it's only a line. Farewell, dear Hermann.[42]

To H. Schauenburg

Basle, (before 14) September 1849

I have been expecting Kinkel's fate ever since 1847; there was simply no talking to him; he wanted revenge, and was bound, sooner or later, to run his head against the wall; if it had not been this wall, it would have been another. He never understood anything about politics or economics, except from the point of view of causing a stir. For years, you know, I was quite aware that he was bound to make an exhibition of himself, and in that I was always the very opposite of him. All this sounds very hard on the poor prisoner, and I only write it to you. O dear heavens, what is to become of the family? His wife's parents have some means, but they won't go very far; I am afraid they will be in real want.

How frightfully ironical the end of *Otto der Schütz* sounds:

Sein Schicksal schafft sich selbst der Mann.

Man shapes his own destiny indeed!

. . . I hope for nothing from the future; possibly we shall be granted a few half-bearable decades, a sort of Roman Empire. For I am of the opinion that democrats and proletarians, even though they make most furious efforts, will have to yield to an increasingly violent despotism, for our charming century is made for anything rather than genuine democracy. A more detailed explanation of all this would only sound uncharitable. It

---

42. The next letter, quoted in Schauenburg's diary, was written after Burckhardt had spent the winter in Rome. S. introduces the quotation by saying it expresses "a part of their old friendship."

is no longer possible to link up a real social organism with our ageing Europe; anything of the kind has been forfeit since 1789.

I am delighted to see that you have achieved a considerable degree of resignation! I have grown so prudent that I now know that the philistines are not the worst; misplaced genius, however, is the very devil. I may not be very much at home in the present world, but I shall nevertheless try to learn to meet it affectionately and gently.

I have never lived a more solitary life than I do at present, but in spite of that I feel a breath of indefinite good luck coming my way, a relative peace: *otium divinum*. . . .

To Eduard Schauenburg

Basle, New Year's Eve 1849

First of all, sincerest wishes for the New Year! Dear Ete, I have not written to you for a long time, because I had nothing to say, and because for a long time past I have been tempted to commit nothing but lamentations and jeremiads to the post. Many a letter, that sounded too complaining, I have burnt and replaced by another! Simply because those I was writing to were either sad enough themselves or were sure to ridicule a sad correspondent. Now I am once more in a better mood, so you see it has all come right and I can wish you happiness on the occasion of your marriage.

Who would ever have thought that you, of all people, were to have such a long period of trial before you! Though I think I can congratulate you on it. Formerly, perhaps, fortune gave me its gifts all too easily, on a plate, and still does so in some respects; my whole life long I have never really exerted myself very much—in return I am worth less, and feel myself hardly courageous enough, or worthy enough, to stretch out my hand for the highest blessings of life.

The struggle against cramping circumstances you are entering upon is no small matter; but I recognize you well in the fact that you don't start back from it and demand to have the happiness destined for you by right. The little span of time allotted to us in our earthly existence must be used to the full if we are not to go unreconciled to the shades and before attaining harmony. Those who know you know that your worth is of the highest and that the greatest happiness can emanate from you. Let the hermit, who once enjoyed such good times with you, sound the trumpet just a little in honour of the great day; after all, no one else will hear it.

What you have, had to be won in a hard struggle so that you should measure its entire worth. The outer circumstances in which the acquisition takes place may be raw and wintery, but that can only raise your inner happiness higher still; you are neither frivolous nor stubborn by nature; what you ask for is your divine right. And to your last breath you will be able to say to yourself that you have fought with all your might to make your life a complete and a beautiful one.

Your dear fiancée has all my admiration for her courage and constancy. She must possess a vivid sense that the happiness of true love will be a lasting one, and is not dependent upon external events. Lay the expression of my devotion dutifully at her feet.

My fate may well drive me to and fro in the oddest way, and not at my behest, for if the decision lay with me, domestic bliss would be my idea of the most desirable happiness. It is not without envy that I see you running into harbour when it is not yet open to me; in the distance, it is true, some beacons beckon to me, but I am not certain of my compass, and a sharp north wind drives me past the rocks.

Will you sometimes think affectionately of me in your new life, although I left you without a sign of life for so long? I'm sure you will. I shall take that hope with me into the new year which I am entering with strange, curiously mixed feelings of anxiety and hope.[43]

---

43. This is the last known letter to the brothers Schauenburg until the letter written in 1869 from which it seems that he and Eduard remained in touch with one another.

To   Emma Brenner-Kron

Basle, 21 May 1852

I think I can descry a talent of some importance in your poems which is worth developing—not for the sake of others, for poetry only occupies a very minor position in the world of today, but for your own inner strengthening. You must save yourself from the seas of feelings and reach art, simplicity, truth; it is worth the effort. Even if upon doing so you were to give up writing yourself, you would find an important surrogate in the solid view of life and of art which a study of that kind gives one. Think how wonderful it would be if you learnt to transform all suffering, all excitement into sheer beauty! Of course, one must give all one's strength to doing so.

Above all, not every feeling, not every mood is fit to be held fast and expressed in poetry; the immediate pain must first be patiently endured before the right high mood occurs which is the mother of Song. Poetry should not be the expression of inner misery; the golden shimmer of reconciliation must already be hovering over things before they can be treated poetically. And anger and revenge above all are very questionable guides! It is not impossible to give them imposing forms, but it requires a very powerful nature, as in some of the Psalms, or a highly finished mastery of style, such as Dante's.

To the same

Friday, 4 June 1852

. . . Now I am going to be obstinate and take these things[44] seriously, though I see quite clearly from your letter that you regard me as an arch-

44. A detailed criticism of the poems, which were sent B. anonymously.

pedant. *Wohl mir!* I am not the silent admirer you mention! I am beyond the orbit of your beauty and your charm, the sight of which might perhaps unsettle me in the matter of artistic superiority, like the man you mention. Nor will it harm you in any way—charming mask!—should there be someone on earth who does not adore you, but merely wishes to be useful to you.

But what good would that do me? You will simply laugh at me. I might propose a theme for you to treat—you would reject it, or conceal such thorns in it that my poor hands would be blood all over. I might, for your sake, treat the theme myself—the moment you had it in your hands you would find it bad in every respect, and I should have to keep quiet, or write half a book in defence of my poem, which would involve both you and me in great *longueurs*. One can never—forgive my unaffected liberty—influence women very much with reasons. When everything has been said, the situation looks well enough, only . . . the question is just where it was before.

So far I have busied myself trying to improve my position—as the known *vis-à-vis* the unknown. For, beautiful mask, such is my weakness, that an anonymous titter behind closed shutters is still enough to excite my interest. However, I am on the verge of falling into "confessions"— forgive me.

What more shall I say? Up to now you have taken my criticism as a personal attack upon all that is sacred; you defend the poems which you love "for special reasons," whereas one must only love a work that, in addition to a special content, also satisfies the requirements of art up to a certain point. In any case that sort of thing does not deceive me. I am not asking you to admit to your former aesthetic mistakes, if only you improve upon them! If you will only learn to use images more warily! If you will only recognize what is ugly and mannered! If you will only take care to avoid reminiscences! For they come of themselves, the whole atmosphere of poetry today is full of them, and if one reads a lot, indiscriminately, one receives them at third and fourth hand.

You think me astoundingly conceited, don't you? So I must grasp that nettle. The thing I have the honour to represent existed long before me; what I am doing is my office, so long as you don't find someone else better able to deal with your charming talent, and at whose feet I too would willingly sit.

In the meanwhile I suggest you should continue to send me a lot, in fact everything you write: I shall not be one whit more gentle with it than I was with the first lot; but that alone can really help you.

To   **Paul Heyse** ★

Basle, 15 August 1852

It is some time now since my view of art (*en bloc*) underwent a complete metamorphosis, about which there will be much to say when you are here. I should not have believed that a rusty old historian like me, who imagined he could see the value of each period and of every standpoint, could in the end become as one-sided as I have. But the scales are falling from my eyes, and like St. Remigius to Chlodwig, I say to myself: *incende quod adorasti, et adora quod incendisti.* On the whole it was really the Latin elegiac poets who gave me the impulse, only I cannot quite explain it, and remain at the stage of good intentions. I have also read all sorts of Greek things and Italian too, *del buon secolo.* Furthermore, the whole thing requires that one should keep one's eyes tight shut to the aesthetic that is preached nowadays, namely against Robert Prutz in Berlin, who will be a tendencious rider of hobby-horses to the end of his days.

But more of all this verbally. It is high time for me to free myself from the generally accepted bogus-objective recognition of the value of everything, whatever it may be, and to become thoroughly intolerant. Where history is concerned I still keep a safety-valve open. But there is also a word to be said on historical research and the way it is carried on, and gradually I am acquiring the right to say it. . . .

To Heinrich Schreiber

Basle, 18 December 1852

There is something painful to me in your *pia vota* for my career, as I am not only obliged to recognize the excellence of the intention, but in almost everything its correctness and applicability; but at the same time I cannot follow your advice. Believe me, I simply must get away for a time! Here, I should certainly go to pieces, unless I could refresh myself from time to time elsewhere. This is my last chance of getting away from bricks and mortar; if I don't take it, I should be condemned for ever to a miserable existence. And then, please observe: I shall come back in a year's time, furnished, I hope, with enough material to work on for a long time. But for the moment I simply must get away temporarily. It is asking too much to expect one to remain fresh in a town without stimulating company and almost without scholarly incitement.

Dearest Friend! You really have no idea of the intellectual climate here. I can feel the best people here going rusty, literally, with my finger tips. So you won't take it amiss if I do not follow your advice; the ground under my feet is on fire. Once I have been away for some time I shall be quite ready to accustom myself to Basle again; but for the present, away!

I hope the new railway-Basle, that seems to be forming, will, in addition to some disadvantages, have the advantage of blowing the controlling clique here sky high, their insularity embitters the life of both natives and foreigners. You too know well enough the mood in which one longs above all things for a neutral face. If only I were already beyond the Alps!

I know quite well, from a previous sojourn of fifteen months, that it is not a bed of roses. My illusions are no longer those of a youth of twenty, who expects to find paradise in the south. But my poor soul expects from time to time to be plunged into a refreshing bath of beautiful forms, particularly the landscape. Perhaps in this I am still something of a fantasist; but what is the use of argument and discussion when one simply thirsts for beautiful things? After all, I give up so much else. And then, what I really want to do is to work. There is going to be no question of expensive sight-seeing; the Florentine libraries are my principal aim, where one has to work in winter in a coat and woollen gloves. You see, I know the darker side too.

I think that there will always be some little place open to me here, where I can make room for myself and spin myself into a chrysalis. Only don't bother about me.[45]

To Paul Heyse

Basle, 6 May 1855

This summer will be spent on various bits of work. In the middle of July I shall go again, if possible, over the Alps and down through one or two Piedmontese valleys with their chestnut trees and pilgrimage chapels, but only for two to three weeks. In the beginning of October I move to Zürich. And in the course of next year I shall come and look you up in Munich. I hope to write more poetry in Zürich than here, as I shall spend most evenings alone. In fact, one of the principal reasons why I have decided I should like to go to Zürich is because I can live there practically incognito. Here in Basle I have to keep up appearances to a certain extent, and lose a lot of time with people. I am not going to Zürich as the only newly appointed Professor, but as one of thirty who will, as a rule, lay considerable store upon being known in society and getting to see a lot of people. Among that crowd one can hide away unnoticed. So come, O golden freedom! I am sure of two or three good quiet friends, and the country is such that I only have to go five minutes away to see really beautiful views in the grand style.

. . . Once grant me that golden freedom and no one can make any

---

45. Burckhardt remained the best part of a year in Rome and returned to Basle in 1853, remaining there till he moved to Zürich in 1855.

St. Peter's, 1847

A street in Rome, 1848

demands upon me, except my professorship; then I shall "turn up my sleeves, spit happily in my hands" and undertake something worth while.

To   Albert Brenner

Zürich, 17 October 1855

Your letter gave me heartfelt pleasure. Although at your happy age one is volatile in many ways, I think nevertheless you will stick to your vocation having once discovered it; some branch of culture, with special reference to the beautiful. You will hurry and worry for years, just as others pant and groan, but on the whole I hope you are safe. What is not yet ripe will ferment. Only do not merely contemplate life; keep the secret promise you have made to poetry. May it precede all your spiritual efforts like a blazing torch.

How few things, ultimately, are capable of giving real value to the life of modern man. We are cut off in a thousand ways from action, which at other times and among other peoples strengthened the nerves and kept the senses fresh. How ill at ease we feel in the present world with its great wheeled machines, if we don't consecrate our personal existence to nobler ends. All this must, however, be as clear to you as it is to me. There is consequently no better support against the spirit of scorn and contradiction that sometimes besets you, than a Dionysian grape-cure in the vineyards, as long as it is not attached to some passing autumn—I say no more. The steady contemplation of the beautiful and the great should make our whole spirit loving and happy. And our ambition should thus rise from the stage of vanity to the desire for fame. Whether we are victorious over others should no longer be a problem, though we should continue to be anxious to conquer our own whims for the sake of the beautiful.

Whatever you may have learnt from me, someone else can teach you better still, in a higher sense, now that you are prepared for it; and in your private studies too, you must cut a path through the undergrowth, now that you have learnt to walk—not that I have taught you, in all honesty—and generally know your direction. I miss our literary discussions as much as you do. Although there are many excellent people here whose society is open to me, that is a point at which I am left in the lurch—because as a rule fate and overwork have deprived them of real joy in these things, and because they do not (as far as I know) write themselves. The atmosphere is full of significant poetic inspiration; but for the moment I am not solidly established enough to be able to think of producing myself. And then I am possessed by a scholarly spirit that is torturing me and may well lay claim to all the powers at my disposal for years to come, the seed of a serious examination into the history of the beautiful. I brought this "infirmity" back with me from Italy last year, and feel I could not die in peace unless I had fulfilled my destiny in this respect.

I regard this as a really important matter, and do not affect false modesty. Once we really break off relations with the great and the infinite, we are utterly lost and caught in the wheels of the present age. Forgive my turning up again with the "wheels" metaphor, but it happens to be so; other centuries recall rivers, storms or flames of fire; the current century, called the nineteenth, always suggests enchanted machines to me. But we must profit as best we may from the *Freedom* of this century, and owe it our objective contemplation of all things, from cabbages to kings—so be sparing with your complaints. In one matter you have pleased me and listened to my advice: I mean your more legible handwriting. Can I now hope that you are attending to the *precepta magistri* in other more important respects? I refer, as you know, to classical literature. It is no mere superstition on my part.

To Albert Brenner

11 November 1855

To my great delight your letter of 27th October reached me, although you had written the word "Zürich" in very small letters. You must learn to be careful in such things; the post is no joking matter. And with that my stock of comments is at an end, and from now on you are very welcome. Your Faust-fever reminds me in a moving way of a similar epoch, not so much in my own life, as in that of my fellow students sixteen or seventeen years ago. To tell the truth, I never went very deep into the speculative side of *Faust,* as my friends did, in part. I must therefore be careful not to try to introduce you to a new conception of that tremendous poem. I only want to say this much: it is the certain, inescapable fate of the educated youth of Germany at a certain age to dig down and explore *Faust,* and you are in the process of fulfilling that destiny. The old gentleman would be deeply hurt if one were to discover *fixed dogmas* in *Faust!* So go to it and make your mistakes. The best minds have all had to follow the same path, because they sought for solid truths; the poem attracted them, drew them deep down into its subterranean and supernatural paths, and left them at long last no *truths,* but a purified *impulse* towards the *truth,* such as preoccupation with spiritual matters ought indeed to evoke.

I have no special explanation of *Faust* ready prepared and filed away. And in any case you are well provided with commentaries of every kind. Listen: take all those second-hand wares back to the library from which they originally came! (Perhaps in the meanwhile you have already done so.) What you are destined to discover in *Faust,* you will have to discover intuitively (*N.B.* I am only speaking of the first part). *Faust* is a genuine myth, i.e., a great and ancient image, in which everyman has to discover *his* own being and destiny in his own way. Let me make a comparison: whatever would the Greeks have said if a commentator had planted himself between them and the Oedipus saga? There was an Oedipus fever in every Greek which needed to be stirred and to tremble after its own fashion *without intermediary, immediately.* The same is true of *Faust* and the German nation. And even if large parts of that overrich work are lost to the individual, the little that really moves him immediately makes a very much more powerful impression, and then becomes an essential part of his life.

The second part has never appealed to me otherwise than as a delightful fable. The speculative thought is mysterious and obscure to me. The mythical aspect is handled with a certain magnificence of feeling, as though one were to see Rafael paint the adventures of Psyche. But what wholly passes my understanding is the way Faust's moral account is finally settled. Anyone who has dealt in allegories for as long as he has, inevitably becomes an allegory himself and no longer interests us as a human being. But there are many sublime things in the second part, and there is little to compare with the ascension of Helena in all the poetry of the past.

And finally it is only right that *Faust* should drive you to some form of production. The same thing happened in our green years. The enormous distance between the desire and the achievement usually results in the burning of these scriptures — unjustly; for even the faults of such symbolic poems are strangely marked with the signature of the writer, and in later years one learns to treasure that kind of thing as a source of self-knowledge.

Let me have a short sketch of your poem; I will go through it conscientiously and not spare doubts and encouragement; I suspect it will contain some quite personal things, belonging to you alone. Read Immermann's *Merlin.* It is a most significant and independent parallel, not to say addition, to *Faust.*

To Albert Brenner

Zürich, 2 December 1855

. . . And now I come to your ultra Byronesque *Faust* character. Believe me, a fellow like that, *if* he really could exist, would be an odious individual, in spite of all the "divine sparks," the "higher impulses," etc. Even if he *"occupies* himself with politics, philosophy and science," as you suppose, he is only playing at it in a literary sort of way and never really works at anything because he is altogether lacking in the genuine *love* of things, and because he is just a sneering ne'er-do-well. I should like to take this opportunity of convincing you that these tremendously interesting, melancholy-sceptical, mysterious beings *à la* Byron are beings of pure fantasy, and have never existed anywhere, and consequently possess no poetical truth whatsoever. (They are the type to which Heine at one time would have liked to belong, till he found pure carrion suited his complexion better.) Blasé, three parts carbonized individuals, originally built on a grand scale, exist in plenty, but THEY ARE NO LONGER INTEREST-ING. Certainly not nearly as interesting as they think themselves. The couple of little smoke-rings they blow in the air now and then are simply the last stink that they give out, even if one is tempted to imagine an Etna of genius boiling within. Into the bargain, individuals of this kind are hopelessly vain. You have obviously never known any of the type, or you would not idealize and respect these "characters." As a matter of fact I should very much like to read you a sharp lecture on the habit of thus consciously anticipating things. Your whole life long you have met with little but love and kindness; at the same time you have a youthful fantasy with a natural leaning towards the extraordinary, which is the preliminary condition of all poetry. You ought really to bring forth great figures, Gods, Heroes, Fortune and Love, in simple and affecting contrasts. Instead of which you catch after anything that is decaying, and shines phosphorescently, clutching at things about which you know nothing, and which you have never experienced. You may say: "I have no experience of Gods and Heroes either." All right, but you have the right to *imagine* them. Your fantasy, at your happy age, has the right to do so—you have not got the right to imagine putrescence. Out of pure curiosity I should almost like to see you carry out your Faust plan, just to see how relatively innocent you would make such a character—in spite of murders, daggers, etc. I should then note in the margin all that you had omitted through innocence—all the spite, the utter lack of consideration, the infamies typical of these carbonized geniuses. Believe me: a man is only interesting as long as he loves something. And then *Non fumum ex fulgore, sed ex fumo dare lucem,* etc. By the way, you have only trusted me with the outline of two scenes: the conversation with the friend, and the oath. The friend's character is unfortunately—I have it to say—all too true of our day; the type who on his "voyage through every point of view" once spent a couple of weeks "at the sign of modern orthodoxy," until a different wind began to blow; who always has a scapegoat ready, that he pursues with vampire-like scorn. I could definitely point out a character of the kind to you. . . .

To **Albert Brenner**

21 February 1856

Your letter of 17th pleased me very well up to a point, and *secundo* did not estrange me at all. Let us deal with the principal point first. So thoughts of your future position in life are beginning to stir? Good for you; so you are no longer dreaming of a poetic existence, with Eichendorff's roast chicken flying into your mouth? (*If* that was your dream, there is nothing to be ashamed of any more.) The man who needs a great and powerful ideal in life is the very one who must, in our times, stand on his own economic feet. Do all you can to form and develop this particular pride as highly as possible! The world wants and takes very little from us, and we must want and take little from it. Above all, you love the Muse too dearly to want to live off her, i.e., on royalties! Even the Great who wrote to live, suffered serious inward harm. No, let the realm of profit be thoroughly prosaic; one can, nevertheless, get very fond of it, and duty, though it costs bitter hard work, can have its agreeable side.

And now I am even going to preach a bit of heroism to you, the sort of thing that I certainly hadn't much use for when I was your age. I mean avoiding expensive amusements, and the society that relies upon them. Among us Swiss, people are very sensible on the point, and one's duty is not made too difficult. But it is very different among German students, where a man will not only study his way through a family fortune, including his sister's *dot*—for if he is fundamentally decent he may perhaps be able to make good most of it—but *fritter* it away and leave a lot of debts behind. The end of the song is a shabby existence at home or in America—or a job as a *fonctionnaire,* where one is dragged hither and thither, kneaded, trodden down and insulted by some charming civil servant, an existence, that is to say, which is in ridiculous and miserable contrast to one's former life of luxury. *Dixi et salvavi,* etc. One must learn in time to stand on one's own feet and to be poor with honour. That is a fundamental requirement of poetry, the shield of character, the one guarantee of pure and beautiful feelings. You will of course be looked after for a few years; it will suffice if you keep your future livelihood in view during your student years, and accustom yourself to the prospect, not as an attractive, but as a pleasant one. Don't aim too high: giving lessons, teaching at a school, and then if possible a permanent job as school teacher. Don't let yourself be drawn too easily to an academic career; it is a game of chance, if only because there are always infinitely fewer positions vacant in any particular line, even if one reckons in all the German universities, and in the natural course of events these posts are often filled by chance or favouritism and not according to merit. There can never be any question of founding a family unless one can live on one's wife's fortune—whereas all our high-school teachers marry at twenty-five or twenty-eight. O, if you had seen, as I have, the misery and poverty that prevails in German academic circles! But the last thing you must dream of being is a journalist. It devours the poet in one, and labour for labour it rarely brings in as much as teaching. I am only reciting all this prose to you in the name of poetry, that likes something solid and calm about its confessors.

To continue: you say you are not satisfied with university life. What blindness! I must in that case undeceive you as follows: The poet does not need a student's life, *qui n'est qu'une espèce de poésie mise à la portée de tout le monde!* He lives and moves and has his being among a different order of images and feelings than those given him by his surroundings. And then what a seedy version of student life has been transplanted into our Swiss universities!

Further, you are dissatisfied with X, Y and Z—I only miss one thing, that you certainly feel, but do not confide to me: you are dissatisfied with yourself. O, you are setting the wrong way about it, if you look to others for exalted moods, or make them depend upon others, and demand an ideal world from the world that surrounds you. And now, for your good, I make the following suggestion: throw your superior attitude, your wit and sarcasm down the drain, and in your relations with others try to bring out all the goodness of heart, the faithfulness, the devotion that is in you, and you will find that you are answered in the same way. Do not upset the society in which you may find yourself with witty, biting re-marks, but give proof of real *esprit* which is naturally gentle and kind, and you will discover real *esprit* in others, timid and awkward perhaps, but kind, willing and loving. Then your relations with others will not indeed be ideal, but in good time a breath of the ideal will touch them. Do you believe what I am telling you? Let me know. When those around you seem dull and stupid, begin by doing penance in your inmost heart for having intimidated some and embittered others, and then be the most cheerful and the liveliest of all, and you will see how greatly it helps. A man with wit who has *completely* tamed himself, is *eo ipso* a man with power. Schleiermacher was a man like that. You see that in spite of your warning I still stick to the "outward consequences."

Now about your work. I am too little of a specialist to help you directly. But this much is certain: if you do not cultivate a high degree of memory you will remain a dilettante. Further, I require that you read the necessary things in folios, if they are not to be had in 4to, 8vo and 12mo. What have you got against the poor folios? There are thousands of wonderful things in them, things that one can read with delight—or even rave about and cry over. Just one example: I don't know whether you were here last winter when I lectured on Saint Severin. The historical as well as the human aspect of this wonderful story—though I neither raved nor wept over it—touched me deeply; but it has only been edited twice in the original, and as far as I know, each time in folio. And, by the by, try and wean yourself somewhat from raving and weeping, which are only fit for hysterical women. It is always the effect of the material, and not of the artistic form. Summa, if you really want to achieve something you must be less shy of books. It is self-evident that only a thousandth part of the contents will be of any value to you, but it is the work of sifting that educates the mind. How else does the miner work? And finally there is one consolation: you will gradually learn to bring that hundredth part to light quickly and accurately.

As regards the influence of study on the observation of life, I don't grudge it you, as long as your study of books does not suffer. You assure me that you apply the study of life to yourself in the shape of self-examination. I should be lying were I to say that all this appeared to me to be suitable to your years. A God has blindfolded the young so that they should think the motley world harmonious, and be happy in that consciousness or madness. But if you want to go on being purely critical instead of enjoying life, that's your affair. By the way, one of the things you tell me gives me great pleasure: "that will is more important in the

world than understanding"—if *that* is how you philosophize, then just
carry on. Put in a slightly different form the saying reads: *Character* is far
more decisive for a man than riches of mind, which is one of my oldest
and strongest convictions.

To Albert Brenner

Zürich, 16 March 1856

Your letter of 11th pained me greatly and filled me with concern for you.
I will answer the second part of it first. If you really regard yourself as a
demoniacal nature, then I only make one demand of you: that you never,
for a single moment, consent to it. At all costs remain good, loving and
kind, compel yourself to wish the best for everyone, and show this in
your daily conversation and intercourse with others, so that if possible
someone should be able to make friends with you. If you knew the terrible clefts and cracks that run through our subterranean life, you would
sooner unlock all the treasures of love and devotion today, than wait till
tomorrow. For that is the only way in which it is possible for that something resembling pure and exalted feeling to develop, which walks on
boldly and confidently over the abyss. You don't yet know what beggars
we men are at the gates of fortune, how little can be got by pertinacity
or wrung by force, or how the greatest gifts and genius itself hammer
vainly on those doors, trying to break in. *Denn ach, die Menschen lieben
lernen, es ist das einzige wahre Glück*—to learn to love men is indeed the
one true happiness.

It is a real pity that you should cloud your golden university years
with such melancholy thoughts. You sit and brood over your "consistent
indifferentism," till the categories "necessity and chance" have eaten
away that excellent daily bread "good and evil." Am I to witness the same
thing happening to you that I saw happening to others sixteen years ago:

as a result of supposed or true "world-historical, or philosophical" axioms, the consciousness of those things which *alone* protect and bring happiness to the individual's existence were totally forgotten. (And above all let me say this *en passant:* These intellectual operations eat away and corrode poetry entirely; they cost us Lenau, who allowed himself to be blinded by the high poetic glamour of a determinist philosophy, till in the end he was completely done for.) If it must be so, then at least look out for yourself; the intellectual pride that develops in the course of that occupation has, for us children of the world, as penetrating and unbearable a smell as religious pride.

The twelfth hour has struck; if you want to remain a poet you must be able to love (1) men, (2) the individual things in nature, life and history, quite personally. If by any chance it should happen to be Hegelian Philosophy, my advice to you is: he is a drug on the market, let him lie where he is. And now think a bit about your future vocation, whether as author or as teacher: you ought to school yourself to make as many different kinds of men as possible love the things of the mind. Is your present brooding a step in that direction? But I am probably talking in vain; I cannot obviously plant a different mood in your soul—and much of what you take to be conviction is really only mood—don't take this amiss.

And now, as to your academic laments. I will not repeat my last letter; I quite believe that the individual traits in your picture of student life are correct. But you betray to me that you yourself act as a solvent and not as a builder. In our time I was neither the one nor the other, but lived a life of fantasy both within the students' club and outside it, and have no wish to flatter myself. But I now have a very lively and painful sense of what I ought to have done, not only there but in many other situations. Later, in Basle, it became very difficult for me to establish links; in most circles you will find one or two scornful, purely negative individuals who are endured by the great majority of decent, rather simple men, and who twist the tails of those who aim at something better. *Don't you become one of them.* How easy it is to destroy, and how difficult to build up again! It requires infinitely little intelligence to apply a very exacting measuring-rod to the actions of others, and to throw into relief the inadequate and ridiculous side, or in a somewhat more exalted style, to emphasize the limitations and prejudices of social life and its *laisser-aller*. I talk about this because I believe in the predominantly positive side of your nature. Just think how lucky you are! No one, for example, obliges you to celebrate the birth of the heir to the French throne who was born early today, whereas at least a dozen unhappy Frenchmen have been chewing their pens for months!

. . . And now, getting down to it, point for point. I take the greatest interest, as you know, in your spiritual life, as you mean a lot to me. But you dissect and picture your own point of view and sensibility as in a journal and—much as I like to read that kind of thing—it is not what I desire; what I want is the poetic expression, the unconscious which breaks forth in conscious form. Take courage for once and perpetuate the various streams of your own feelings quite simply, in different figures, and fuse them with their personality in a necessary artistic relationship. Your real and lasting journal, in the highest sense, will be poems. When you philosophize, I listen till it's over, as at a sermon, and make no comment. I have nothing against that way of passing the time, if you will only promise one thing, namely, at moments of high philosophical emotion (and they will not be wanting) to repeat three times under your breath: "I am, after all, only a miserable atom *vis-à-vis* the powers of the external world." And "All this is not worth one drop of real contemplation and feeling." And "Personality is, after all, the highest thing there is." And after mumbling these three sayings, you can go on philosophizing in peace.

To   Paul Heyse

Basle, 3 April 1858

Your and Ebner's letter left me greatly dismayed. It never occurred to me when I wrote to Frau Clara (Kugler) that that sort of invitation was on the cards.[46] All things considered, I simply cannot undertake the work.

I am entering upon a purely historical professorship, in every respect exacting, where *an enormous amount* is expected of me. Perhaps I shall have to postpone my own work,[47] for which I have been making notes for two years, indefinitely.

Furthermore, for a long time past, I have been out of touch with so many forms of art; I am no longer able to travel for study's sake; I shall hardly leave Basle for a single day this year. I only have a fading recollection of things outside Italy. So just think what sort of a continuation that would mean to a work begun with an unequalled knowledge of detail, as well as depth and solidity of mind. Not to speak of the impossibility of procuring the illustrations. Just think seriously of your own responsibility to the work.

I must admit I have nobody else to suggest, if Lübke[48] won't do it. And I presume you don't want Springer. I can't name any other. How is Eggers getting on?

If there is absolutely no one to be found, then my good or bad advice is this: print what there is of the history of architecture, simply adding a brief general view of the Renaissance and modern architecture. I could, if need be, take care of the supplement, only it would be necessary to tell the public it was a work making no claims, which had been forced on one. In that way one can at least see that no *spropositi* occur.

46. Kugler died on 18th March 1858. Burckhardt had been asked to complete and edit Kugler's "History of Architecture," and edit a third edition of his *Handbuch der Kunstgeschichte*, published by Ebner.
47. The *Renaissance*.
48. A friend of Burckhardt's lecturing in Zürich.

Lübke *must* supply the missing parts of the *Handbuch*. I would have modern art printed directly from the second edition, somewhat revised. If absolutely no one can be found to do that, then I will undertake the revision. But someone else must see to the illustrations.

If I were still in Zürich I could do something more, though not very much. There are in fact lacunae that cannot be filled, and to which we must reconcile ourselves. I am still overwhelmed by the heavy blow which fate has dealt your family.

To   Heinrich Schreiber

Basle, 1 August 1860

My holidays, three-fifths of which have already expired, have been given to polishing and correcting my book, of which twenty-one sheets are already printed, and about fourteen outstanding. My anxiety grows as it goes to press, i.e., is irrevocably babbled out. The title is to read: *The Civilization of the Renaissance in Italy.*

As soon as the printing is completed, I will send you a copy. My dear old friend will no doubt smile and shake his head at such dilettante work, but will surely concede that the author has not spared trouble and sweat. It is an altogether wild plant dependent upon nothing whatever already existing. One eulogy I should like to receive from your lips, namely, that the author firmly resisted many opportunities to let his fancy wander, and virtuously stuck to his sources. And I also think I deserve some praise for not having made the book three times as thick as it is. It would have been the easiest thing in the world and would probably have gained me more respect among a lot of people; I had only to give in to my natural talkativeness, and there would have been a hundred instead of thirty-five sheets. . . .

To Paul Heyse

Basle, 16 November 1860

O, dear Paul, my surprise is beyond belief, and I have been preoccupied all day long—so now I have to make a conscious effort to realize the full extent and manner in which *you* have dedicated this masterpiece to *me*.[49] I believe you would laugh out loud if you could see how it contrasts with my existence here; I am the complete philistine, play dominoes with other philistines, and go for walks with philistines (and colleagues who are equally intent upon being philistines), drink my glass of wine *sans prétention*, coffee-house about politics, and regularly spend Saturdays with my relations, lecture and teach in my classes in a plain and honest fashion—and behold, the most charming bombshell flies in through the window! O Paul, think of all the jokes and the ridicule which your myth about my singing will expose me to among people here, who have never heard me sing except in the fifth act of our University Guild dinners and other festivities—but it is a bitter pill for me to swallow when I recollect how egoistic and unfit for company I must have been in 1847. Of course the reckoning has had to be paid, and I have reached the point when the least sign of friendliness sets my heart in a mood for thankfulness. Since then I have had difficult times. I don't ask for any special good fortune, as long as things continue as they are.

Deeply moved, I began dipping into your little book at a number of places and am for the moment confounded to realize how very far I still am from knowing the real hallmark of the Italian spirit. I feel as though any number of passages in my book[50] ought to be rejected and rewritten; I must have been blind never, in the whole course of my work, to have recognized the quite peculiar fusion of spirit and passion.

49. Paul Heyse dedicated his *Italienische Liederbuch* to Burckhardt, recalling their friendship in Berlin and the times when Franz Kugler and Burckhardt took it in turns to accompany one another at the piano in German and Italian songs.
50. The *Renaissance*.

But then, try to write cultural history without anyone at your elbow to shake you up and pinch your ear. Ofionide[51] certainly helped me a great deal without knowing it, by giving me the measure of a completely healthy, charming, age-old Lombard, with a wide knowledge of literature; only he is not accustomed to our carefully filtered point of view, living as he does naïvely and unreflectively. What qualities I have, I got from Kugler, who had a feeling for essentials, even in those spheres where he was a dilettante; and then he knew how to awaken an interest in them. My God, how easily satisfied and conceited most (even) *great* specialists are compared with him! A panoramic outlook such as his would naturally only disturb them and spoil their sort of work. And they liked to ignore the quality of his learning even in his special field. But enough of that! They will do the same to my book, and I and my publisher are prepared for it! Fair-minded people, with something in their heads, will perhaps acknowledge that the book *had* to be written from sheer inner necessity, even though the world ignores it.

To   Otto Mündler★

Basle, 5 January 1862

. . . The position in regard to my book is not, unfortunately, what friend Lübke supposes it to be. The melancholy truth is that we have not sold 200 copies. That kind of thing is no longer bought in Germany. I had warned the publisher, who is a close friend of mine and who had not even covered his costs for the (handsomely rewarded) *Cicerone,* not to print more than 500; he printed 750 and now holds the surplus in bales in his store. With that experience behind me, I have decided only to work out a skeleton for *The Art of the Renaissance,* about twenty sheets, and simply to use the occasion to communicate results that seem to me new.

51. Picchioni. Ofionide was his "nom de guerre."

Of course, that will not make a readable book, but however readable one is one can't break the ice in Germany. And even so short a work will have to wait a good while, until my very exacting duties are to some extent simplified.

I can only say yes and amen to the translation of the *Cicerone,* and beg you to recommend me to Mrs. Perkins and her collaborator, but I fear that under present circumstances the work will hang fire indefinitely.[52]

With your improvements, it would, of course, cut a different figure! I am really very ashamed sometimes when I look at the article "Painting" and recall the authorities on the strength of which I baptized and commented. But there is nothing to be done about it; we German brooders scratch together what we can in our neighbourhood, and then creep away and write, without being able to call on anyone's advice. The result always smells provincial, hardly even German.

I am most desirous of making your personal acquaintance, and would drop all my work any day you chose to come here. For it would be of great value to me to have your opinion on a certain picture of the Milanese school, belonging to a manufacturer here.[53]

To   Paul Heyse

30 November 1862

PS. I have still not thanked Bernhard Kugler[54] for his dissertation on the Princess of Antioch, as I did not know where he was. It is an important critical study, that promises well for the future. For me, arch-dilettante,

---

52. It failed. Finally trans. by Mrs. A. H. Clough, 1873.
53. Probably the picture Burckhardt had bought and sold at the same price to Felix Sarasin, and which he thought at one time was a Leonardo. The money he got for it was given to Böcklin, to enable him to study in Rome. The picture now hangs in the Museum in Basle.
54. Franz Kugler's son.

it contained some humiliating things, and I saw what Sybel means by method and imparts to his students. I shall never found a school!

To   Friedrich Salomon Vögelin

Basle, 15 February 1863

Unfortunately I am not in a position to suggest any publication in which you could publish the results of your archaeological studies. I myself am so out of touch with Journals and periodicals that I should not know what to do were I to find myself in the same situation. On the other hand, Professor Lübke in Zürich knows all about them; if you will give him my kindest regards he will tell you all you want to know. And with "S. Francesco in Assisi," you are sure to make him anxious to help you.

Your father told me about your disaster, though when he was here your valise was still in Leghorn; you have my sincerest wishes for its prompt recovery. I am one of the few who can sympathize with your fears and hopes in such matters, as I lived for four weeks in Northern Italy (it was in 1854), in perpetual anxiety that the Austrian police would seize my notes, because the Swiss *in genere* were being pestered at that time, and my passport had just expired.

If Lübke cannot suggest anything to you, I would certainly recommend you without hesitation to make a temporary book out of your researches with some such title as Christian Art, or Fragments of Christian Art, or Mosaics, or something of the kind. It is true that one makes little or nothing out of it, but gets a good deal further *per ora hominum*. It is quite easy to give research work of that kind the sort of form which would allow you to take your doctorate wherever you like.

I lament your theological direction with all my heart. I saw the same sort of thing facing me, and turned away in good time by changing over to history.

In the last few years I have thought a lot about the fate of the Protes-

Burckhardt on his way to the University (undated)

Burckhardt, photographed by Hans Lendorff, *c.* 1890

tant Church. Man does not seek freedom in this sphere, but dependence, which the Catholic Church, as everyone knows, offers him *satis superque*. His manner of picturing a personal God grows and is formed according to his grief and suffering, and in this way all the rest—the Bible and doctrine—acquire a new hold on him. Had I had the luck or the fate to be near you, I would have tried to urge certain things upon you, probably without success. But one cannot discuss such things in a letter. I know quite well that the great breach in the Protestant Church is bound to become official in the next decade, but I also know the modern State: and when the time comes it will display its ruthless omnipotence in evident and most practical form. It will simply take the rough level of feeling among the masses as a standard and take its measures accordingly. In France, as I see it, the break up of the Huguenots can only lead to the growth of Catholicism. In fact, we have not yet experienced the full impact of the masses, of sheer numbers, on religion, but it may yet come.

To Paul Heyse

Basle, 5 April 1863

. . . As far as I am concerned I live here like a hard-working Professor of History, and am content if everything remains as it is; not that everything is perfect, but with advancing years one no longer expects any special gain from changes. I too have had some heavy sorrows, of the kind that do not make men young. I worked out seven-eighths of my *Art of the Renaissance* in the winter of 1862–63, but then found it inadequate both in principle and in execution, and put it back in my desk, probably for ever, as I can't hope to make good the lacunae with only six months in Italy. Here we never have more than four or at the most five weeks' holiday at a stretch, and that does not allow of a journey such as I need. My consolation is that at least I was not afraid of a great work.

I now consider my modest literary career as finally closed, and feel much better and more content reading sources, as I only study and make notes for teaching and not for possible book-making. The historical market is tremendously overcrowded as things are, and it will be worse if peace lasts. Then, my good kind publisher died ten days ago, and my *opera omnia* of which there are cart-loads, are to be moved *en masse*, i.e., they may perhaps be bought by some wholesaler in Leipzig, and offered for a time at reduced, indeed, very reduced prices, and then pulped, all of which I look upon with stoical calm and a genuine secret joy. My cure is: after eight in the evening I go to the café (*scil. Weinkeller*) or into society, to gossip. Saturday evening to some nearby village, and Sunday afternoon I walk a little further. For years now I have avoided concerts, because of the slavery involved, which is balanced by the fact that I have acquired a pianino, and make my own music.

Some years ago I asked you to look out my letters to Kugler and after having read them if you wished to, to destroy them. I should be pleased if that were to happen, as there are quite a lot of things in them that are not meant for the uninitiate. Let me know what happens!

To Paul Heyse

Basle, 6 December 1864

In all haste and not to keep you waiting: I simply cannot do it.[55]

I find it more and more unbearable to have to describe what I have not seen with my own eyes simply from other people's books, and owing to the incompetent way in which our holidays are arranged I cannot travel abroad. My duties, as I have come to conceive them since 1858, absorb me entirely, and my dislike for going into print grows from year to year, proportionately.

55. This refers to the proposed completion of Kugler's *History*, which was to be re-edited posthumously.

The best demonstration I can offer you of the sort of author I am was given last Friday when I gave Lübke,[56] who was here, the MS. of my *Kunst der Renaissance* which is seven-eighths finished for him to do as he pleased with, and so that he could at least use part of the material for a fourth volume to Kugler's *History of Architecture.* I was not satisfied with the work, and cannot pursue my studies, so gave it away on condition my name only occupied second place on the title page — though I should prefer it not to appear at all. . . .

So now you see how I behave towards my very own children. . . .

To   **Otto Ribbeck**

Basle, 28 October 1867

Leave us Dilthey a little longer, I *beg* you![57] He is still young and youthful, and he can prepare himself so well in Basle for a career in Germany. I think he will look back on his time in Basle as the happiest in his life. And then perhaps you wouldn't keep him long in Kiel, who knows! For the intellectual material is really *very considerable,* that I must say, in all honesty and truth. I am quite worried by your enquiries and only foster one feeble hope, that perhaps my delay in answering will help to determine his remaining here. You know perhaps that owing to his poor health Steffensen looks to him for assistance; and lo and behold the students were enthusiastic about Dilthey and we had the consolation of seeing that we had made an excellent acquisition for our *botteghino.* Is all that to be destroyed so soon?

I write no more on the matter, as I don't know enough about his

56. Lübke, a friend of Burckhardt's who had succeeded him at the Polytechnique in Zürich.

57. Ribbeck, whom B. had known while he was lecturing in Basle, had moved to Kiel. Wilhelm Dilthey, the philosopher and historian, followed him there for a short time.

books in detail. To judge by his conversation and his inaugural lecture, his culture is exceedingly solid, and then there is a superb literary vein in him. You simply must leave him to us, whatever happens!

We have now reached a total of 120 students, *without inflating ourselves,* but wait submissively for further propitious changes in our academic destiny.

Many thanks for your ὕβρεως.[58] Unfortunately hybris will always reproduce itself. And as Geibel says: *Wer Gewalt hat, braucht Gewalt,* whoever has power uses it. Wednesday last I saw Franz Joseph entering Paris with Napoleon—which gave me to think.

To Eduard Schauenburg

Basle, 5 December 1869

An invitation to lecture in Krefeld does me great honour! I didn't think I was known that far away—but it is more likely "one of your jokes," as the *Zeitgeist* says in Raupach.

But in itself it shows the high level of culture in a manufacturing town such as your prosperous Krefeld, if people are ready to make the sacrifices you indicate, in order to devote a series of evenings to the cultivation of their minds. But I have never hawked my lectures beyond the gates of Basle in spite of more than one invitation to other towns, and mean to stick to that rule. Honestly, I should regard myself as robbing Basle if I were to act differently. My whole nervous energy belongs solely to this piece of ground, and lectures, if they are what they ought to be, cost nervous energy.

I envy the celebrities of Bonn and Heidelberg their appearance within your and other walls, but I cannot compete. In any case, I desperately need every day of preparation for next summer term (once again "An-

58. Ribbeck's lecture on Hybris.

cient history excluding Roman!"). And so I beg you to express my best thanks to your committee for the confidence shown to me, and make excuses on my behalf for the reasons given above—sheer want of time. I have already spoken here twice this winter in the evening *coram publico*, and there are still three Saturdays before me, the 4th, 11th and 18th. It is a sort of moral duty for us lecturers born in Basle, to preach before large mixed audiences; and anyone born abroad who joins us is doing a good deed. We guarantee the public a great series of 38 to 40 lectures every winter, and a series of fourteen pitched a bit higher for a more discriminating audience. And side by side with these quite a number of courses prosper, worldly, religious, etc. Briefly, I am convinced that if there were a lecture every evening in the winter, it would be well attended. The young business men's Society, to mention no other (I am a member and am booked for two evenings), runs an educational establishment the size of a respectable institute. You see that every minute can be put to use here.

How much I should like to see you, your house, Julius, your son Stift, and everything! But I am driven along by the winds, and my one consolation is that my life is made up of the daily duties of my office. Addio!

To Otto Mündler

Basle, 15 February 1870

As I no longer know your address in Paris, I must trespass on the kindness of Herrn von Zahn [59] in order that these lines of sincerest thanks should reach you.

Yesterday I received the "Beiträge zum Cicerone." The Preface in which you mention my work (far too kindly) moved me and shamed me,

---

59. Von Zahn, who with Mündler and others prepared the 2nd edition of the *Cicerone*, was at the time director of the museum in Weimar.

and then as I read the text, and realized the enormous howlers I had boldly perpetrated, I felt it was a real duty on my part to excuse myself to you as best I could.

The *Cicerone* was not only undertaken upon an extremely inadequate aesthetic basis, but also in very difficult circumstances, with very modest means and at a moment when I had lost my position here and did not really know what was to become of me. In point of fact it came faithfully to my help and got me the Professorship in the Federal Polytechnical School in Zürich, so that I shall always owe it an honourable mention.

But a work which called for at least three years' leisure, for relations with those on the spot, and local assistance of every kind, was hastily carried out and finished after thirteen months' travel and four months' subsequent work, proof correcting included (of which three weeks of my earthly life were spent on the index), quite in the style of our hasty nineteenth century. Just one little detail: As Switzerland was at the time officially on bad terms with Austria, I was in continual danger on the way home from Ponte Lagoscuro, where I entered the K.K. States, and only obtained a *carte de séjour* with difficulty in Venice; on the way back I was, indeed, allowed to stop in the towns on the direct route, but not to visit Mantua. And what is more it was Lent, and the pictures were covered! And added to everything else I was condemned to strict economy.

Those are some of the little earthly inconveniences of my quondam authorship. And to that you must add the arbitrary, dilettante outlook on art which I could not shake off. Further, the lack of almost any kind of technical knowledge—and the permanent danger of taking secondary and borrowed works for primary, and the school for the original! I can still remember quite well what a desperate decision it cost me in Rome in April 1853, to treat classical sculpture according to type and subject. You must know many a place in the book where in one way or another I have been obliged to make a virtue of necessity.

Finally, there is this to be said in my favour, that from sheer prejudice and mistaken industry, local Italian studies very often led the observer on the wrong track. But what I still cannot forgive myself are all the awful mistakes, especially in the Venetian school, which I helped to originate and perpetuate. And then, not to have gone a single step north of Venice was pretty stiff! I now see from your supplement, and from Max Lohde, among others, that the whole of that great province conceals a world of important things in every branch of art.

But if anyone had told me in 1853–54 that later on, as a respectable Professor of History, I should thank Heaven if I completed my daily *pensum* in books and printed matter, and that I should leave the study of art entirely on one side, I should not have believed it; yet that is what has happened.

All things considered, I wish a better man than me had written a *Cicerone* (according to the plan I had before me)—but *what* was there excepting Murray, in 1853, in the way of a guide to art which made any attempt to take in the whole of Italy and all the forms of art?

To Bernhard Kugler

Basle, 30 March 1870

The great theme you have consulted me about has more than once been the subject of discussion between me and other younger scholars. It is difficult to give advice, for a great historical subject, which is to be one of the principal elements of a whole life of study, must needs cohere sympathetically and mysteriously to the author's inmost being. But apart from that, we differ on one point: you are looking for a theme which should, if possible, find favour in the eyes of the times, and appeal to the mood of today. So thought I at your age, but not so later, fortunately for me. There are, in the first place, always a number of mediocre and slap-dash fellows after a theme of that kind; they get in sooner than we do, exploit the moment, and disturb our view and vision; or else we arrive much too late when the mood and the fashion have already changed. On the other hand one may find unexpected applause with a theme that no one else has thought of, that takes the reader into a different neighbour-hood to the one he knows, or than he had, with his desires and passions and fantasy, anticipated.

In concreto: in my opinion, though perhaps this sounds rather impor-tunate, you should, in selecting a theme, free yourself entirely from ev-erything which has anything to do with the Prussian Monarchy and its (more or less) providential career, the preparations of 1815 and 1866, the constitutional hair-splitting, the confessional quarrels and all that kind of thing. Your theme, which may well condition your happiness in study for a number of years, and your inner growth, ought by its very buoyancy to float above the floods like Noah's Ark. Now, of course, it is said that that is precisely the sort of scholarly contemplation that makes bad citi-zens. To that it might be answered: Where are we getting to exactly, as a result of the tendency of present-day historical work to turn into journal-ism (or material for it)? On the contrary, ought not History and Philoso-phy and one or two other beautiful things to assert themselves as being among the few dry rocks that the flood of time and of the age cannot touch, because they offer knowledge as such an asylum?

And then the very readers who are in a position seriously to decide the fortune of a book have had enough, and more than enough, of ques-tions of the day; they long for something refreshing from distant lands.

Furthermore, one writes and works differently when the theme is not sustained by the interest of the moment. One knows one is master of one's fate, and can only save oneself by awakening, as can be done, an inner interest in the subject. Then one is protected against journalistic prolixity, *currente calamo,* against the perpetual thrust and parry, and the allusive style that makes a book quite unintelligible in a few years' time.

But for all that I allow that in one respect the public ought to be taken into consideration in the choice of a subject: I advise you to choose an historical episode of general significance, the very name of which inter-ests as many people as possible. I have twice done disproportionately well on that score.

I further advise you simply to omit the refuse of mere facts—not from your labour—but certainly from the presentation. One really only needs to use such facts as are characteristic of an idea, or a vivid mark of a time. Our nervous strength and our eyesight are too precious to waste on the study of external facts of the past, unless we are archivists, county historiographers or something of the sort, expressly appointed for the purpose. There is always enough stuff of that kind that has unavoidably to be included.

And finally never go beyond one volume and remember the silent despair with which you and I regard some new three-volume monograph or biography, whose spiritual and intellectual contribution could have been put on four or five pages. The concentration I recommend need not lie in the form of expression, which on the contrary must be easy and smooth; it is much better to save space by limiting the above-mentioned refuse to the absolutely necessary.

On getting your letter yesterday, I spoke to my colleague Wilhelm Vischer, and got from him that a theme which I had, at his desire, suggested to him earlier on, had been entirely given up in favour of another, which he mentioned to me. I had advised him to take "The age of Charles the Bold," so that it is now free.

To someone else, who also seems to have stopped on the road, I once recommended "The Age of the Council of Constance," as a great motley coloured map of the period and countries and minds at that time. As you see, I like themes that are *à cheval* on the frontier between the Middle Ages and modern times. It is truly exhilarating to depict the variety of life in those times, for the sake of its many different forms and its vitality. And long before the dustmen have got their refuse carts moving, and shout disagreeable things after us, we are already over the hills and far away.

As far as your humble servant is concerned, I now only work for myself, i.e., for my office. But at your age one must of course write books, so as to show others, and oneself get to know, the dimensions of one's powers. At present I am mostly making notes for a course of lectures which, in the most favourable circumstances, will only be given in a couple of years' time, and that now preoccupies me in just the same way that preparing a book used to do. If you come here, I will tell you what it is.

I have written at greater length and more incautiously than I ought to have done. But I felt as though I was talking with your dear father.

Put the letter on one side, and come very soon to Basle, to one who has not seen you since you were twelve years old.

To von Preen*

Basle, 27 April 1870

First of all my warmest thanks for the magnificent photographs! The staircase [60] must produce a wonderfully mysterious effect; the ceiling of the lower hall (which is normally open where there is a double staircase) corresponding to the gorgeous anteroom above, with the stairs giving on to it, is unique of its kind; moreover, the decoration is of the finest Rococo, and the ceiling of the kind I love quite particularly in South German Palaces, evidently by a hand similar to that of the *Treppenhaus* in Meersburg. I must see it one day at close quarters, and we will examine the clerical symbolism and the symbolized diocesan clergy together, for one cannot really enjoy such things alone.

As you seem unable to forget Lörrach [61] and its surroundings, I shall enjoy calling on you one fine day in Bruchsal, first of all to thank you personally, and then to bring you some gossip from the Oberland, but my only outing these holidays, otherwise wholly dedicated to toil and

60. In the Bishop's Palace at Bruchsal.
61. The town in Baden, not far from Basle, where von Preen first made Burckhardt's acquaintance.

work, is over; it was a day spent in Thann,[62] which I had not visited for more than twenty years, whose Cathedral I saw again with wonder and astonishment. More and more I am coming to see so-called degenerate, late Gothic (as indeed other styles, in their final form) in a highly heretical light; the presumed degeneration consists for the most part in drawing the final consequences, and in the brilliant pursuit of these developments. As a rule styles die at their height, otherwise a vigorous style could not follow immediately on the one that died. I myself no longer purvey my heresy among strangers; but each time my friend Lübke[63] is here, I am more than delighted to find that he holds similar views.

Which reminds me (heaven protect us!) of another friend, who died twelve days ago in Paris: the admirable Mündler. God forgive me the association of ideas, but it's not altogether our fault if the thought of our few remaining possessions at once calls to memory the losses we have suffered. In addition to what M. achieved with the *Cicerone* (and as you have condemned yourself to read it, I must mention it), Zahn and Mündler published a special supplement, in the preface to which Mündler referred to me most affectionately and I was deeply touched. And it was destined to be his last publication! When a naturalist dies in the middle of important studies and experiments, one consoles oneself with the thought that mother nature will offer the identical forms and problems to a successor and to a subsequent generation to investigate; but who can replace a man who has acquired such a vast general view of the works of art strewn all over Europe and that are only present once? An irreplaceable piece of knowledge that no one can inherit died with Mündler, as with Waagen two years ago. And he was a South German, from Kempten in Bavarian Swabia, just as Waagen's best qualification was the fact that he came from one of the Hansa towns and not from Berlin. Our good old friend from Lörrach, who visited you recently, has felt obliged, since

62. In Alsace.
63. Lübke was lecturing in Zürich during these years.

his return from Berlin, to find the character of the people there agreeable, though in Berlin people would be quite satisfied with political sympathy. For brother Berliner knows in his heart of hearts that he is an altogether unbearable individual. And I, who lived there for four years, listen, and think my own thoughts.

You ask me what to read! Alas, in the midst of the confusion of my library I have become a man *paucorum librorum*. I should like to have Flaubert's *Education Sentimentale,* but it's still too dear for me, and I shall wait for a cheaper edition, though I have not got patience enough for the quite cheap ones *à 1 Fr. le volume.* The review in the *Augsburger All. Zeitung* was certainly written by a master hand, and I should very much like to know whose. By way of introduction some German novelists get one or two truths told to them in the most respectful form. I can't help it, to me novels and poetry are two utterly distinct species; in the novel, on the rare occasions when I take one up, I demand realism, and what is more I can stand unmerciful realism, as I apply little of it to myself. In poetry, on the other hand, I demand the ideal completion, and in the first, encouraging days of this month I made myself a present of Mörike's *Poems* (fourth edition), that I had long wanted to possess. That wonderful man is one of the most comforting phenomena of the age; one sees how a nature born for beauty can unfold happily, magnificently even in the most constrained surroundings and conditions. . . .

The day before yesterday fat old Alboni gave a concert here. She brought an excellent company with her; a tenor (Hohler) *hors ligne,* a pianist so sublimely beautiful that people went mad at the mere sight of her naked arms, the soprano, Battu, from the Opera in Paris, etc. In addition to a medley of all sorts they sang a selection from Rossini's *Missa posthuma,* and only then did Alboni herself appear. My dear Sir, whenever that woman crosses your path, hear her at any price! During the last ten years, which was the last time I heard her *aux Italiens* in Paris, she has not, to my ear, lost in the very least; the majestic organ-like tones high and low are the same, and her calm and perfect art remains unaltered!

Her singing of the final cadence of the *Agnus Dei* made the air vibrate, and our miserable theatre shook. But perhaps you had the same pleasure in Karlsruhe or in Baden, where she has certainly sung.

To von Preen

Basle, 3 July 1870

One really gains something from your epistles! Don't for a moment imagine that I am provided with society like yours from any other quarter; I have no other correspondence except with Professor Lübke, and in the evenings I hawk my conversation round the cafés. It is no doubt largely my fault if I prefer to live *par distance* with clever people when I am not assured of real goodness, as I have come across some very curious specimens in my life. It may be that I ought to trust some of them more than I do; but life is short and I haven't time to make experiments. . . .

Like me you find everything in old Europe looking out of the true this year, and what is more judging from an entirely different knowledge of everyday affairs. I really no longer know what can be the value of German culture in making the individual inwardly happy; all those small centres of culture, where the German spirit was sitting pretty *next door* to German philistinism, are being blown sky high with *éclat,* and after all, the chief consequence of centralization is spiritual mediocrity, made most unpleasing by the increasing vexation of "hard work." The latter, reduced to its simplest terms of expression means, in my opinion, roughly this: will anyone who has not got, or does not earn, enough money to cut a figure in a large city kindly cease "existing." If the German spirit can still react from the centre of its truly personal powers against the great violence which is being done to it, if it is capable of opposing that violence with a new art, poetry and religion, then we are saved, but if not, not. I say: religion, because without a supernatural will to counterbalance the whole power and money racket, it can't be done.

During the last few days I have been looking at the two first volumes of *Kritische Gänge,* which contain the quintessential extract of all the discontent and enthusiasm of the years 1840 to 1844. Those years surely seemed to promise more than has since been fulfilled. But what exactly happened? After people had been played about with for two decades and always egged on to will and to want something, suddenly a really firstclass "willer" appeared at Sadowa;[64] and since then, exhausted by their former effort of will, they have collapsed at his feet and want what he wants and just thank God that there is someone to give them the direction.

À propos of Sadowa: did you notice how boldly Ollivier[65] made out that the successful plebiscite was a French Sadowa?

There is something very consoling in the fact that armed with a culture and a life of the mind independent of one's business, one is also a different man in business, and that people guess that there is someone quite different behind the Herr Oberamtmann, who, for all their profane education, they cannot get at. This is where government business and financial business divide sharply, the latter consumes a man entirely, and hardens him to all else. Here, indeed, we still have a class of business men that makes a splendid exception owing to the part they take in life outside their work and yet I see so many individuals who have formally forsworn every kind of reading. They say "with regret" that they have no time, and really just don't feel like it, and what with the present pace of work in businesses, one can really hardly blame them. Now and then I get an inside view of the life of men in "big business," of the perpetual rush they live in, always standing to attention ready to telegraph, and of their utter inability to stop talking shop even in the evening or—were that possible—to free themselves from the whole business. Now and then one of them says to me: you teachers are lucky, you get holidays. To which I answer: With three or four partners in your business you too

64. Bismarck.
65. Prime Minister during the last years of Napoleon III.

could make time for holidays, in rotation; but it's within you, in your souls, that there are no holidays.

You are only making one mistake in your reading: the fact that you are really reading the *Cicerone*! When, with my former insouciance, I wrote the book, I little thought that I should be taken so seriously, as so many excellent people have since done. Only recently an American climbed up to my room, in order to develop a complete theory to me, which he linked on to some passage in the *Cicerone* (about the asymmetry of Roman architecture). I had the greatest trouble imaginable in making it plain to him how entirely divorced I am from art and the literature on the subject. I am delighted that you like the *Cortegiano* and *Galateo,* a complete world of *Courtoisie,* long since departed, and yet it is no longer the Middle Ages, but intelligible to us. I can only enjoy the *Decamerone* if I force myself to enjoy the beauty and limpidity of the style consciously, by reading aloud to myself; the stories are either too long drawn out (compared with our present fashion: telling old stories in brief, just reporting on them); or else, as regards the spicy *genre,* they have been outdone by newer relish. But if you want something really stimulating, get yourself given Vasari's volumes, containing the biographies of Brunellesco, Signorelli, Leonardo, Rafael, Michelangelo, etc.; just skip anything technical that you don't understand; Vasari is the most refreshing reading, one gets such a sense of the very visible growth of the people he is describing.

But if you must know about my reading, well, I am writing this letter between two of Pindar's Olympic Odes, which I have to go through as part of my duties. Here and there, and despite all my admiration, the most disrespectful thoughts occur to me, and from time to time I catch sight of a lot of festive philistines, and Pindar with all his great pathos in pursuit. Pindar had obviously to deal from time to time with boors. But there is a tremendous amount of every sort of thing in these poems that I must know about. It is quite possible that three out of my four weeks' holiday may go on them, as it is no use reading piecemeal, one has got to master the whole Pindaric drapery at one go. Before that I hope to enjoy a week in the Schwarzwald.

To **von Preen**

Basle, 20 July 1870

My warmest thanks for your cordial greeting, before the frontier is closed! Under what auspice shall we one day greet one another again? Whatever happens we ought not to forget that it is good for us children of the world to know that, even in tolerable health and in fair circumstances, we live over an abyss, etc. — that is the sermon I preach to myself. And then, as it seems to me, this war, far from originating in specific troubles, really has its roots, justification and inevitability in the depths of the nature of the peoples (which are only human nature raised to a higher power). The last scenes point to a long prelude. In the end L. N. found out what had occurred between A. and W.[66] in Ems, and I don't fancy the Russians were kind enough to tell him. Then up went the *ballon d'essai,* the Gotthard question, in which the French Ministers played the innocents in a masterly fashion, *doux comme des agneaux.* Upon which the others thought: aha! he doesn't care, and threw out the Candidature for the Spanish Throne. And when they were well out on the *glacis,* he let down the portcullis, and could not be persuaded to raise it again. We now have to go through with the rest. I say *we,* because I don't believe very much in the lasting neutrality of Austria, and ours infallibly collapses with theirs. Your worthy compatriots are rushing their possessions here — very softly, I ask "Why?"

There is one minor historical consolation: how far is a great war followed by a long peace, i.e., the clear proclamation of real and lasting

66. Louis Napoleon, Alexander II and Wilhelm I.

powers? I do not want to plead that that is what has been wanting in recent wars, but presuppose a great war, with the resulting lasting peace. But what a horrible price to pay! For only a long destructive war that rouses nations to their very depths (and despite all the wrath, that is still far from being the case) produces that result.

The final end might quite well be an *Imperium Romanum* (only when we are dead, to be sure), and after numerous Assyrians, Medes and Persians. That sort of *Imperium,* as we know, will not be a dynastic one, but a centralized administration with (thanks to its soldiers) a *beata tranquillitas.* In large sections of society the men of today have gradually and unconsciously given up nationality, and really hate every form of diversity. They would readily give up all their individual literatures and cultures, if it had to be so, for the sake of "through sleeping-cars." What I am writing sounds fantastic now, no doubt, and yet it's profoundly true.

O, if only we could avoid the unavoidable with sighs and tears!

To von Preen

Basle, 27 September 1870

. . . Since receipt of your letter I have been waiting and waiting to see whether a pause, an armistice, might not give me time to bring some kind of clarity into the whole problem. But events move on. France is to drink the dregs of misery and disorder, before being really allowed to speak. O, my dear friend, where will it all end? Does no one realize that the pestilence from which the conquered are suffering may also infect the victors? This frightful revenge would only be (relatively) justified if Germany were in fact the completely innocent victim of unprovoked attack that she is given out to be. Is the *Landwehr* to go right on to Bordeaux and Bayonne? Logically the whole of France would have to be occupied by a million Germans for many years. I know quite well it will not happen, but that is what one would have to deduce from what has happened hitherto. You know I have always had a mania for prophesying, and have already met with some astonishing rebuffs; but this time I simply must try to picture to myself what seems to be coming. Now supposing that, after the occupation of Paris and possibly of Lyons, the German Army Command were to let the French vote on the government they wanted. A lot would depend on how it was staged; the peasants and a section of the workers would certainly vote for Louis Napoleon again.

There is a new element present in politics that goes deep, and which former victors knew nothing of, or at least they made no conscious use of it. They try to humiliate the vanquished profoundly in his own eyes, so that he should never again really trust himself to achieve anything. It is possible that this aim will be achieved; but whether things will be any better and happier is another matter. What a mistake the poor German nation will make if once home it tries to put its rifle in the corner and devote itself to the arts and the pleasures of peace! In point of fact it will be a matter of military training before everything! And after a time no one will be able to say what they are living for. Then we shall see the Russo-German war in the middle of the picture, and then gradually in the foreground. In the meanwhile, we can both thank Heaven that at least Alsace and Baden are not to be soldered together: it would have produced a fatal mixture. That has been rendered quite impossible owing to the fact that Baden troops were given an essential role in the siege of Strasburg. For I take the liberty of presuming that that was not arranged by mistake. One of two things must happen: Alsace will either become purely Prussian or it remains French. Precisely *because* German dominion in these new *Länder* is so difficult, it can only be administered directly by Prussia, and any intermediary form of guardianship or tutelage under the German Empire would not be feasible. There is one other extraordinary sight to which the world will have to accustom itself: the Protestant House of Hohenzollern as the one effective protector of the Pope, who from now on becomes a subject of the Italian Kingdom.

But enough of politics! Heaven grant us a tolerably quiet interval. The Philosopher's[67] credit has risen again these last weeks. Living here is one of his faithful, with whom I converse from time to time, as far as I can express myself in his language.[68]

And so, Greetings! We shall have to reorientate ourselves spiritually in more than one respect. Europe without an amusing, decorative France! Phew! And quite a few more things that Europe has forfeited and that have been emphasized for a long time in Renan's work.

To von Preen

Basle, New Year's Eve 1870

. . . What has not happened in the last three months! Who could have believed that the struggle would have lasted far into a horrible winter, and would still show no sign of ending on the last day of the year? I shall remember the end of this year my whole life long! And not as regards my own, private, fate. The two great intellectual peoples of the continent are in the process of completely sloughing their culture, and a quite enormous amount of all that delighted and interested a man before 1870 will hardly touch the man of 1871—but what a tremendous spectacle, if the new world is born in great suffering.

The change in the German spirit will be as great as in the French; at first the clergy of both confessions will look upon themselves as the heirs of the spiritual disintegration, but something quite different will soon make itself felt, to one side. The shares of the "Philosopher" will rise sharply, whereas Hegel, after this year's jubilee publications, may very possibly make his definitive jubilee retirement.

The worst of all this is not the present war, but the era of wars upon

67. Schopenhauer.
68. Nietzsche.

which we have entered, and to this the new mentality will have to adapt itself. O, how much the cultured will have to throw overboard as a spiritual luxury that they have come to love! And how very different from us the coming generation will be. It may well be that, to the young, we shall appear very much as the French *émigrés,* intent on a life of pleasure, appeared to those to whom they fled.

Just think how much of all that has been written up to now is going to die out! What novels and dramas are people going to look at? Are the authors, loved by publisher and public alike, because they met and flattered the needs of the century, indeed, of the year and the month, going to survive? Anything that is to live on must contain a goodly portion of the eternal. And if anything lasting is to be created, it can only be through an overwhelmingly powerful effort of real poetry.

To me, as a teacher of history, a very curious phenomenon has become clear: the sudden devaluation of all mere "events" in the past. From now on in my lectures, I shall only emphasize cultural history, and retain nothing but the quite indispensable external scaffolding. Just think of all the defunct battles in the note-books of all the VV.EE.[69] in their Professorial Chairs! Fortunately for me I never went in very much for that kind of thing. But I see I am again talking about myself, when the times may well laugh at all our personal hopes and activities.

We are hourly expecting a battle in the neighbourhood, somewhere between Besançon and Belfort, and hourly expecting a great decision, who knows where, in France. The position of Switzerland, however strong our determination to maintain a strict neutrality, will not remain what it was, even though peace were signed today. The rest must be left to God.

"Put your house in order," etc., is the wisest thing we can all do, in central Europe. It is going to be different from what it has been.

And with all that I am dreaming of a little tour this summer in Southern Germany, in the course of which I might call on you in Bruchsal. How incurable our optimism. . . .

69. *Viri Eruditissimi.*

To von Preen

Basle, 6 March 1871

My one and only longing is for a profound reaction in the mind and spirit of both peoples. I know wishing often makes fools of us, and we think we see light when it is only the flickering of our eyes, and yet it must come some day. But, the less people feel at home in these two states, the more certain and the more violent the change. The great majority will naturally be satisfied with the mere pleasures of relief, but large numbers will demand something new and better.

In the meanwhile we shall see the *viri eruditi* in their Chairs of History in Germany rearrange their facial expressions from what they have been during the last four or five years and not, perhaps, without a prod from above. Perhaps talent and hard work alone and not just enthusiasm will once again carry one through. For the audience, whether they were in the field or not, will in the interval have been through a whole process of fermentation, and what was future is now past. Certificates of baptism read quite differently now from what they did eight months ago.

At times all kinds of mad ideas come to me. . . . I wondered recently whether, in order to reduce his civil list, the King of Bavaria might not stop payments to Richard Wagner, who would then leave sadly—for Berlin.

What do you say to the old Jew Crémieux, who has headed the subscription list with 100,000 francs in order to pay off the 5,000 million at once?

To von Preen

Basle, 2 July 1871

Now that the terrible days, under the impression of which your last letter was written, lie a month behind us, what you say gives me once again to think. Yes, petroleum in the cellars of the Louvre and the flames in the other palaces are an expression of what the Philosopher calls "the will to live"; it is the last will and testament of mad fiends desiring to make a great impression on the world; from all that one has read since in intercepted papers, etc., the mainspring of it all was, at bottom, Herostratic.[70] And now they are building schools. Those who arranged those things could all read, write and even compose newspaper articles and other literature. And the ones in Germany who mean to do the same sort of thing are certainly no less "educated." But just look at England, bursting with wealth, and secretly kept in a state of siege by analogous elements! Up till now, for two hundred years, people in England have imagined that every problem could be solved through Freedom, and that one could let opposites correct one another in the free interplay of argument. But what now? The great harm was begun in the last century, mainly through Rousseau, with his doctrine of the goodness of human nature. Out of this plebs and educated alike distilled the doctrine of the golden age that was to come quite infallibly, provided people were left alone. The result, as every child knows, was the complete disintegration of the idea of authority in the heads of mortals, whereupon, of course, we periodically fall victim to sheer power. In the meanwhile, the idea of the natural goodness of man had turned, among the intelligent strata of Europe, into the idea of progress, i.e., undisturbed money-making and modern comforts, with philan-

70. Herostratus, an Ephesian, set fire to the Temple of Artemis at Ephesus on the night Alexander the Great was born, 356 B.C. He confessed under torture that he had fired the temple to immortalize himself. His name was condemned to oblivion, but seemingly Burckhardt could count upon von Preen knowing the incident. "The Philosopher" is, as elsewhere, Schopenhauer.

thropy as a sop to conscience. But the day before yesterday the victorious Prussians found it necessary to declare a state of siege in Königshütte.

The only conceivable salvation would be for this insane optimism, in great and small, to disappear from people's brains. But then our present-day Christianity is not equal to the task; it has gone in for and got mixed up with optimism for the last two hundred years. A change will and must come, but after God knows how much suffering. In the meanwhile you are building schools—at least you can take the responsibility for that before God; while I instruct my pupils and audience. I make no great secret of my philosophy to my students; the clever ones understand me, and as at the same time I do everything in every way I can to honour the real happiness that study and knowledge give one—however little it may be in itself—I am able to give each one some degree of consolation.

To von Preen

Basle, 12 October 1871

Art and scholarship, my dear Sir, will continue to be sick and sorry. We now shall see what Hartmann's *Philosophy of the Unconscious,* which I have ordered and await in pain, brings forth. Though our former Philosopher would really suffice. Think what he could have written on recent events in a supplementary chapter on the "will to power"!

"Who are you, after all, that you should long to be happy? Just tell me!"

In four weeks' time I am giving a lecture here in the University Aula on "Fortune and Misfortune in History"—in which I shall discuss as smoothly as possible the impropriety, in most cases, of the term "good fortune," and conclude as comfortingly as possible so as to reconcile people to fate. If one alarms people one cannot win them over, and the cleverer, cheeky ones just ridicule one. . . .

To von Preen

Basle, 23 December 1871

I am afraid that the thirties and forties of this century do not appear more agreeable to us merely because we were young then, but because they were incomparably more enjoyable times. We ought never to forget Renan's words about the period of the July Monarchy: *ces dix-huit années, les meilleures qu'ait passées la France, et peut-être l'humanité!* The fact that we are enjoying what is neither more nor less than an uncertain armistice is proclaimed as clearly as possible in Bismarck's decree of yesterday's date. . . .

Fortunately I shall have both hands full if I am to be anything like ready by the beginning of May with my new course of lectures for next summer (the history of Greek culture). I no longer get any time for out-side reading—even with my coffee and during the short siesta that fol-lows (it restores my strength wonderfully), I read the Greek Tragedians, etc., lying on my sofa, so as to devote every moment possible to the daily routine practice of Greek. My consolation is the assurance that I have gradually wrung a goodly portion of independent knowledge of antiquity directly from the sources, and that I shall be able to present by far the greater part of all I have to say as my own. But for that pride, I simply could not do anything else than say *Vale* to my Professorial Chair.

The *bonbon* I encourage myself with is a six-weeks' tour in Italy, from the end of September to the beginning of November 1872. In the mean-while I picture that heavenly reward to myself in such delightful colours that in the end I shall be able to forgo its realization. Sometimes I debate earnestly with myself whether I would not do better simply to go to the Riviera, to Spezia for example, and spend four weeks lying in the sun, or, say, take up my quarters in Sienna—and then suddenly the thought of Palermo strikes me. And in the end I shall be satisfied with an outing or two to Rheinfelden and Lörrach, and save a mint of money. . . .

To von Preen

Basle, 17 March 1872

First of all my best thanks for having drawn my attention to Konstantin Frantz's important book.[71] He certainly has his head above the mist. He is of course obliged to leave the reader to draw the most serious conclusions, and I very much fear that they run as follows: If, as a result of the increasingly felt lack of balance and topsyturviness, things get out of control, the one resource will be another foreign war. Of course, as you know, I am unteachable and unconvertible in these matters, and trace the last three wars to the wish to deal with internal difficulties.

To Arnold von Salis

Basle, 21 April 1872

. . . You could perfectly well have kept the Calderon; in fact I do not need either the Schlegel or the Gries translations at all this summer, and at a word from you I will send you all five. I have other worries; as the French say: *J'ai d'autres chiens à fouetter.* Unfortunately, much more is expected of my new course of lectures (on the history of Greek culture) than I shall be able to offer, and my one comfort is that there will be an end to September in anno 1872. Except for the necessary minimum of recreation I sit assiduously at my last, seeing only one thing: how unpolished and amateurish the whole series promises to be, although I spend all the scholarly effort I can on it. . . .

Herr B. will tell you in detail all about Nietzsche's lectures (on the work in our University); he is still in debt to us for the last, from which

71. Konstantin Frantz, author of several books on Europe and the German question written from a pro-Austrian and anti-Prussian point of view.

we awaited some solutions to the questions and lamentations that he threw out in such a grand and bold style. But in the meanwhile he has gone to the Waadtland to recuperate for ten days. He was quite delightful in places, and then again one heard a note of profound sadness, and I still don't see how the *auditores humanissimi* are to derive comfort or explanations from it. One thing was clear: a man of great gifts who possesses everything at first hand, and passes it on.

What you say about this being a transitional period is felt by all thinking people about everything. But there is one particular point I want to draw your attention to: the worries and troubles in store for all spiritual things within the next few years, resulting from the ever-increasing emphasis on material things, from the general change in mundane affairs that is bound to follow on the coming rise in the cost of living (one and a half times), and from the fact that we are at the beginning of a series of wars, etc. Things have reached the point at which first-class minds, which ten years ago devolved to scholarship, the Church or the Civil Service are moving over in appreciable numbers to the *business* party. And as to the extent to which the Universities are feeling the lack of *timber* when they have to stop a gap (that is to say of sufficiently respected young scholars who are neither deaf nor blind from special research), on that score I have heard quite incredible admissions from a well-informed source.

If I am not mistaken, I told you my fundamental beliefs during the last war: something great, new and liberating must come out of Germany, and what is more *in opposition* to power, wealth and business; it will have to have its martyrs; it must be something which of its very nature will swim above water and survive political, economic and other catastrophes. But what? There you out-question me. It might even be that we too should fail to recognize it if it came into the world.

In the meanwhile let us attend assiduously, and where we are concerned, learn and learn till we bust.

To von Preen

Basle, 26 April 1872

. . . I am not being unfair. Bismarck has only taken into his own hands what would have happened in due course without him and in opposition to him. He saw the growing wave of social-democracy would somehow or other bring about a state of naked power, whether through the democrats themselves, or through the Governments, and said: *Ipse faciam,* and embarked on three wars, 1864, 1866, 1870.

But we are only at the beginning. Don't you feel that everything we do now seems more or less amateurish, capricious, and becomes increasingly ridiculous by contrast with the high purposefulness of the military machine worked out to the last details? The latter is bound to become the model of existence. It will be most interesting for you, my dear Sir, to observe how the machinery of State and administration is transformed and militarized; for me—how schools and education are put through the cure, etc. Of all classes, the workers are going to have the strangest time; I have a suspicion that, for the time being, sounds completely mad, and yet I cannot rid myself of it: that the military state will have to turn "industrialist." The accumulations of beings, the mounds of men in the yards and factories cannot be left for all eternity in their need and thirst for riches; a planned and controlled degree of poverty, with promotion and uniforms, starting and ending daily to the roll of drums, that is what ought to come logically. (I know enough history, of course, to know that things do not always work out logically.) Of course, what is done will have to be well done—and then no mercy, whether for those above or those below. In the paper yesterday or the day before the programme of the carpenters' union in Berlin was given, which you will easily find in the Berlin papers. *Lisez et réfléchissez!*

The development of a clever and lasting sovereign power is still in swaddling clothes; it may perhaps wear its *toga virilis* for the first time in Germany. There are still vast uncharted seas to be discovered in this sphere. The Prussian dynasty is so placed that it and its staff can never again be powerful enough. There can be no question of stopping on this path; the salvation of Germany itself is in forging ahead. . . .

To von Preen

Basle, 28 June 1872

What Dr. Kaiser wrote you is the truth.[72] For Curtius's sake I buried it in deep silence, but four weeks later the matter was noised abroad in Berlin and Leipzig and reached here. I denied it to three-quarters of the students, so as not to have to acknowledge any visible compliments. I would not have gone to Berlin at any price; to have left Basle would have brought a malediction on me. Nor is my merit in the matter great; there would be no helping a man of fifty-four who did not know where his modest portion of (relatively) good luck lay.

Had I accepted, I should be in a suicidal mood, instead of which people here are really grateful to me and here and there quietly shake me by the hand. Officially nothing is known of the matter as I wanted to avoid all fuss. On the other hand, it is a great triumph for Treitschke — good luck to him!

Why am I so devilishly pressed by my lectures? Because I shall not be spending my summer holidays (middle of June to middle of August) at my writing-table, but in Vienna. Friend Lübke was here recently straight from Vienna and warned me to see Vienna before the exhibition, whatever happened, as it would soon be out of the question owing to rising prices. So now I am going to Vienna at a time when it is usually deserted, so as to have a thorough look at the Belvedere, etc. Nothing but toil and work; I would really sooner go somewhere in the mountains: and now I

72. Ernst Curtius had enquired confidentially whether Burckhardt would accept the Professorship of History vacated by Ranke. Kaiser lived at Lörrach.

must make all haste to look to the gaping holes in the last part of my lecture; what I can't heal I must patch together and what I can't patch together I must stop up with moss. Only pray don't betray me to my students. Up to now the sixty(!) who have signed on have remained faithful.

You will certainly find me here in the late summer, as the golden phantasmagoria of the Riviera or even Palermo is naturally incompatible with the Vienna project. . . .

To von Preen

Basle, 3 October 1872

. . . Vienna, which I think you know, was quite wonderful; three weeks of undisturbed enjoyment and any number of friendly meetings with unknown people; and once again I found out that, provided the air and the water are good, great heat is not only not harmful, but exhilarating. I really have nothing precise to recount; one day passed like the next as I more or less assiduously harvested my observations and notes on Art and Antiquity, and enjoyed a comfortable and agreeable existence. Politics were hardly mentioned; where the conversation happened to take this turn I encountered a really astonishing thoughtlessness. One thing became very clear to me: the growing dislike for the all-powerful Jews and their utterly venal press. The whole Gabriel Affair[73] in Linz was simply a machination on the part of the Viennese Jewish press, whose patrons cannot do without that sort of thing, even for their own safety's sake. There is a regular duel going on between Israel and the so-called Ultramontanes. It's fairly easy to see who is seconding it from outside.

Politics may disgust one altogether, only they have the power of beck-

73. The Jewish press had accused a Carmelite priest of unsettling the mind of a young girl in the confessional.

oning us to the window, even if we don't want to listen. The latest thing they are frightening us with is a possible resurgence of the Commune, "foreseen" by Bismarck, who is supposed to have got *carte blanche* at the meeting of the three Emperors, to go on "experimenting" with France. To this I add the following certain fact: a considerable number of workmen of the better, quieter sort from France (Frenchmen *nota bene*) have been applying for work at one of the large works here, stating expressly that they saw the Commune coming, and did not want to go through it again.

And then there is the frightful exodus from Alsace! A lot of people are saying that if Prussia had known that, it would never, etc., etc.—but Prussia need only have asked any old Basler who knew Alsace, and it would have discovered what was going to happen, for example, even in 1867 (when I met a Prussian "reporting" on the state of feeling and conditions in Alsace—not exactly an agreeable individual. He must have carried quite a lot of news back to Berlin!). But they wanted a Poland, and now they have got one; without a running sore South Germany simply could not be kept in order.

Eduard von Hartmann, who writes a little much in the newspapers "for a philosopher," has recently written a curiously pessimistic article in Lindau's *Gegenwart* on the general political condition of Germany. And now along comes old Rosenkrantz with some remarks on the increasing uniformity of our civilization. One begins to feel as though one were going to Evening Service on a rainy Sunday—but for the time being the most prudent thing is to be as cheerful as possible, and not to behave as though there were bad omens in the sky. If the evil does not occur, then our behaviour will be sheer profit.

Further, I have provisionally sworn never, not at any rate wilfully, again to undertake a large pressing work, such as the last series of lectures, but merely to go on working diligently at the already existing ones, the usual classes. Further, how miserable I should feel if I were on my way to Berlin with all I possessed. As it is, I employ any fine afternoon in quiet and contemplative expeditions to certain good inns in Oberalemannien. I spent the day before yesterday *ad Cervum,* where Kaiser talked a lot of a letter he had had from you. The postmistress is solemnly rejuvenating herself, as in fourteen days' time her work and troubles will be over. With the years, indeed, we shall none of us, in the end, put in an appearance—*isch's Gottswill, so sterbe mer alli!* If it's God's will, we'll all die, as Hebel says.

To Bernhard Kugler

Basle, Wednesday, 20 November 1872

. . . My heartiest congratulations on your position in Tübingen. Anyone lecturing without notes to an audience of 100, and economically provided for as you are, my dear Sir, can afford to laugh at everything. It doesn't matter a bit whether you are "on the Staff" or not, or what a certain number of place-hunters in the North think, or pretend to think about your views; you are bound to be wanted and offered a job; just take no further steps in the matter, and show a gentle breath of contempt for certain people; then they will be polite.

It is most diverting to stay outside the cliques and claques, and not requiring them, to watch them and as the occasion arises, to let people know that: "you can neither boil nor roast me, and one fine day I shall be carried above your heads." That in fact happens quite unexpectedly, while the *viri eruditissimi* are all peering into their almanacs to find out if there isn't someone who has reached seventy-five and is ripe for a pension.

So courage! Give more and more of your time to lecturing without notes, and see that even this term your lectures are quite untied to paper! One gets quite other ideas than one does lecturing from notes, and becomes quite a different man! What one produces is quite different too and one reads sources quite differently. . . .

To Bernhard Kugler

Basle, 11 December 1872

Your proposal gives me the greatest pleasure,[74] and I take it as an omen of the very best quality that the names Kugler and Burckhardt should once again appear on the same title-page.

I give you sovereign powers to lengthen and change the text. You could say something like this in a short preface:

"The original author, being somewhat estranged from the subject owing to other work, has given the editor a free hand, not only with reference to the material, but also as regards the standpoint and the judgment of things. As a result of the work devoted to the subject during the last thirteen or fourteen years, and to the great changes both in the North and in the South, opinions have altered in many respects, without the author being in any way to blame."

What do you say to lengthening the book and making two volumes of it, perhaps two little volumes? Of course, Seemann would have the last word on this point.

À propos Seemann: he is the sole proprietor of the book, and I have no shadow of ownership. I write this to you so that you should lay him heavily under contribution, as he richly deserves for the slovenly and incorrect way in which the second edition was prepared.[75] I repeat: above all no *égards* on my account, for the book no longer concerns me at all from the pecuniary point of view.

The idea of putting my book into your hands is too good to be Seemann's; that jack of all trades Lübke must have devised it.

It is understood that I give you full permission to rearrange the material entirely as new, the arrangement of the principal subjects, etc.

74. The third edition of the *Renaissance*.
75. Prepared by Burckhardt himself for the publisher Seemann.

One doesn't only need to have one's hands free, but one's elbows too, and to be entirely free.

In all haste *Glück auf!*

To von Preen

Basle, New Year's Eve, 1872

I have just read your melancholy pages again and am beginning to feel tempted to preach you the following sermon: You may thank God if you are ignored, i.e., if mankind gives you to understand that others have become the fashion; put your trust in contemplation, *nota bene* on gathering your views of the world and the age together, and on written observations. Your career has been sufficiently active and many-sided to make you familiar with innumerable spheres of existence, and yet you have not had to go so far out on the high seas that you were bound to lose your delight in studying things.

I have acquired the whole of Grillparzer and now realize with astonishment from reading the Dramas, Autobiography and note-books of every sort left by this fugitive from the world, how useful and fruitful a secluded life such as his can be for posterity. . . .

With regard to the failure of spontaneity in Germany, you will probably find a prophecy on the point in one or other of my letters of two years ago, if you should by any misfortune have preserved them. Things can only be changed by ascetics, by men who are independent of the enormously expensive life of the great cities, far from the atmosphere of company promoting and from the horrific luxury to which official literature and art are falling victim, by men, that is, who will be able to help the national spirit and the popular soul to express itself. For the moment Richard Wagner occupies the whole forefront of the scene. People have tried to promote him to the rank of Fool, which he is not, but bold and ruthless, a man who has caught time by the short hairs in a masterly fashion. The fools are the ones he has trampled under foot and compelled to give him unreserved homage. Let us try to remember that once upon a time Bismarck was called a fool. In the meanwhile, a very important aspect of his music is becoming quite clear to me: one can in fact keep clear of it and of a great crowd of nervous people who cling to it. Instead I play very beautiful things very badly in my room and need render an account to no man.

Why Filius should not have been called up for military service is a complete mystery to me; but I congratulate father and son on the liberation, which is a great and real benefit for higher education.

I neither read nor know any works on recent history (under which title our delightful century is no doubt intended); since Gervinus I have lost my taste for such books, and where the thing itself is concerned, namely the said century, I look at it through my own one-sided spectacles. In your position I should take the first good short book that deals with the facts superficially in some way or other; for the interpretation of the facts is going through a complete and thorough moult, and one will have to wait some years before the history of the world, beginning with Adam, has been painted in victorious German colours and orientated towards 1870 and 1871. They will certainly win the next war too, but the national-liberal foundations of their point of view may in the meantime have begun to show some thought-provoking cracks.

May the year 1875 bring you, my dear Sir, and me, peace, quiet, resignation to the will of fate and a clear head with which to observe the world!

To Friedrich Nietzsche

Basle, 25 February 1874

In conveying to you my best thanks for sending me the newest part[76] of *Thoughts out of Season* I can, for the moment, only reply with a few words after having read rapidly through your powerful and weighty work. I really have no right to do so yet, as the work requires to be enjoyed bit by bit, and maturely considered, only the matter concerns people like us so closely that one is tempted to say something at once.

In the first place my poor head has never been capable of reflecting, even at a distance, as you are able to do, upon final causes, the aims and the desirability of history. As teacher and professor I can, however, maintain that I have never taught history for the sake of what goes under the high-falutin' name of "world history," but essentially as a propaedeutic study: my task has been to put people in possession of the scaffolding which is indispensable if their further studies of whatever kind were not to be aimless. I have done everything I possibly could to lead them on to acquire personal possession of the past—in whatever shape and form— and at least not to sicken them of it; I wanted them to be capable of picking the fruits for themselves; I never dreamt of training scholars and disciples in the narrower sense, but only wanted to make every member of my audience feel and know that everyone may and must appropriate those aspects of the past which appeal to him personally, and that there might be happiness in so doing. I know perfectly well that such an aim may be criticized as fostering amateurism, but that does not trouble me overmuch. At my advanced age one may thank heaven if one has discovered some sort of principle in teaching for the institution to which one belongs *in concreto*.

This is not meant as a justification, which you, my dear colleague,

76. "On the Advantages and Disadvantages of History."

would be the last to expect of me, but simply a brief summary of what one has desired and attempted up to now. Your friendly quotation on p. 29 makes me uneasy; as I read it, it occurs to me that the image at the end is not entirely mine, and that Schnaase might well have expressed himself similarly at some time or other. Well, I hope no one will bring it up.

This time you will interest numerous readers because the book puts a really tragic incongruity right before our eyes: the antagonism between historical knowledge and the capacity to do or to be, and then again the antagonism between the enormous heaping up of knowledge acquired, and the materialistic motives of the age.

With renewed and best thanks. . . .

To von Preen

Basle, 31 May 1874

My heartiest congratulations on being liberated from Bruchsal,[77] a very interesting place in its way, but really not at all suited to you and to your family. . . .

Once again last year I spent a couple of hours walking about Karlsruhe after leaving you; what could be done in a plain has certainly been done, and quite a few things, such as the new baths, are really very good. And from a social point of view you will certainly find all that you could desire. Do you know that a few years ago it was quite on the cards that I should go to the Polytechnical School in the place of Woltmann? We should then have been compatriots and colleagues in the Service. Moreover, since then I have had to take the same decision more than once: that I do not move from here. For many years now I have foreseen developments here which do not promise to be exactly pleasant, and know

77. Von Preen had been appointed to Karlsruhe.

there is going to be no "peaceful old age" or anything of that sort for me, but I never wanted to give the signal for emigration. Come what may in Basle, I want to be there.

In April I spent sixteen days in Paris buying engravings, lithographs and photographs for my new work as Professor of the History of Art, which I have since begun. People would like *la république des honnêtes gens,* and speak favourably of Thiers, but in private they sigh: *ce qu'il nous faudrait, ce serait un gouvernement fort,* and in business circles, that is spoken from the heart. At present I am lecturing five hours a week on history, three hours on the history of art, and in addition have kept my class, the third, in the Pedagogium, which involves four hours. Nobody can now say that I eat my bread in idleness and sin. Although indeed I only lecture three hours a week on the history of art, I find I have to retouch my lectures much more than I thought; I no longer find my note-books, dating from Zürich (1855–1858), good enough for my present audience (nor perhaps do they satisfy the greater maturity I have since, as I flatter myself, attained). I have to proceed taking very general views and be clear and brief. And if conditions here do not get too troublesome, it looks as though I should have to take six months' holiday in Italy and make a little outing as far as Athens, which means that a respectable sum of money will be spent.

It is good and kind of you to honour my old and forgotten "Constantine" with your attention. If I had not lost my job here in 1852, soon after finishing the book (which threw me forcibly into the history of art), I should have written a series of cultural-historical descriptions of the Middle Ages, of which "The Culture of the Renaissance" would have been the concluding picture. As it is, I have grown old without doing so, occupied with other things, and have always had enough to live on.

To Bernhard Kugler

Basle, 14 June 1874

To undertake Spanish History for Heeren and Ukert would entail a tremendous specialized work for a number of years, allied to a by no means insignificant slavery, which might easily have a harmful effect on your teaching. Of course I do not know how you look upon these matters; anyone who overvalues teaching to the extent that I do, ought not, perhaps, to join in the discussion. If the publishers gave one time, and one could make an *opus vitae* of it, and could let everything ripen as it should, there could be nothing better; only one forms part of a series, and Perthes Jun., or whoever the publisher may be, wants to produce so and so many volumes a year. Moreover, most important of all: one is tied to a particular style, to a definite amount of material, and has to deliver a certain quantity of erudition *in rebus hispanicis* to the doors of German learning, all neatly prepared. Now, to anyone as self-willed as me, that would be quite unacceptable; in books I talk solely of what interests me, and treat things according as they seem important, not to the learned Kunz or Professor Benz, but to me. Now I will try for once to put myself in your place and talk in character: "Along comes the publisher and offers me work that will not leave me a moment's peace for six to eight years, if I am to complete it in the manner required by the erudite specialist circles in question. But the theme itself is a fine one, and tempts me. Then suddenly an idea occurs to me! I am so situated in worldly things that I don't need to sweat myself to death; I shall leave Perthes' pig-skin history of Spain to another, and go off on my own to Spain as soon as it is safe, and study Spain and write about it exactly as it pleases *me*—two volumes instead of six, just as *I* please."

And now, pray, forgive my impertinence. I am far from wishing to spare you mental effort and strain, but only slavery to norms fixed by others without any action on our part.

And what about the poor "Council of Constance"? Well, if you don't want it, I shall advise somebody else to take it up, and if nobody else will, I shall end by treating the wonderful theme myself.

My congratulations on escaping from the Tübingen *Jubiläumsschrift*. That sort of thing is work for mossy-heads and old war-horses, and not for those who still have to sail out on to the high seas. . . .

To Bernhard Kugler

Basle, 5 October 1874

I for my part, who have unloaded my works on to the shoulders of others, and don't write books, enjoy good health which I no longer have any rights to, though I am prepared to see it gradually decline any day now, and will patiently acquiesce. But however that may be, in my experience learned authorship is one of the most unhealthy, and mere teaching (however troublesome it may be, and however circumstantial the studies and preparations need to be) one of the healthiest *métiers* in the world. To be always standing, walking and talking, and to go for a good hike once a week whatever the weather, now and then a bottle of the best, no overheated rooms in the winter, and an open collar, that is what is good for one. The one thing I take great care to avoid is wet feet. Now just look at my *Cicerone!* Shortly after working on the second edition the splendid Mündler dies; towards the end of the third edition it cost Zahn his life; that fine, spiritual, gentle character Bode will, I hope, take over the fourth edition, but he is sickening, and I, the original begetter of it all, am still in rude health. But I have a heavy winter ahead of me with eight lectures a week (some of them new), four hours in the classroom, and six evening lectures for the general public. But it has to be so. . . .

To von Preen

Basle, 30 December 1874

. . . I envy you one thing: you are only now, in the full ripeness of experience, reading Ranke's *Popes,* while I devoured them in my student days, and knew parts of them by heart, and can now no longer feel the old spell. That, and the first volume of his *German History in the Age of the Reformation* are, in my opinion, his masterpieces, whereas much seems to me to be lacking in the *French History,* and in his *English History* there is a certain tediousness even, because there he loses the sense and the measure of universal history. On the other hand, I think a lot of his much abused *Prussian History.* The latest things, since Wallenstein, are indeed astounding performances at his great age, but I have caught him out in a certain amount of party-feeling against the House of Austria and no longer trust him on certain questions. In conversation he is still said to be unbelievably vivacious; this summer he gave someone who told me about it an appointment from ten to twelve at night, and left him in the same old state of sheer wonderment.

To von Preen

Basle, 31 December 1874

The famous dispatch[78] has startled a lot of people who are not easily startled; it is simply Philip II's policy from another angle—he thought he could not go on existing unless everything around him were utterly feeble. I have nothing against the press being bought on a scale hitherto unknown, expressly founded, or at any rate obliged with articles *gratis* (whether they are dated from Rome, London or Paris); that is simply how

78. Bismarck's dispatch on the Arnim case.

power behaves in the nineteenth century, but what I find unbearable in certain papers is the unasked for, over-zealous servility with which they perform the task of policeman for the Master. *Surtout pas de zèle!* as one of Napoleon's ministers said. . . .

To Robert Grüninger

Rome, 1 April 1875

As I arrived here yesterday evening, and have since run through the Rafael Frescoes, the Pinacotheca, and the Sistine this morning, I want to write to you before I start on my evening visit to the Colosseum, etc., for during the next few days time may be short in which to fulfil my promise. Elegant as the Albergo Centrale may be, I have a shaky table so you will have to put up with my hand-writing. . . . The night journey through the Mont Cenis with a good *chaufferette* and a full moon, was quite tolerable; at a quarter to five I woke from a refreshing sleep in Turin and so, like Odysseus coming to Ithaca from Scheria, landed in Italy in my sleep. (Prosaically that means: I slept through everything.) I had two and a half hours in Turin, and walked about the town while the last gas lamps, the full moon and the grey morning light played one against another like the three orchestras in *Don Giovanni*. I went right up to the Cappucini Terrace to await the sunrise; from there one sees the whole chain of Alps over the Po and the whole magnificent town; I just had time enough to see the mountains begin to redden and shimmer. But there was ice and snow everywhere down to Alessandria; it was fabulously beautiful then to descend into the warm spring air of Genoa which gave a real impression of spring with its predominantly evergreen vegetation, although one saw quite well that really fresh green was rare even here.

. . . The crowds in the churches were enormous, *le donne per divozione e gli uomini per veder le donne,* and there were some very pretty women among them, whom one hardly sees at all the rest of the year. Unfortunately almost all of them were dressed *alla francese;* the national dress, which I used to see worn by the entire middle class, is now only normal among the poor. The line from Genoa to Spezia is more tunnel than landscape, but wonderful in places, reminiscent of Sorrento and Amalfi. On the other hand, Spezia would not come up to memories and expectations, although I spent a very enjoyable evening talking politics to three Italians; and I really must praise my traveller's luck, as I have not had to spend a single evening by myself and without my *conversazione.*

To   Max Alioth★

Rome, 5 April 1875

. . . My respect for Barocco grows hourly, and I am almost disposed to regard it as the proper end and main achievement of vital architecture. It not only has means for everything that serves the end, but also for beauty of appearance. On which more when we meet.

I am in excellent health in spite of running to and fro; among other things, I am enjoying not having to know *ex officio* who painted the reredos in the *x* chapel in St. Thingummybob. I poke my snout in everywhere and now realize how very different Rome is from, e.g., Genoa, which looks as though children had stuck up some fourth-rate theatrical scenery obliquely, on the top of every rock. What I saw of the early Renaissance on the way moved me deeply, namely St. Catherine's in Sienna and its façade, the little staircase, courtyard and hall and out-buildings. On the other hand, the Palazzo del Magnifico fooled me completely; I had in the past only seen it from outside, and thought, from the bronze torch-holder, that the interior must contain something dating from the age of the Tyrants, but found nothing but a stinking little courtyard with a vaulted, arcaded cloister along which, presumably, the late Tyrant went to the closet.

. . . Rome is greatly changed, the Corso is a bit of Paris in the evening and at night; at every step one notices the invasion of Italians with all their dialects; I hear Milanese and Neapolitan, etc. Some things are expensive, though not so dear as I feared. Many things are decidedly more convenient than formerly, and food and drink as good as ever. Last year's red wine, even in *trattorie* like the Tre Ladroni and the Archetto, is as fiery and magnificent as a Burgundy, and if I were capable of solitary drinking on a large scale, I should become a soak. At the coffee-stalls one can get coffee for fifteen centimes that puts our miserable Basle *cafetiers,* with their dish-water at thirty, into the shade. And, *N.B.,* coffee does not grow in Italy either, and without doubt pays higher customs dues here than in Switzerland. I always look out now, in the smaller cafés, to see what they have in the alcove above the buffet; occasionally it is still the Madonna with the little lamp in front; somewhere or other it was still the Madonna, but instead of the little lamp a number of select old liqueur bottles were displayed in front of it; instead of the Madonna you find the bust of Vittorio Emmanuele in the enlightened cafés, usually covered in dust, which settles on his forehead, in the eye sockets, on the enormous snout and on the top of his upturned moustachios, which looks very odd. By the by, I shall be thoroughly ministerially minded in Italy, and until my return.

The thing that particularly characterizes Rome for me at the moment is the numbers of Germans; today in the Palace of the Caesars they were in the majority. In the Vatican, a few days ago, I followed along after a party of Germans who had a decrepit old Austrian as a *cicerone;* you ought to have heard all he told them! Today, in the great hall of the Museo Capitolino where the Centaurs stand, a charming thing happened; it was a free day, and there were some of the poor of Rome walking about; a nice old woman with a child asked me, quite alarmed, where such creatures were to be found; and I had to reassure her that they were only *immaginazioni de' scultori, perchè,* I added, *sarebbe troppo l'intelligenza dell'uomo insieme colla forza del cavallo.* But isn't it wonderful to sculpt for a people that think even the boldest thing real? Who still perhaps regard female allegorical figures as *Sante persone?* Whereas, of course, in the North every child knows *a priori* that Art is a mere joke.

. . . I am already living in a morass of photographs and yet am only at the beginning. Certain doubts are gradually forming in my mind, not for me but for those who come after us: they will fade, while even the smallest lithograph will last; everyone has now gone in for photography, and people will say, if they fade we can make a thousand new ones—only the objects themselves are not eternal! And I found a lot of the Camposanto in Pisa much more damaged than formerly, and also in the Palazzo Pubblico in Sienna.

To Robert Grüninger

Rome, 13 April 1875

You can imagine what pleasure your letter gave me. Then too the copy of the *Allgemeine Schweizer Zeitung* arrived yesterday, and this very moment, on my return from a long expedition, comes a letter from Max Alioth, which I must also answer, to whom in the meanwhile my thanks.

What an ideal picture of Italy you paint, whereas my behaviour in Rome is so commercial and flighty that I haven't even been to S. Pietro in Montorio, or so much as on the Pincio. The only thing I have allowed myself was S. Paolo; the day before yesterday, Sunday morning, tempted me out to some of the more distant churches, and among other things to S. Sabina; and then I walked a little further on the Aventine between garden walls and suddenly saw a large bit of Campagna in front of me, to the west, as far as the sea it seemed to me, and S. Paolo almost at my feet. So I toddled along and for the first time fully realized the gigantic proportions of the interior, and made a mental note of some general observations on problems of colossal size in architecture which are useful to me. You see how prosaic one becomes.

The sad thing about it all is that the gentlemanly leisure necessary for real meditation, such as I enjoyed in the winter of 1847 to 1848, is entirely lacking, and I have to snatch and snap my observations at full speed. On the way home from St. Paul's a seventeen-year-old girl from the Campagna by the door of an Osteria, wretched and dirty but of an indescribable, soul-stirring beauty. All in all I must say that during the twenty-nine years since I first came here, the people have not declined physically at all, although peasant colouring is becoming rarer. On the other hand, foreign tourists are much more awful than they used to be, and the sight of the Piazza di Spagna, as it is now, makes me despair. I can stand the English, but a certain other nation somewhat less.

Bode is here and so we meet now at one place, now at another, and go through a whole gallery, for example, the Vatican Pinacotheca or the Borghese critically, discussing genuineness, condition, etc. He really has a most astonishingly good eye, and when I think that he might die over the nth Edition of the *Tschitsch,*[79] I am tempted to say: Dear Bode, Mündler died over the Second, Zahn over the Third, spare yourself!—But an enlightened North German would simply laugh in my face. And moreover it would be a pity not only on account of his knowledge, but on account of the dear fellow himself. Like other good people I know, he comes from Brunswick. He is the only German I know, though I see crowds of them in the galleries, etc. The majority belong to the modern class of penitent pilgrims, who don't visit the Privileged Altars with peas in their shoes and weals on their backs, but do penance by boring themselves to death in front of works of art from which they gain nothing. Italians never make that impression on me in galleries; they either go away or look properly at a thing. I think I may flatter myself that I am grasping a great deal that formerly remained concealed from me in works of art, and that my capacity to observe has grown substantially; it would be worrying if that were not so. If only I had three months! Instead of thinking things over, I have to run from one *Bottega di fotografo* to the

79. The *Cicerone.*

next, and bargain, which is very much against the grain, and if I achieve something it's not much.

. . . I spend the evenings either in the Teatro Quirino *chez* Pulcinella, or more often in the Teatro Rossini near the Minerva where I particularly enjoyed Petrella's *Precauzioni,* Fioravanti's *Don Procopio* and Rossi's *Falsi Monetari.* In the latter, the composer, who is at present in Rome, was called for, and the audience in the stalls thought he was not on the stage but in the centre of the front tier of boxes . . . where two large, painted courtesans sat taking the applause amid general laughter. *Aida* was given twice, but was sold out each time, so that I had to give up; it is quite deliberately rarely given here; the owner of the score and the opera (Ricordi) will not allow anyone but a certain Nicolini to sing the tenor part—whereas I must be in just the right mood to go to the theatre, and be able to decide, half an hour before it begins, whether I am going or not; and then I am quite ready to put up with a good deal, standing for three hours, for example.

Italy is *Italia aeterna* and they still ride bare-back, as they did twenty-nine years ago, not only because they have balance and a firm grip, but because they are firmly baked into the dirt on their beasts, and so it is in everything; meeting and talking to people is always amusing, and they are still men and will remain human. In the meanwhile I have greeted Rome on your behalf from my balcony window, looking towards the Villa Medici and Trinità de' Monti.

All my best wishes to you and to the gentlemen at "The Mill" and all the other initiates, to whom you may show this letter if it interests them.

To **Max Alioth**

Rome, 16 April 1875

. . . As for the rest, Rome is pretty well intact in all essentials with the exception of the neighbourhood of S. Maria Maggiore, and still possesses that galaxy of proud architectural perspectives which no other town on earth can rival; it is by no means always the classical beauty of the individual building that is decisive, but whole groups of buildings seem to have been put together at different periods as though according to one great homogeneous plan. For naturally, if people spit in their hands and work for twenty-five centuries, something grand may well emerge. (It occurs to me that twenty-five centuries spitting into their hands does not give a very beautiful picture of the whole thing, though at least it's less funny than *les quarante siècles censées de contempler l'armée Française le jour de la bataille des pyramides.*) And what is new is quite as good, if not better than elsewhere. God knows I like the station better than the Gare du Nord in Paris with its *néo-grec;* Podesti's frescoes in the Vatican are better than most of Kaulbach's, and even the monument to the Immacolata in the Piazza di Spagna, apart from its significance, is worth looking at from an artistic point of view, and the Prophets are by no means bad. The most ridiculous monument I have seen on my journey is unquestionably the fountain in Chambéry with four huge elephants emerging from the four sides of an obelisk, which means to say they are all joined together inside the obelisk. And just think of the joint "motion." On the other hand, in Turin I was delighted by the most glorious of all equestrian statues, Emmanuele Filiberto.

I have been able to avoid Germans up till now, with the exception of my good Bode; the place is still crawling with them, although the trek to Naples has already begun, and the photographers are busy day and night and can hardly supply souvenirs enough. My chief supplier, Crippa, a comic Milanese, maintains that "la fotografia, sinora, non e che una fanciulla," and will be quite different shortly.

To Max Alioth

Dresden, Hotel Stadt Wien, 24 July 1875

By gossiping to you and telling you what has happened to me up to now, I shall rest and restore myself after my toil and effort. And then, too, I am fortunate in having a table that is of exactly the right height in relation to the chair, whereas in Rome I had to write at a wretched little *Katzentischlein* that was two inches too high into the bargain. But then Rome is Rome, and Dresden is glorious, but only Dresden.

Early Saturday, after a tolerably good night's sleep in the express, Frankfort. Furious building of Palaces by Jews and other company promoters, and what is more, in *German* Renaissance, which our friend Lübke has made the fashion. Clumsy ornamentation of every description, naturally, has been smuggled in under that rubric; people who are incapable of producing something beautiful are unable to do so whatever the style, and all the "motives" and "themes" in the world don't help a man without fantasy. Most of what is built in Italian Renaissance is hideous, despite its richness, e.g., huge windows framed by projecting pilasters and pediments without any attempt at a pedestal. And you should see the classical buildings!

> *Denn die reichen Jüden*
> *Baun mit Karyatiden*
>
> *The wealthy Israelites*
> *Build with Caryatids*

which must show up to good advantage when Kalle and Schikselchen and Papa with their famous noses, appear on the balcony between females borrowed from the Pandroseion. Then there are façades broken up into a mass of harshly alternating smaller scenes, like a scene by Richard Wagner. If only it were unclaimed, but at least genuine, fantasy! Instead of which there is no lack of skill. Here and there one comes across some-thing really brilliant, but the predominating effect is as I have described it.

In the afternoon to Marburg, a three-hours' stroll, and a visit to St. Elizabeth's which confirmed me in my old respect for the men of the thirteenth century, whose buildings seem to grow up out of the very ground, like living plants. Late in the evening to Cassel, where I remained five days, till yesterday evening, and studied the picture gallery. As on this journey I copy my pencil notes at once on to a number of separate pieces of paper as soon as I get back to the inn, the day is spent most industri-ously: I have to work it this way, because I should never find the time to copy out my notes after my return to Basle. More later about the as-tounding treasures of the gallery; but I don't think you know Cassel at all, and you ought to see it. . . .

Tonight the *Postillon von Longjumeau* is being given and I am deter-mined to go at any price. But the interim theatre is small to be sure, and I am rather doubtful in some respects about the big Semper theatre, the outside of which is almost completed, and fear that in spite of its being larger and richer it will never replace the former one.

To von Preen

Basle, 19 September 1875

Kaiser tells me you found "the Philosopher" as widespread among edu-cated people in Austria as he is elsewhere. I am more and more convinced that he had a special mission for our age. As the illusions of the "Prog-ress" which had dominated since 1830 come to disappear it is essential to have someone to tell us all that belongs to the kingdom of illusions and how to give up our vain hopes in time. Only compare it with the terrible kingdom of this world, the merciless optimism that is springing up every-where, even among the workers who live in the mad belief that they are going to be able to insist on a life of comfort that bears no relation to the

state of society. In the end there will be a pitched battle between optimism and—not pessimism—but "malism" (forgive the silly word).

All that is no mere dream. There were times in the 3rd and 4th
centuries when, without counting the influence of the *Völkerwanderung*,
pessimism had become an almost generally recognized attitude, theoreti-
cally at least. What a face "Progress" of the 1830 variety will make one
day when, if, ever, it realizes that it simply served: (1) to draw men together and mix them (through the railways); (2) as a demolition squad, so
that a very different type should be able to build on the cleanly swept
ground? But I shall at the most only see the beginnings of that, and certainly have no great longing to assist in the work.

To von Preen

Basle, 27 February 1876

. . . I don't any longer hear very much music except what I produce
myself on my pianino. I entirely share your taste for good dance-music,
and am quite carried away by some of it, specially the Viennese things,
while other Viennese productions betray only too well that they are
merely a tracing of what has already been. As to Offenbach, I too say: *à
tout pécheur miséricorde;* some of his things are delightful and witty. There
is only one I have no wish to hear about, the murderer of present-day
opera: you know whom I mean. . . .

To von Preen

Basle, 17 November 1876

Put forward any idea, any proposal whatsoever in the Conservative's
sense, and in practice nothing comes of it; only disintegrating and level-

ling ideas have any real power. You will find the point we have reached illuminated in the same sense in our *Allgemeine Schweizer Zeitung*, but there is nothing to be done. Our Federal and Cantonal Referendum sometimes frustrates one of the ideas of MM. Homais and company, and for a time they are puzzled what to do, but in itself it is really one more solvent. No amount of uneasiness could any longer plug the source of the ill, which is the leadership of the masses, who are so easily led, and the utter lack of respect shown by Radicalism—not for the old, conservative political forms (since I don't expect piety from it on that score), but for the laws and regulations of their own creation. That's what makes the situation so hopelessly insecure. In the meanwhile duty and policy require that though we may not smile on everything we should at least not look sour-faced. For my part I have long since simplified my outlook by relating every question to the University of Basle and by simply asking whether this or that is good or not good for it. As long as I am neither guilty nor an accomplice of anything that does it harm, I shall be satisfied with the outward course of my life *in globo*. Term has now been going on for four weeks, and the additional public lectures have begun, of which two are behind and two before me. Further, I have been to the Opera six times already, and it's been very good, all things considered. On the 2nd December our simple and beautiful Concert Hall is to be inaugurated with the Ninth Symphony, etc., so I shall see that I get a seat, as the Society in question will almost fill the 1500 seats. Does anyone, nowadays, feel the *Freude, schöner Götterfunken?* Those who do so must be very young. All the same, our Concert Hall is a more pleasing building than your Festhalle, and the programmes it is likely to offer.

To   **von Preen**

Basle, 13 April 1877

. . . The abdication and return of the great man[80] gives me the feeling
that he doesn't know what to do next; he has pretty well overshot the
mark in all important internal questions, and one may certainly believe
him when he says his health is wrecked. He could of course be asked to
come back again, but would he really be much help? He might possibly
still set the tone in a great European crisis, if there were to be one as a
result of the Turkish war which seems imminent, but internally he can
no longer save the Empire. . . .

Among recent books Taine's *Les Origines de la France Contemporaine*
is undoubtedly to be recommended, indeed worth possessing: Tome I,
L'Ancien Régime (Paris, Hachette, this volume 550 pages). The author has
two great qualities; he sees the spiritual contours and colours very clearly,
and writes unexpectedly well and simply. Presumably (according to the
preface, page v) there will be three volumes: *Ancien Régime, Révolution,
Régime nouveau.*

To   **von Preen**

Basle, 30 May 1877

. . . Since I last wrote I have been exploring the Oberland assiduously on
Sundays and Holidays, but I cannot rival the feeling for nature which you
obtain from the delights of the landscape and a detailed knowledge of its
history. My feelings in youth were always for things distant and far away,
and it is only in the last few years that I have become thoroughly indige-

80. Bismarck.

nous. And then, unfortunately, I am altogether innocent of botany; I delight in every pretty little flower, but I have never learnt anything about them, and so have to take nature more or less *en bloc*. Even my knowledge of the noblest plant in the Oberland is only very sketchy, so that last Sunday at the "Hirsch" in Haltingen I stuck my fingers in a hornets' nest, by making the innocent mistake of calling Isteiner the best wine above Schlingener in the presence of Beck. I had to listen to a lecture about Isteiner being a wine of no importance, that was prized too highly in Basle because certain old gentlemen argued from the same premises on which certain other old gentlemen overvalued Pisiatello in Italy. I also called in at Liel again since I wrote; I can't help being interested in the proprietor of the old library there, and the picture by Angelica Kaufmann is perhaps one of those in which she is the most enjoyable of that generation of enfeebled classical imitators. Only I suspect that a friendship there might cost me part of my freedom, and in future I shall hurry quickly by. . . .

Evening

The steady rain has stopped; the sun is shining warm and close, and the rain will soon begin again, but nowadays one accepts every hour's sunshine with thankfulness. The general feeling here is no doubt little different from yours or anywhere in the West. The ground is not yet quaking with bankruptcies, as in Zürich, where panic is ruling, but things do not look good here either. Add to that the irresponsible undertakings decreed by our present majority and the way the moods of the "working" classes are exploited. (If only we could get rid of that infamously unjust term, once and for all, something would have been achieved.) And of course we are getting ready for a Festival. . . .

To Max Alioth

Munich, 7 August 1877

The old Munich of Ludwig I is very stale. If one looks around as I do, in second-hand bookshops, at the publications of that period, the tender piety of the line engravings, the romantic portraits, and sees all that low-bred romantic architecture, painting and sculpture pass before one's eyes—how utterly dated it all is! I went one evening to the Ludwigs-kirche; Cornelius[81] still makes a certain impression on me, but the building is a wretched affair, and the only question is whether the interior or the exterior is worse. On the other hand, how glorious the majestic Thea-tinerkirche and St. Michael's are! They make all the modern buildings here so dull and feeble by comparison that one feels "relatively sick." However, I except the Triumphal Arch,[82] the Propyläen and the Alte Pinakothek. In fact there is nothing great about the new things, and the Frauenkirche has had its Gothic "purified"—the Frauenkirche that I knew twenty-one years ago, with its marvellous Baroque wrought-iron gates in front of the side-chapels, and the exquisite triumphal arch over the tomb of the Emperor Ludwig in the middle of the nave (which it served to break in the lightest and most beautiful way); and of course, the vaulting is painted blue with gold stars, so that it doesn't look half as high as it did, and the octagonal pillars are painted *cream,* etc.—instead of thanking heaven that a building with only very modest Gothic decoration had been taken in hand and cured by a cheerful Baroque.

81. A painter of the Nazarene School.
82. In Schwabing.

To Max Alioth

Munich, 11 August 1877

You are, unfortunately, only too right in your opinion of the Maximili-aneum; it is a *papier mâché* concoction and is very feeble when one sees the other side. Though I am rather thankful for the building because at least outwardly it leads up to the forms of the Renaissance and sets one's spirit free from the miserable Gothic of the Maximilianstrasse. . . .

Today I allowed myself to be driven with a whole stream of people through the rooms of the Residenz, that you surely know. I will say noth-ing of the frescoes: though I had to admit, on reaching Ludwig I's two *Schönheitskabinette,*[83] that in spite of Stieler and the dreary court-painter's "almanach" style in which the portraits are carried out, it was in itself a royal idea, and only a King could have carried it out. The Archduchess and the shoemaker's daughter could never both have been persuaded to sit for their portraits even for the richest private individual, or have agreed to an entirely neutral beauty competition, not dependent upon station. The way the custodian told us where all the ladies lived and whom they had married was heavenly. On the looking-glass of a pilaster in one of the rooms, dated 1856, hung the portrait of Lola Montez with her timid and beautiful eyes; the same was now replaced by Frau X "ge-borene Daxelberger," the daughter of a copper-smith in "Minchen," the custodian went on. The Throne Room with the twelve golden statues is the only one that has anything grandiose about it, although the golden Wittelsbachs are lighted from behind. And then came the principal thing, which perhaps you have not yet seen, the Emperor Charles VII's rooms dating from 1730–1740, the loveliest Rococo on earth, superior in inven-tion, freedom and elegance even to the staterooms at Versailles. As it is, one is driven through with a whole swarm of people, but I shall have

83. Two rooms hung with portraits of the famous beauties of the day.

myself driven through a couple of times more so as to impress the wonderful forms deeply on my mind. And what is more it's a crescendo from the anterooms to the bedroom and the fantastic magnificence of the *cabinet de toilette*. . . .

To   Max Alioth

Munich, 15 August 1877

Today the shops were closed because it was the Assumption (and of course my shop too, Helgen); instead the Opera opened. I don't know rightly what the ideal relationship between them may be, but I went round to the Opera house where twenty-eight years ago I heard several operas that have since then slept the sleep of the just (Chalard's *Macbeth*, Lachner's *Caterina Cornaro,* and the *Earthquake of Lima* and that sort of thing), and among other things made the acquaintance of *Tannhäuser.* Today was Verdi's *Aida,* with full pomp and Egyptian décor; the Third Act with its palm grove and the little temple by the Nile in the moonlight was quite fascinating. Nachbauer as Radames was in wonderful voice, and both women at least beautiful to look at; among the three basses was Kindermann, whom I had heard twenty-one years ago, as Wolfram among other things, so entirely unchanged that I had to ask my neighbour whether it wasn't a son of the old man. But no, it was him. A good deal of the music is sophisticated and strained and learnt from various quarters (even Wagner and from Spohr's *Jessonda*), but there is also some really wonderful, inspired Verdi; and in the Second and Third Acts he is sometimes his old self, though the form is more severe. The captivating rhythmic melodies of the early Verdi are wanting, but it still has a good deal of soul, and from the finale of the Second Act, right through the Third, it is quite beautiful, and the duet between Amonasro and Aida, *Tu verras cette terre adorée,* is so beautiful that like no other Verdi it moves me to tears; he is full of new things, all his own. At sixty, he still had something to give that I had not suspected. There are some fine moments in the Fourth Act, but not the sustained beauty of the Third. Hear it whenever you can, though if possible not in Basle! It needs the great spaciousness of the Munich stage. The little blackamoors who do burlesque dances in the various ballets had been given shining cats' eyes by attaching green glasses to them, no doubt. Friday *Fidelio,* Saturday *Lohengrin.* . . .

To **von Preen**

Basle, New Year's Eve 1877

. . . The bronze plaque you told me about is highly entertaining. We too have people wanting to try out that form of immortalization of I know not what, but they are still shy of public ridicule and laughter. There is always a certain quota of "public characters" trying to set something or other *en train* from sheer inner emptiness and loneliness, simply in order to convince themselves that they are still alive. Something must happen, and when they can't think of anything else, they agitate for a memorial. In the course of last year one of the most disastrous local Hotspurs suggested I should put myself at the head of a society for a monument to Hebel, at the same time naming the proposed site (the most absurd imaginable). I withdrew at once from the affair, and wrote him an earnest moral letter, pointing out the heavy responsibility one incurred by proposing monuments at inauspicious moments which came to nothing for ages, and perhaps for ever. Whereupon the fellow left me in peace and began agitating for something else.

To   von Preen

Basle, 21 February 1878

. . . The excessively long hours that your admirable youngster has to accustom himself to at school arouse one's entire sympathy. But as a nation we are bound to be weighed down to the ground by learning. Sometimes I develop the most heretical views, which no teacher ought to express. Considered purely as a business, the schools are one of the least paying propositions that exist, from the A B C to the highest ultra-academic heights, because so unbelievably little of what is learnt is retained and really used. In the upper classes of the Gymnasium there is surely a great deal of unnecessary and excessive sweating, the only point of which is to show the young beforehand, allegorically and symbolically, what (in most cases) life is really like. Only its importance is not as a rule understood or realized because the alluring freedom of the University sparkles before their eyes as an indemnification. And so they only see the torment of the last terms at school. All too often the Lycées are unable to find teachers for the difficult subjects, who attain an even mediocre level; for good teachers are by no means frequent. . . .

To   von Preen

Basle, 7 July 1878

Just recently a Pastor of the Reformed Church has been chosen, by a show of hands, by those who do not go to church, and to the misery of those who do. As you know, I do not belong to the latter; once upon a time I studied theology for four whole terms with the greatest interest, and then found I did not have the faith required for the pulpit, and thereupon transferred to the historical side. But what I can't understand is the cheek of a Reformer occupying a pulpit and even performing rituals in the meaning of which he does not believe! How can he force himself upon a congregation after getting the office as a result of a *malentendu,* as a result, namely, of the vote being given to everyone on the assumption of their belonging to the congregation but in fact and truth to a non-existent congregation? . . .

To Max Alioth

Gravedona, Lake Como, Tuesday, 30 July 1878

Early yesterday, in a delicious and much-needed fine rain, I reached Lake Como. *N.B.* on the box, with the Postillion, who put his rug over my knees, so that with my umbrella up I kept quite dry. Then from Colico I took the steamer to Gravedona, where indeed I found the so-called "good" hotel closed, but find myself installed instead most comfortably in a genuine Lombard Albergo. From my bed I can see no less than four mountain chapels through the window, the top one of all at a giddy height. Up till now the only meat I have eaten in Italy has been *côtelettes,* which in this pub have attained the supreme degree of excellence. With them I eat *minestra di paste,* large beans baked in butter (a *délice!* tastes like chestnuts), and drink a warm though excellent Barbera. In either of the dirty little cafés here I have found coffee (*N.B. nero*) at twenty centesimi, so that it's a mystery to me how such good coffee can be brewed in a country with import dues such as Italy has.

There are in fact two curious Romanesque churches in Gravedona, and other things besides—but what is that compared with the majestic Villa on the rocks directly above the lake, which Cardinal Tolomeo Galli had built, and by Pellegrino Tibaldi, what is more. Square, with four powerful Loggias at the corners, and in the middle the huge room that occupies two storeys and opens through three windows on to a portico giving on to the lake. From the portico, framed between two pillars, with pilasters of red marble on either hand, there is a view such as one can only get on Como. Tibaldi's best front is the garden front, where the principal floor on the lake front becomes the ground floor, because the garden lies higher. I know I have drawn the forms hideously, and the open central part of the building has come out much too narrow-chested, and then I draw Ionic and Tuscan columns like elongated sausages, but you will forgive me.

The building was never finished inside, and it would be a wonderful task to paint and decorate these *volte a specchio* and stucco vaults of every kind. The building itself is sound and in a perfect state of preservation. It passed from the Cardinal to the Duchi del Vitto in Naples, who only came here rarely and could not prevent *certi gentiluomini del paese* from occupying the ground floor from time to time and holding undoubted orgies. It was only in 1819 that the last del Vitto sold the thing to the grandfather of the present owner, the lawyer Pero, and now the whole building is filled with cocoons for the silk trade, and the familiar smell (my almost dry ink-pot has been refreshed in the good Italian style with some red wine, and I continue) that comes back to me from anno '46 from Naples, where I met with cocoons as the stock-in-trade of a Palazzo near Portici, under the auspices of a Major who had not long since finally managed, with no inconsiderable trouble, to drive out the last Maîtresse of the Duke of San something or other. In the centre of the vast room, sitting enthroned at an enormous table between four women spinning cocoons, was the mother of the present owner, a huge old Donna Lombarda, with imposing, and at one time, certainly, dazzlingly beautiful eyes, and round about her other tables occupied by cocoon spinners, and as I sat and sketched in the garden, a stately song sounded from the working women's room, through which one heard one of those deep alto voices that you have to look for with a lantern among us. In the evening Signor Pero came to the inn, i.e., we sat *all' italiana* in the kitchen talking endlessly and drinking a very good *vino nostrano,* that is not to be despised even by comparison with the Barbera, as it doesn't tear one's nerves to bits as much. It was the first time in my already long life that I had drunk with the owner of a great classical building, and the fellow seemed positively venerable to me. . . .

To Max Alioth

Bologna, 13 August 1878

Yesterday, driving into Bologna in an open carriage, I had to confess that this city of arcades possesses a greater number of beautiful and picturesque street views than any of the other four or five large towns in Italy, though they may be superior in individual buildings. The same evening I saw a brand-new restrained Baroque palace looking just like one of the splendid old ones; a rich Marchesa (Lambertazzi or something of the kind) built it as a speculation and lets it at high prices, herself living in a smaller old Palace near by. That sort of thing is only possible in present-day Bologna, with its many officials and the rich crowding in. Quite a number of the streets, which were formerly cobbled, are now paved with good smooth stones. Of course the jug and the municipal finances are both going to the fountain till they break. I love magnificence, but a folly such as the new palace, the *cassa di risparmio,* is beyond the limit, and reminds me of the fine railway station in Zürich that lies so heavily on the stomach of the bankrupt Nordostbahn. (In Florence, which is bankrupt, the banks didn't pay out for five days last week, until someone came to their rescue.)

The Italians are the same as ever; last night *Norma* was given in the huge open-air theatre, in perfect weather, to an audience of at least a thousand, Platea 50 cts., seats 1 lira, etc. The singers were so-called third class, but quite respectable nevertheless, and then you should have seen the public, the small artisans, manual labourers, business people, etc., and how much better they behaved than the public in a superior, expensive theatre very often does, where they chatter, beat time with their sticks and join in their favourite tunes, etc. Here we had absolute silence except for applause in the right places; the modest public really wanted to hear its favourite old opera. The only pity was that the moment Norma began her great aria, *Casta diva,* the brilliant full moon chose to go behind a cloud. The auditorium was very adequately lit with some ninety gas burners; no reliance was placed on the moon.

There is one thing that is awful here; the perpetual spitting. In the train I counted the number of times a man smoking a *Virginia* spat: about fifty times. In church people saying their prayers spit the whole time; and there's a wet or dry puddle under every priedieu. The fact is, this cheerful and pleasant people is periodically transformed into a vast crowd of expectorating figures. One thing I do envy them: their beautiful teeth! A man like that can say he will count the heads of his loves, and by Jove! not one is missing. It's a positive pleasure to see them yawn. . . .

To Max Alioth

Bologna, 15 August 1878. Evening

. . . Today is *Assunta* so, alas, I found one of my favourite churches here, San Salvatore, entirely draped inside with those disgusting *Ornati,* the pillars being dressed up in dirty reddish-purple trousers with bedraggled gold fringes, like clowns in a tight-rope act at the circus. It is in brick, the most beautiful, simple Baroque I know, colourless inside—but for the trousers. Earlier I had been to the baths; there is an arm of the Reno that flows into Bologna, on an island in which Augustus, Antony and Lepidus agreed the Triumvirate, anno 42 B.C., i.e., decreed the letting of blood which cost 4000 Romans of all parties, Conservative, Progressive, Centrum, National-liberals, their lives. Now we bathe in little stone rooms into which the said river flows, bringing its mud with it, and I am afraid I came out dirtier than I went in; and I was almost afraid some old *crotte* from the days of Caesar Augustus would come floating in through the opening, and my veneration for antiquity does not go to such lengths that I should have welcomed it.

In Italy, as everywhere, the agitators are working to produce the same disintegration; a really mischievous Socialist paper is published here, *la Stella*. Things have reached a point that even so-called respectable papers have to concede almost everything in advance, as though it were self-evident, which in itself is a serious matter. And the sound of the boys shouting *la gahzittah! la stellah!* with their shrill voices goes right through one. Ever since it has become known that the Socialists have got their candidates recognized in all the principal towns in Germany, the majority among the urban masses is no secret.

It is hot, but there is a little movement in the air—and it's so clear and so beautiful! I only wish there was a way of measuring blue, so as to convert those who do not want to believe in the Italian sky. Now, towards seven o'clock, that wonderful soft greenish hue is beginning to mix in near the horizon; in the distance I can see the massive superstructure of S. Petronio through my window, shining and flaming above the roofs in the evening sunset. But I am looking forward to the Adriatic, where I shall be able to wash off the mud of the Reno. Rimini and Fano are, of course, bathing resorts.

Once upon a time there was a certain Abbé Trublet who enraged Voltaire by writing a treatise "On the true causes of the boredom of the Henriade"; now I am studying the true causes of boredom in the Caracci pictures—not all of them! But I have identified the point at which Ludovico Caracci degenerated: it was when he only served out his general knowledge, and no longer felt any psychological struggles over individual characters and their actions; finally, in the colossal Annunziata above the apse of S. Pietro he noticed this himself, fell into a melancholy and died. . . .

To Max Alioth

Bologna, 25 August 1878

I got here twenty-four hours earlier than I intended, and begin by getting a letter to you in reserve. Since writing the Thursday before last from here, I have grazed my way through every miserable little hole on the railway line: Imola, Forli, Cesena, Rimini, Pesaro, Fano, Ancona and Loreto, not of course in that order, but some going and some coming, leaving only Sinigaglia aside, because it was *fiera,* and Faenza, because I had really seen enough miserable little holes, and badly needed a larger, more comfortable town. There is plenty to see and to meditate upon everywhere, and even the most miserable of holes, Imola, contains something or other, and a revolting form of stucco into the bargain. Moreover, it was gradually getting hot again, though by tolerable degrees; one cannot strike up an acquaintance in the little cafés of those miserable holes, that usually have no ice. By great good luck I never lost sight of a really wonderful wine all the way from Forli to Ancona, a Sangiovese; one sits in a narrow street in a delicious evening breeze, and sips it slowly for hours, chatting at the same time. As a matter of fact I have never been at all short of conversation on this journey, and even the day before yesterday, in Fano, conversed from eight till after midnight with a rich business man from Bologna who had been in Germany and all over the place and was a zealous Wagnerian; Mariani, the late director of the Opera in Bologna, was an intimate friend of his and had managed to get him into all the rehearsals for the Bolognese performance of *Lohengrin*! For the first time in my life I heard an educated Italian talk outrageously objectively about Rossini, Bellini and Verdi; it made my hair stand on end. He approached Wagner from a mystical-psychological angle; he can only be enjoyed if one gives oneself entirely to him, and sinks oneself in the music, i.e., the diametrical opposite of what normally passes for the enjoyment of the theatre in Italy. At that I gathered fresh hope in the thought that the

Italians would never agree to having that presupposition forced upon them. Of course he was able to point out that all the present-day young Italian composers go to school at Bayreuth. At which I thought to myself: no wonder they hardly produce one bearable opera a year between them, they all disappear quickly after a *succès de réclame,* one or two comic operas at the most excepted. But—in any case—I was inwardly protected against his eloquence by a talisman, for on the Thursday as I wrote to you, I had again heard *Norma,* and in company with at least one thousand four hundred absolutely silent spectators, it being a holiday (*Assunta*).

I had to see Forli, on account of the frescoes; in Rimini, San Francesco and the Arco d'Augusto, of which I possess your drawing, are the most astonishing; I was able to get quite a number of photographs of San Francesco (monuments, pillars, chapels). In addition I was busy sea-bathing, and realized that bathing in the middle of the day, in glorious water, is a very serious matter, and makes mortals lazy and shy of work for the rest of the day. (The town of Rimini, by the way, has spent a million on luxurious bathing-establishments and hotels, etc., that don't pay, and day after day one can read about it all in the local rag. Ancona, too, has been overbuilding and is now howling.) In Ancona, as in 1847, I was once again enchanted by the arch of Trajan, and the Loggia de' Mercanti; and I would have sketched the two fantastically magnificent Baroque gates at the Arsenal if only I had not lost all taste for sketching. One of them, the Arco Clementino, is the absolute *non plus ultra.* There must be a Porta Pia somewhere in Ancona resembling the Roman one, of which I only got a photograph; I really couldn't force myself to go from gate to gate in the heat. Loreto, where you don't seem to have been, is most instructive; first of all the delightful hill and the cool fresh air, and the running fountains, then the church, begun in Gothic, on which every conceivable style has been superimposed, and finally the sculptures! The photographs of the Santa Casa, absurdly cheap; and the fifteen prophets and Sibyls, that can be got separately, only fifteen centesimi.

From Pesaro I went to Monte Imperiali, which I didn't want to miss, and which, as you know, is worth while, for the view alone. If only *it* had been completed! Someone really ought to have attempted something gigantic, but since her late Majesty, the architect Semiramis, who built the hanging gardens, no one has dared. But I am not going to make any more expeditions into the country; it's too unsafe. The night before last an hour after sunset, quite near Bologna, Count Aldrovandi was set upon in his little chaise by a couple of Camorristi, taken to his Villa and relieved of more than a thousand lire. Some very curious things are happening here: the Romagna is undermined by the International. Though elsewhere, too, in Italy a systematic *laisser-aller* and *laisser-faire* have brought some very strange blisters to light. Today's *Epoca* (from Genoa) appears with the following tragic caricature: a man holding up his decapitated head to three terrible Crowned Heads, saying: *Insensati,* do you think you can cut off the head of socialism by doing this? Instead of this you ought to force the rich capitalists *di associare il loro denaro al lavoro!* (i.e., give their money to the workers). It will certainly be some time before the deeply rooted optimism in this country sings its *Pater peccavi.*

If only they weren't so cruel to animals! For example, there are the fat old men driving about on two-wheeled carts drawn by donkeys! They whack their animals continuously (which are obviously not strong enough, and will certainly give their owners the necessary lesson by dying early). Then, on Sunday evening, the Signor Marchese drives down the Corso in Bologna as fast as possible with a team of horses, lamming into the sensitive animals ceaselessly with his whip, so that His Honour should be seen by the female population of the town in a perpetual *prestissimo.* I think I may say that such a spectacle would be impossible anywhere in the North. Then in one Bottega there was a giant tortoise to be seen, and I thought perhaps it might be a well-preserved animal, and paid my ten *centesimi.* In fact it was a colossal beast, with a head as large as a child's, caught in Corsica on 6th July. Only of course in the process it had got a blow or a shot in the back and as the owner explained to one man, the joke wouldn't last long as it had a *cancrena* (gangrene). I thought of the warning *tat twam asi,* in Schopenhauer, and would like to have given the fellow one in the face. . . .

Monday, 26 August

Bologna is divinely beautiful and charming; yesterday I only did the palaces and churches in the via Galliera, one by one, taking a good two hours, just strolling along, as I no longer make notes. My favourite is the Palazzo Zucchini, immediately behind the Hôtel d'Italie, with a really fantastic courtyard and one of the most exquisite staircases in existence, decorated in the finest Louis XVI, an oval landing above with a light painted ceiling.

To Max Alioth

Milan, Friday afternoon, 30 August 1878
In a café on the Corso

It's a delightful, rainy day, not a drizzle, but real country rain; the sun made one or two infamous and vain attempts to fool us; it was a complete failure.

ARCHITEKTURLIED AUS ITALIEN

An manchem schönen Vestibül
Verstärkt' ich schon mein Kunstgefühl,
An manchen schönen Stegen;
Es ist ein wahrer Segen.

Ich bin im Welschland wohlbekannt,
Jetzt durchgeschwitzt und hartgebrannt,
Und tu mich nicht genieren,
Krummkrüpplich zu skizzieren.

Denn neben Dir ist alles Tand,
O Du, halb Dreck- halb Götterland,
Wo alles hoch und luftig
(Der Mensch bisweilen schuftig).

Und mein Programm ist bald gesagt,
An allem was da schwebt und ragt,
Gebälk, Gewölb and Kuppeln,
Mich noch recht vollzuschnuffeln,

Damit mir Atem übrigbleibt,
Wenn Basel mir den Angstschweiss treibt,
Und enge Häuserreihen
Ob mir zusammen keien.

To von Preen

Basle, 9 December 1878

. . . For almost six weeks in Italy (end of July till beginning of September) I had a most lovely and enjoyable time, but the air was so thick with revolutionary miasmas that one could almost catch hold of them, and uncertainty, too, was on the increase. Nor am I surprised, after that, at what has happened since, and shan't be surprised at what is coming. Italy wanting to be a great power and a centralized military state is such a colossal untruth that it is bound to incur punishment step by step. The present situation in Rome, with one man sitting a voluntary prisoner in the Vatican and the other an involuntary prisoner in the Quirinal, surely belongs among the great ironies of history! And being only half an hour apart across the roofs, they can see and talk to one another. Heartiest greetings from afar! It only depends on very little—whether the dynasty can maintain itself. One can no longer attain security simply by driving out one's equals and inheriting the land!

I opened my winter term with three special evenings *coram publico*, and preached on Talleyrand, not without sounding a cheerful note here and there, that the public is said to have appreciated highly. But I've had enough of public lectures; I am entering on my sixty-first year, and consider Talleyrand to have been a very suitable swan song to my public appearances. The trouble and distraction that one feels as a "lecturer" is too great for one's other work. . . .

The older I get the more I turn away from highly spiced things, and the more I like the harmless ones and the things one is accustomed to. Yesterday I heard *Martha* from the first to the last note, with childish delight. It has, of course, its superficial moments and some very ordinary goods in it, but much that is touchingly beautiful into the bargain. Gradually I am acquiring a whole library of piano scores (of operas, oratorios, songs, etc.) that are towering up around me, and they occupy my solitary evenings when I don't want to work after eight o'clock. I wonder whether the cheapening of so much that is beautiful (specially the Peters Editions) will not prove to be noticeable and appreciable in the last two decades, if anyone should ever write the history of taste in the nineteenth century. . . .

10 December

By the way: have you noticed that in his last book[84] Nietzsche has completed half a turn towards optimism? Unfortunately his state of health (very weak sight, constant headaches, with violent attacks every few days) is in no sense the occasion of this change. He is a man out of the ordinary, he has an individual, personally acquired point of view in almost everything. . . .

84. *Human, all-too-human.* See next letter.

To Nietzsche

Basle, 5 April 1879

. . . I got the supplement to *Human* from Herrn Schmeitzner safely, and read and chewed it, marvelling anew at your fullness and freedom of mind. I have never, as is well known, penetrated into the Temple of genuine thought, but have all my life taken delight in the halls and forecourt of the Peribolos, where the image, in the widest sense of the word, reigns. Now, your book caters most fully, in every respect, for the very class of careless pilgrim that I belong to. So where I can't follow you, I watch, with mingled fear and delight, to see how surely you walk about on the edge of the giddiest rocks, and try to form some image to myself of what you must see in the depth and distance. What would happen were La Rochefoucauld, La Bruyère and Vauvenargues to get your book in their hands in Hades? And what would old Montaigne say? In the meanwhile, I have found a number of sayings which La Rochefoucauld, for example, would seriously envy you. . . .

To Max Alioth

London, Thursday, 31 July 1879
Paris and Europe Hotel, Leicester Square

The journey was simple and there were no disasters; early on Tuesday, three hours in Paris, then Tuesday and early Wednesday in Amiens, then Calais, and a glorious crossing in ninety-three minutes to Dover, and yesterday evening by six o'clock I was here in my hotel.

Today the South Kensington Museum, from half-past ten to half-past five, so arranged that I thoroughly enjoyed the good restaurant in the

Museum itself, and then consumed a small cigar outside before beginning my inspection again.

It was high time I saw London again; there is a gap in one's teaching of art if one does not know this astounding maze of collections. The building itself, in the completed parts, is incredibly opulent; there are whole sections of the building where the pillars (and what is more outside) are decorated with three tiers of medallions with richly figured reliefs, while the corresponding hall inside may only conceal a collection of coloured tile-stoves from the Black Forest. In fact, there is a good deal of trash on show, among other things Schliemann's entire boot, and a complete exhibition of the art of the Japanese vase. But upstairs are Raphael's Cartoons, and *La Vierge aux Candélabres* among other things. Quite a number of the original Michelangelos, among them the Cupid, and more in casts. Almost as much della Robbia as in Florence, a magnificent selection of the great Florentine sculptors in the original, the complete screen from a sacristy by Brunellesco, whole altars and tombs in plaster; complete gates in the original, and finally a colossal plaster cast of the gigantic entrance to Santiago de Compostella. A huge Natural History Museum is being built near-by in a powerful Norman-Romanesque style, with four towers like a Rhenish cathedral. It is certainly high time the British Museum was relieved of its Natural History collections, and devoted entirely to antiquity.

The rise in prices here is not enormous, and once my preliminary purchases and arrangements are over, I hope to get along on twenty francs a day, and perhaps be able to afford my half bottle of so-called Bordeaux. But London is no place for you, one has to put up with a lot of discomforts in the course of the day.

This evening on my way back from South Kensington at six o'clock, I came upon a little restaurant in the middle of the crowded Strand, called the Cleopatra Restaurant, because from there one can see the recently erected Cleopatra's Needle through a narrow little street looking down towards the Thames. After some delicious oxtail soup and a ditto sole, I went down and examined the obelisk at close quarters. As far as I could see, deciphering the hieroglyphics with difficulty, they read, on one side: Be anything in the world in Egypt rather than King or Viceroy, it doesn't pay; (2) That I led a life of debauchery is one of the many lies of history; (3) In Alexandria the dogs cocked their legs here; they don't in London, though it was more amusing in Egypt than it is here, among a lot of Mr. Smiths, Hodgsons and Dobsons, etc.; (4) unreadable.

To **Max Alioth**

London, 1 August 1879

As I was dog tired yesterday, I must supplement a few things from memory. The façade of the Gare du Nord in Paris is a scandal; the Ionic pilasters of different sizes, the slopes of the roofs which rise up from the ornamental tops of the smaller ones to the higher ones, and the huge round-topped windows that go hop-hop-hop, cutting into the wall surfaces in between—all in all it's the most infamous architectural achievement of the century, which is saying something.

The inside of Amiens Cathedral leaves one gasping, it's so sublime and where would Cologne Cathedral be but for this model? The view, from the nave across into the choir, branching out so magnificently into the side aisles, gives one the feeling of one's lungs and chest expanding; and everywhere that *will* to carry everything into the heights.

On the train between Amiens and Calais was a man who talked very sensibly, connected with well-to-do farmers in the neighbourhood of Paris, so the time passed quickly till Boulogne, where he got out. When I let it be known that I was Swiss, I became conscious of genuine sympathy dating from the time of Bourbaki.[85] I have in fact noticed more than once that since then we have been in people's good books.

For the rest of the time I journeyed in the company of a resolute

85. The general commanding the French armies on the Swiss frontier in 1871.

femme de chambre, who was engaged by the Duchess of Newcastle. She will, I think, make a career in England.

The boat from Calais to Dover was one of the new-fangled kind really made out of two boats, with the engine in the middle, which greatly reduces the motion; we hardly felt anything, though we saw little ships quite near us pitching quite a lot. People talk of the *Tunnel sous-marin* as of a certainty; of course the tickets will be expensive, but on leaving for England the philistines will have to promise their wives not to go on board ship; they will complain of the price, but pay. The wiser ones are already lamenting in advance that the excellent boat service that now exists will be cut down.

In London I took a *cab* at once, and drove from *Gasthof* to *Gasthof* till I found what I wanted. The cabman was "quite a honest man" [*sic*] and was satisfied with quite a small tip; I looked him in the eyes and thought I recognized a Methodist or some such strict and Godfearing man. The hotel is really French, but my servant is from the Ticino, from Aquila, Val Blegno.

I discovered yesterday evening that I could drink quite a good French red wine at two shillings a bottle (almost a litre), and smoke at the same time, which I can't do in the better "wine-stores." Briefly, I am content.

If only I could decipher the fourth side of Cleopatra's Needle, but it is a Herculean labour. Yet all hope is not lost.

To Max Alioth

London, 2 August 1879

I meant to go to the British Museum yesterday but found the Elgin Marbles and almost the whole of the Greek department closed. Thereupon I made my decision at once and went by bus, *outside,* into the thick of the city and looked at St. Paul's and one or two other things; I shall not willingly go again into that crowd unless forced to do so. Then I took my interim fodder in one of the oldest city pubs that I had visited nineteen years ago (The Bell, Old Bailey), and went by Underground to the South Kensington Museum again.

My wonder increased considerably. Where will our history of art lead us, if people go on collecting at the present rate, and nobody tries to take a really general view of it? If I had a year to spend here, I would turn up my sleeves, spit on my hands and do what I could, with the help of others, to formulate as clearly as possible the living law of *forms*. However, I can't change the course of my life for the sake of such splendours. And what good do these great aesthetic incitements do the Londoner, if the look of the town is to be ruined all the same by a colossal horror on purely utilitarian grounds, by comparison with which our new bridge is perfectly innocent![86] A disgusting, high, straight, cast-iron bridge has been built slap across the main vista of the town, a main-line railway laid across it, and a hideous great round-topped lady's trunk built above it (the main station at Charing Cross). As I strolled in the moonlight yesterday evening, on Waterloo Bridge, and saw how the wonderfully picturesque view of the Houses of Parliament, Westminster Abbey and Lambeth Palace was cut in half, I could have cried. The evening light and the full moon rising made it all the more painful. Further down too, towards London Bridge, there is a similar monstrosity in cast iron, also leading to a colossal terminus. O Lord! what is not going to be sacrificed to the *practical sense* of the nineteenth century! And what will London look like in a hundred years' time, or even in ten years, if more and more of these terrible decisions have to be taken on account of the growing population? I am daily astonished, in the meanwhile, that the crowds don't crush one another to pieces, and that the supply and maintenance is so orderly.

Tomorrow in, I hope, fine weather, to Hampton Court.

Queen Victoria gets off lightly; her face on stamps and coins remains the same as at the beginning of her reign, whereas in truth it must be looking a bit rough.

86. The new bridge in Basle that Burckhardt strongly disapproved of.

Diary Jottings

6 August

In which of the strange books of destiny is it written that one should only be able to form an opinion on some of the most important developments in Italian sculpture and painting in London? Let me tell you this: in the *Catalogue Raisonné* of the National Gallery it is stated, quite regardless, which Italian *Nobili* and which officials have sold their pictures under the counter to the English, mostly, *N.B.*, since the Regno, since 1859–60. The catalogue must make very painful reading for a patriotic Italian. And after all I can follow things as far as London; but anything the Russians and the Americans may have abducted, I cannot possibly reach. Here in London one at least feels that the leading people who direct the buying have really wide views. This is particularly true in the case of the directors of the South Kensington Museum, who must reckon that the spirit of this highly gifted and still relatively vigorous nation will one day awaken, appropriate these wonderful things, and follow them up in its own way. O, if only earning one's daily bread didn't cost such awful labour! What is lacking is leisure, the mother of contemplation, and the inspiration that springs from it. Art in its great periods has never spared itself exertion, but the intense effort must alternate with inner recollection, which in this island can only be the privilege of "the happy few."

In the meanwhile, there is some gain for art, and at least people are once again building façades, without worrying whether, in ninety-nine years' time, the house reverts to the Marquis of Westminster or the Duke of Bedford. The above Marquis is said to have increased his enormous property not long ago when a large number of leaseholds expired, or to have seen it grow larger, in so far as he can still see it all. But what more can he do than eat, and perhaps his digestion's weaker than mine. And my bed in the Hotel Europe and Paris is quite excellent, so he can't sleep better. So what remains? Perhaps he has to be careful and cannot smoke cigars, which I still can. No doubt he has a box in the best theatre, and gets bored in it. The finest thing he has, is his magnificent collection of pictures, but I don't know whether he gets real pleasure from it. And then there are the sessions in the House of Lords, which can, in certain circumstances, be painfully boring. And presiding at God knows how many sporting events, which possibly disgust him to the point of nausea!

Evening

I am just back from the most splendid coffee-house in London, "Spiersandponts," which ought presumably to be spelt Spears and Punts; but no, it's called Spiers and Pond. To begin with a huge hall, entirely decorated in majolica which "all can be washed" — if only the damned ceiling were not in *papier mâché!* The Buffet twice as long (though not nearly so high) as the stalls in our St. Martin's, and all the panels of the Buffet too in majolica, and then a side room — the most charming little high room you can imagine — aren't you envious? — and the whole upper two-fifths of the room covered in floating majolica goddesses — with a ditto staircase leading from it; tomorrow I shall dine there, cost what it may. Add to that the sorcery of the concealed gas lighting — and who could resist it.

. . . At last I have seen Rubens' wonderful picture *le chapeau de paille* for the first time; only it's a felt hat with a feather, and is really called *le chapeau de poil,* which some drunken English art lover misunderstood. Under the felt hat lodges Rubens' second wife, Hélène Fourment, probably painted as a bride. With the exception of the edge of the right cheek everything is in the shadow of the broad-brimmed hat, but at the same time in a full pale light, the devil knows how — and everything lit up by the quite marvellous dark blue eyes.

Thursday, 7 August. Evening

I went again to the majolica coffee-house Spiers and Pond. The bar, roughly sixty feet, is served by six *dames du comptoir,* who wear a uniform, a black dress and their hair done *à l'enfant.* This time I saw the dining-room as well, charming, but the vestibule between the café and the dining-room is the most beautiful. A friendly *sous-chef* gave me the name of the architect and spelt it out to me in French; he is called Werity—I thought at once, that sounds Belgian or Flemish, and on getting home asked my host and discovered that at least one of the proprietors, namely Pond, was a Belgian and is the brains behind it all, while Spiers is said to be a cypher (presumably he supplied the capital).

In addition to this magnificent café, a mere bagatelle to them, they both own:

1. One of the largest wine-import trades in England;
2. an enormous butcher's business;
3. the buffets on the line to Edinburgh and Aberdeen; and

4, 5, 6. any amount of other things.

One can only ask in astonishment: *who* can possibly make money beside these people?

But I return to the subject of the *dames du comptoir*. If one wears one's hair *à l'enfant* and has tremendously developed jaw-bones, or chewing apparatus, as well, the upper part of the face looks short by comparison with the lower. This weighed on my heart. One or two of them brushed their hair back from their foreheads and at once looked much prettier.

The misery of London—I am now only speaking for foreigners—is the rarity of the sort of place one can stretch one's legs out under the table and stay on as long as one likes. The above-mentioned café possesses that characteristic, and though the majority stand at the bar, there are lovely divans on the other side for those who want them.

. . . The only question is whether, with cigars as expensive as they are, I shall not have to accustom myself for a time at least, while I'm in my room, like almost everyone else, to *brules-gueules* with Turkish tobacco. Cyprian tobacco is already to be had; a result of the recent *conquête*. I know the rot-brain Cyprian wine from Venice, and won't drink it.

If only I knew my way about in the papers here! But whenever I buy one of those voluminous rags, I find the spokesman is English Radicalism. It is really miserable not to be able to consult an educated Londoner, and in the end I shall have to make some acquaintances. My translator is sure to be away travelling, otherwise I should have looked him up at his Club, where I could have got his address. But I repeat, it was high time to come to London; in a year's time I should no longer have risked it.

Tuesday morning, 12 August

"I speak some English" — *Ich spucke einiges Englisch* would probably be the best translation; it comes very hard to me, and I really haven't the will to acquire the accent in this language, whereas in French and Italian I give myself the greatest possible pains to pronounce properly. And then, even where one might expect a knowledge of French, very few Englishmen speak it. It may well be through aversion, even when they understand it, for what happens to me with English pronunciation happens to them with French: they don't want to learn it, and know that they are gauche and ridiculous when they speak French. Though in Italy I have heard quite a number of English people speaking Italian very well and even elegantly.

In the National Gallery one even meets Moors; yesterday there was a pitch black one and a café-au-lait coloured one both of whom seemed to be communicating their views to one another most excitedly, though I only saw them in front of English paintings, whose "actuality" must have attracted them. But I should really like to know what remarks they made in front of Rafael. The "Lazarus" in the big Sebastian del Piombo must have pleased them, as the Oriental is half-way to being "one of us," only more pretentious than the two good Museum Moors.

On the other hand it occurred to me that there can be no German philologists or archaeologists here, as I should certainly have recognized them from afar in the British Museum. That lot have their one long vaca-

tion now; but I imagine there are German archaeologists here and there
who behave as though they had been in London, though they haven't
ever crossed the stream. For my part, I can do very well without them.

Wednesday morning

. . . If only I had something more interesting to write about! But when
one only has to do with things, and hardly at all with people, as is my fate
here, one can only write about things, while of course people would really be the interesting part. Even though a voice from the past does speak
to us from some silent work of art, as for example Cleopatra's Needle.
But I hardly dare to go in its vicinity; yesterday—I was dead sober—I had
taken no spirits all day, as I put off drinking till evening—I deciphered the
following clear and terrible words, and what is more it was no ordinary
Egyptian, but a dialect, probably from the lower Delta: "Get away from
here." I hadn't the courage to ask: Majesty, do you mean me specially?
but turned my bowed head away.

Saturday night

. . . Today I visited the Houses of Parliament; now that Parliament has
risen one is again allowed in. I can still remember the impression the
building made upon me in 1860, and how few people shared it, but since
then the study of Gothic, and in particular of English Gothic, has made
such progress that a great deal is felt to be wanting in all that rich wood-
work; in a word, utter lack of feeling. One or two things will remain
magnificent for all time, especially the octagonal Hall in the centre; the
fact that the light comes exclusively from above in the rooms and the
corridors produces a fine solemn effect, the walls being solid below and
only having window openings above. The Victoria Tower, where the
Queen arrives, with its colossal Hall, is very grand. But all the corridors
inside are narrow, simply because they had to be Gothic. I should like to
hear the contempt of an Italian on that point.

I also went yesterday to Westminster during the hours when they drive a herd of mortals through the choir, ambulatory, etc., and to Henry VII's Chapel (in point of fact a quite magnificent second choir). There, at the very back, the Royal Family bury their guests, as for example, the brothers of Louis Philippe, who died young in England—so one of the niches at the back was closed off and workmen were chiselling and hammering away—that is: for Lulu.[87] All decent Englishmen realize that that is the proper way to behave towards princely families with whom one exchanged formal visits when they were on top of fortune's wheel; and the radical writers are left to yap, and people do not immediately start asking how far "one can agree with their ideas. . . ."

Sunday morning

At last a day of solid rain, and what is more a rainy Sunday, and in London, what's more! Perhaps I shall force myself out this afternoon on a third visit to Hampton Court, if it gets just a little finer. Otherwise I shall stay at home and arrange my notes and photographs. How infinitely better they are done here than in Munich or Dresden! All original photographs, a good size larger than cabinet photographs, and only a shilling each—while in Munich and Dresden the cabinet size mostly cost three to four shillings and are usually taken from engravings and lithographs. That is simply because there is no monopoly here.

As to the Royal Aquarium, I must observe that everything that I have seen in the form of *café-chantant,* music-hall and *Tingeltangel* is dwarfed by comparison. The Aquarium is not a glorified "tingeltangel" but a genuine Crystal Palace, otherwise of course I should not have mentioned it. We Londoners overlook mere bagatelles.

Delicious food! In all my life I have never been fed so completely in accordance with my taste, and yet luncheon and dinner together only cost me barely six francs. If my lodgings were not dear, I should call living

87. The tablet ordered by Louis Philippe for his brother.

here cheap for a modern metropolis. The system of eating is closest to that of Vienna, which I know is high up on your list. With soup and a meat course I am chock-a-block; then black coffee, *ecco tutto*. The great thing is that one is not obliged to drink wine or beer; beer has to be fetched from across the road, from the nearest pub, as the English only drink quite fresh beer—instead of which the excellent coffee that they make in the restaurants is regarded as an equivalent. Wine is only consumed by me in the evening. I met a respectable, but rather drunken Reverend in the majolica café, who wanted to convert me to his Church, a thought I could not entertain.

Thursday morning

. . . Pale ale is certainly very good, but on principle, or rather from habit, I only drink *spirituosa* in the evening. The drunken Reverend has found some new friends, obviously equally semi-clerical, and I am delighted to forgo his company.

You may have had it cold in Basle these last few days, but Sunday with the uninterrupted rain, it was certainly colder here. Yesterday, thank God, it was at least warm, although raining. Today, God willing, it's going to stay dry. Indeed, I am hoping for some sunshine in the South Kensington Museum, which I shall immediately apply to Rafael's Cartoons and the *Madonna de' candelabri*. That is something you haven't yet come across, London's parsimony with sunlight, and the way one watches out for every passably bright ray of sun, so as to hurry off to certain works, before the heavens are sealed again.

London, 30 August

I have just seen Stähelin down to his cab; he expects to be bathing this evening off the Isle of Wight. What we succeeded in doing, entirely

through him, during the last three days, it will be my duty to reveal in all
its greatness, as he will probably only write very modestly about it.

Listen and marvel! On Wednesday, St. with the help of his distinguished English appearance and his bold tactics made it possible for us to
visit the famous Bridgewater Gallery, where we were dazzled by at least
two genuine Rafaels, and several Titians of the first rank. On Thursday
he led me to the Duke of Wellington's, where the entry is exceptionally
difficult, with its valuables and pictures of horrifying worth, among other
things Correggio's Gethsemane! Then to Lord Dudley-Ward, where we
saw Rafael's Three Graces and the Vierge à la Légende, Titian's Three
Ages of Man, an enormous Murillo and other incredible things. Then to
the Grosvenor Gallery, with Titian's Jupiter and Antiope, ten (10) Claude
Lorrains, Spaniards according to taste, a unique Rubens, etc. Friday he
took me to Lord Northbrook's (formerly the banker Baring), where our
astonishment began again from the beginning; Rafael's early Madonna,
Murillo's great self-portrait with the shooting-dog,[88] and with at least
two genuine Jan van Eycks (miniatures of inestimable value), Pordenone's beautiful Herodias, etc.; all this flanked by Ruysdael, Hobbema and
and all that is great and famous. After lunch we visited the Earl of Lansdowne, only "second class," still, with two Murillos, a sublime Sebastian
del Piombo (a colossal portrait), etc., etc., and a whole gallery of antique
sculpture, among which an example of the Berlin Cresilas Amazon, fairly
well preserved. I am sure that if we had had more time, he would have
got me into the famous private collection belonging to the Queen in
Buckingham Palace. He is in possession of certain secret magical arts
where concierges and custodians are concerned. Something was also due
to the favourable moment as the *Herrschaften* are in the country now that
Parliament has risen and yet are probably prepared for another short visit
to town before the pictures are covered in dust sheets. You can imagine
my expression as these treasures were revealed. And perhaps I shall be

88. The portrait of Andrés de Andrade.

able to see the Grosvenor Gallery once more on Sunday, now that I have
been introduced there by St.

But now it will soon be time for me to start packing, and on Wednesday I leave for Calais, if the sea is not too awful. I remain undecided
whether to go to Belgium, or directly to Paris. I shall write at once from
the continent.

Now I must close, as I still have to go to the South Kensington Museum, and throw the letter into the post-box on account of the Sabbath;
if I leave it about today, it would not go until Monday.

My head is as full as a house; these last few days were really too full
of marvels. Yesterday evening, from Lansdowne we went to Regent's
Park, to see the animals, to restore ourselves, and found a number of
likenesses to men, which couldn't be helped.

To   von Preen

Basle, 2 January 1880

. . . I managed to slip through 1879 without serious inconvenience, and
without grave imprudences; at bottom the most humiliating thing of all
are the false front teeth I have worn since the end of March. In my family
circle, one or two agreeable things, and no loss; among friends and acquaintances nothing forfeit, but continuity and, I hope, a solid future.
Travel to be renounced for 1880, and in its place a serious work—only no
drudgery—to be undertaken on the assumption that for the time being
the world in general will hobble along as before, at any rate for this year.

The prospects in general and in particular are certainly melancholy; a
financial crisis is raging with us, as with you, and even if we don't have a
bad year, this year will not differ appreciably from last, now that certain
quotas and classes of men, who cannot possibly know anything about
credit, have without further ado been drawn into it. O, what a vast crowd
of mortals ought, for their own sakes, to be placed under guardians! The

traditional legal system and the constitution were guardians of a sort, bad enough in their way, but at least guardians.

At the moment, I should recommend great prudence and moderation to the Semites, and don't myself believe any longer that the agitation is going to die down. Liberalism, having up to now defended the Semites, will not be able to resist the temptation to shake off that particular odium. It will not be able to look on for long while Conservatives and Catholics hold the most popular trump that exists and play it against them. As soon as it becomes safer for the State to step in than to look on, there will be a change. The Semites will then have to do penance for their quite unjustifiable interference in everything, and the newspapers will have to give their editors and correspondents notice, if they want to remain alive. That kind of thing may easily become contagious from one day to the next.

You were quite right to go for the summer into the fresh air of the forests of Herrenalb, while I tramped about in the filth of London, and on the 17th of August, a shiveringly cold day, celebrated the most ghastly Sunday of my visit. However, it had to be, on account of my job, and I saw an enormous amount. If I had waited one more year I should never have had the resolution to make the journey. . . .

If there was an agreeable *augurium* for the New Year in the last days of the old, then it was the thaw and the south wind. Like you, I did, in fact, feel very well during the cold, but one suffers all the same at the thought of the great general want, and a species of calamity fell upon me too, namely the freezing of a certain pipe. As you know, I now live with two no longer young spinsters. Diplomats might have been present at our joint conferences on the subject, and would have admired the equilibrium that was maintained between clarity and delicacy of feeling. Now that the temperature has risen seven or eight degrees, everything has come right of itself.

Here, too, charitable works have been on a large scale, though perhaps the great sympathy shown might have been better had it been partially concealed; it would not, after all, have been necessary to reduce the subscriptions. Curiously enough the nearest Alsatian villages that had to be fed and supplied with clothes did not enter into the reckoning this time.

The effect of the news of the Madrid outrage was frightful, following, as it did, so quickly on the one in Moscow. (*Ad notam:* a few days ago, a Slav nihilist is supposed to have said that people would hear more within twenty days—perhaps it was only bounce.) I only know one parallel in history, namely the century and a half during which the Assassins threatened all rulers in the Near East, and despatched a number of Seljuk Turks and Sultans. Anyone who is, represents or possesses anything, ought to say quite clearly to himself that the Princes who are now being stalked like game, are merely the forerunners of the lot. Peter the Great's system of compulsory westernization imposed upon the nation for almost two centuries, is now taking its revenge. The Russian national character would have been much better off and much healthier under a tolerable barbarism, and Western Europe too, i.e., not under its own barbarism, but if Russian barbarism had continued.

To **von Preen**

Basle, 3 December 1880

I feel impelled to give you a sign of life once again which at the same time conceals an egoistic desire to receive something in your hand towards New Year. We are jogging along as usual; the University term is marked by a higher attendance—nearly 250 students! There are very often no more at Freiburg.

I for my part am beginning to feel the complaints of old age, specially asthma. The doctor to whom I confidently trust myself, says that there it is, and one can live to a ripe old age with it, which I don't even want. The thing that bothers me most is that I shall have to moderate my long Sunday walks very considerably. And asthma is accompanied by a disposition to sweat very easily, i.e., disposes one to catch cold; in short, I have begun the chapter where one has to take care, and consequently one is only too pleased to give up writing books.

Basle is buzzing with music; Rubinstein thumped his heart out on two evenings, but I missed him both times; I have gradually allowed myself to form a prejudice against hearing any virtuoso. The last I heard was Sarasate, and now when I recall it, I have nothing whatsoever to say about him. It is another matter with voices, and I shall remember Vogel as Faust, whom I heard three weeks ago, for a long time. Today there is a concert, but tomorrow is *Armide,* and I shall go to it; I heard it twice, forty years ago, in Berlin, but not since. I admire the courage of our impressario; he must be counting on several performances, as he even boasts of a new *ad hoc mise en scène.*

To Eduard Schauenburg

Basle, 12 January 1881

On receiving your little note I made enquiries at once, and discovered that Fräulein Anna would be staying with a family I know well and who are friends of mine, and received an invitation from them for Saturday evening. I went first to the rehearsal and heard a voice in the *Erlkönigs Mutter* that was like organ tones and the sound of bells, and that entirely reassured me about the performance. I met your charming daughter afterwards during my evening's visit, and was astonished by the similarity of certain tones of voice and expressions. Then on Saturday came the performance, and immediately after the aria by Saint-Saëns, which she sang with unusual freedom, power and beauty, the fairly considerable public broke out into three salvos of applause. I must observe that our audiences here are normally on the cold side, and have before now rewarded quite well-known artists with hardly any applause. Afterwards, your daughter was much finer in the *Erlkönigs Mutter* than at the rehearsal.

In short, from what I have heard here I can wish you every kind of luck, and the time cannot be far off when Fräulein Anna will become an indispensable specialist in the great German concerts wherever a powerful, well-trained, born contralto is needed.[89]

To von Preen

Basle, 19 February 1881

. . . *In politicis,* you have said very clearly what I only feel darkly. Will a "strong, serious government" be possible in future? In any case the limitless, bottomless irresponsibility which the *laisser-aller* in our urban populations has produced would, to the astonishment of the world, shrink away into corners if ever it was firmly tackled. Among us the irresponsible malice of a few miserable guttersnipes disgusts decent people, the ones who are ready to make sacrifices in office, or secretly leads them not to take office, so that they limit their activity to charity and that kind of thing. O, there is a lot to say on that score.

So the great man in Berlin has given notice that he will remain at his post come what may; that means to say, even if the majority in the Reichstag and the Landtag were to be against him, and he had to fight it out again. The great test could only come in some material form, not as in 1863 ff. — and the whole thing was settled for the time being when the purposeful bean-feast in Cologne was postponed. As you say, "everyone has been nibbling at power," and found the titty-bottle sweet.

The economic advantages which the great man promises are, the Parties venture to think, attainable without his kind help, though the fact that they all want something different is naturally to his advantage. As you rightly say, this is "a generation which knows not Joseph and the fathers," that does not think and feel either historically or purely politi-

89. Schauenburg's daughter died not long afterwards.

cally, that splits up endlessly into fractional parties, and *in summa* is good for nothing, not even for itself. Such are the parliamentary bodies which are capable of reaching the most unexpected majority decisions from one day to the next, like the girl and the baby. . . .

To von Preen

Basle, 1 May 1881

In the last few days Radicalism has lurched another step forward all over Switzerland, and unless everything deceives me, there is a European movement at the back of it, and your country will soon experience something of the kind. I feel deep down inside me that something is going to burst out in the West, once Russia has been reduced to confusion by acts of violence. That will be the beginning of the period when every stage of confusion will have to be gone through, until finally a real Power emerges based upon sheer, unlimited violence, and it will take precious little account of the right to vote, the sovereignty of the people, material prosperity, industry, etc. Such is the unavoidable end of the Constitutional State, based on law, once it succumbs to counting hands and the consequences thereof. You must forgive me, my dear Sir, if I importune you with views which I do not want to make known here.

To Max Alioth

Basle, 14 June 1881

. . . I should like to see the Salon in your company; I am not afraid of going unaccompanied among any number of old works of art, but I have a horror of the new when I am quite alone, and in front of the most important painters of our time I am as a rule swayed between admiration for their ability and aversion for the actual performance. Among many French and European painters ever since Eugène Delacroix one has had to put up, first of all, with a personal insult to one's sense of beauty and yet say what one could for their representational talent without making a face. None of the great masters of the past affront me in this way except perhaps Rembrandt.

15 June

Today is close and mild. If my health remains as it is, I shall spend August and September in Italy, which I simply must see again before I die; in September, with any luck, as far as Rome, which the likes of us ought to visit regularly.

Fortunately the surroundings of Basle are still beautiful, and once again I took great delight in them last Sunday on a long solitary stroll. *Les environs de Paris* are really feeble by comparison.

To **von Preen**

Genoa, 5 August 1881

... Why did I really come to Italy? Principally in order to refresh certain great artistic impressions once again before I become incapable of such journeys. This time everything is going splendidly; I limit myself strictly and pass many things by which I could only see at the cost of too much sunburn and sun-blindness; I crawl about where in former years I ran; am very moderate where my food is concerned, and rejoice instead over the wine of the country.

What an impressive people! The first-born of Europe! It does not matter what happens to them; in politics they may be wicked and child-ish—Alfieri's words are still true: *l'Italia è il paese, dove la pianta "uomo" riesce meglio che altrove;* anyone who won't believe that need only look at a company of Bersaglieri going past at the run. Yesterday, on the train between Savona and here, where I travelled third, a plump but most beautiful woman got into the carriage with a violin and sang a popular song in a clear voice, to her own accompaniment and—O my envy!—one could see her thirty-two teeth, all of them in perfect condition.

It is very hot again, but quite bearable in Genoa, with its high narrow streets. The nights are divinely beautiful, and fresh; it gets quite cool and one even pulls up the light blanket over the sheet—*nota bene,* of course with the windows wide open. There is probably no sensation more perfectly delicious than the wonderful feeling of the cool morning air in the hot south. In Savona I once woke up and saw a flaming star that I took at first to be a meteor, till I realized it was old Venus, only in the clarity of a Mediterranean night.

Now I shall crawl along to the Stock Exchange, not to do business, nor even particularly for the sake of Galeazzo Alessi's noble and beautiful building, but because there is a photograph shop near by, where I shall offer up some money. I shall reward myself for that magnificent sacrifice with a *sorbetto,* in the café close by *della Costanza* which I visited yesterday with some emotion. It was there, as a young student in the 'thirties, that I got my first inkling of Bellini, in fact through hearing a harpist and a clarinettist playing a Potpourri out of *Romeo*—and last night once again from a near-by *Birreria* came the sound of the same pieces from *Romeo;* a thing German musical criticism in 1845 would have declared impossible.

6 August

Are the few drops of Italian blood that have come to me through several marriages, ever since the sixteenth century, moving in my veins? However that may be, everything I see seems so natural to me, so related to me. I have no complaint against my destiny; I have become a not altogether useless Bâlois, and would only have made a very inadequate Italian; all the same, I am very happy that I no longer have the feeling of being a stranger here. I feel quite as much at home here as in Frankfort or in Dresden and I find it easier to meet and talk to people. Only one has to compliment the Genoese at once on their new buildings and the growth of the town, which are in fact astonishing, and then they open up on other matters. The present antipathy for the French is very great and they will hardly be reconciled unless the French give up their rights to Tunis, which they are not likely to do in a hurry. In my foolish estimation, France really ought to thank God that some other European nation, a prolific one of course, is ready to occupy the whole of Tunisia, and expel the Arabs step by step. The French, who have not even got men enough to colonize it properly, are meant to "educate and civilize" the Arabs in Algeria—and nothing could be more useful to them than that the Italians should make a thorough breach in Islam, in Tunis—instead of which the French have got a second Algeria round their necks, have fixed a chain round their foot to Germany's great delight, and are making a nation angry who in certain circumstances would at least have covered their flank.

To Max Alioth

Basle, 10 September 1881

. . . It is just the same in Italy as in France; the growth of business and material things, and a marked decrease in the political security that goes with such business and the pleasures in question; the good liberals and even those in a radical way of business, may fall on their knees before the leaders of the people and beseech them not to commit any follies. But in order to be re-elected, the leaders of the people, the demagogues, must have the masses on their side, and they in turn demand that something should always be happening, otherwise they don't believe "progress" is going on. One cannot possibly escape from that *cercle vicieux* as long as universal suffrage lasts. One thing after another will have to be sacrificed: positions, possessions, religion, civilized manners, pure scholarship—as long as the masses can put pressure on their *Meneurs,* and as long as some power doesn't shout: Shut up!—and there is not the slightest sign of that for the time being. And (as I lamented long ago to you) that power can really only emerge from the depth of evil, and the effect will be hair-raising.

Today, I begin my classes again in the Pedagogium (four times a week), although I have the right to completely free holidays. But one sets a good example thereby, and the labour is not great. In addition, there are my photographs to be sorted, given to the book-binder in series, subsequently labelled and finally arranged in portfolios. That has been my autumn occupation on several occasions, a very agreeable little business. Unfortunately the Rector's speech has been foisted on me because Professor Miaskowski has gone to Breslau in the middle of his term as Rector of the University, and with Steffens being ill, I am now the eldest in the faculty concerned. It does not entail much work, but a lot of worry.

To Max Alioth

Basle, 6 March 1882

. . . There was recently a circumstantial article in the *Figaro* about the cat painter Lambert. It is really disastrous that the good fellow should have to work his cat vein to death so quickly; had he been a Dutchman living two hundred and fifty years ago, he would have developed one cat motive after another, evenly and quietly, into extreme old age, and would have seen that the thirty-odd real friends of art living in Holland at that time waited patiently and were served in order. His last picture, however, would probably have been as valuable as one from the middle period. But nowadays things happen quite differently. . . .

I only knew the Nike of Samothrace when it was exhibited in its very unpropitious setting in the passage from the hall of the Caryatids to the central hall; there, in the half dark, it was hardly intelligible. In any case it's a work of capital importance, given by a King of the Diadochi period. I am in the process of discovering other things of the same period which are very powerful and full of movement; they belong to the Pergamon Altar, photographs of which I had sent me. The archaeologists are already busy comparing them with Phidias and denigrating them. They are never happy till they have proved a thing decadent. How splendid your beginning to see the light where Prud'hon is concerned; he was an oasis under the Empire. Those disgustingly boring contemporaries of his sometimes had an inkling of their own inner *néant;* once when David was sitting in silence with one of his pupils in front of his Leonidas, he at last got up and said: *Vois-tu, c'est toujours le vieux chien!*

To **von Preen**

Basle, 13 April 1882

. . . Stick to your frivolous happiness; I do the same with all my strength, and do not allow the prospect of what is to come (although it's pretty clear) get the better of me. Each and every cheerful mood is a genuine gain, and then you have your sons to translate the things of this world into youth and hopefulness. My circle of friends is limited to cheerful people, for there is nothing to be got from those who have gone sour. Nor do I think that anyone in my neighbourhood could complain that I had damped their spirits; and then, as old people are wont to do, I am really beginning to love solitude (linked to a bit of music).

Everybody has the right to think as they please about the situation, peace or war. There are still, of course, diplomatic secrets on the question, but they are no longer decisive; the danger is in the full light of day, for everyone to see. One principal difference between the present and former years lies in the fact that the Governments of great countries, for example France, are no longer capable of secret negotiations, because the ministries change so often and no form of discretion can be assured. The same is true of Italy; who would dream of trusting or confiding anything to Signor Mancini and his friends?

But the incredible insulance which is spreading everywhere in Russia, far beyond the control of the Cabinet, is very significant. It is not the nihilists who are the most dangerous, but the impertinence of those in high places. I am not surprised that everything points to direct elections with you; parties all over the world are of the opinion that there is perhaps something to be won in that lucky dip, and that anyway there is nothing to be lost, so full steam ahead!—in a mood of despair.

It has long been clear to me that the world is moving towards the alternative between complete democracy and absolute, lawless despotism, and the latter would certainly not be run by the dynasties, who are too soft-hearted, but by supposedly republican Military Commands. Only people do not like to imagine a world whose rulers utterly ignore law, prosperity, enriching work and industry, credit, etc., and who would rule with utter brutality. But those are the people into whose hands the world is being driven by the competition among all parties for the participation of the masses on any and every question. The *ultima ratio* of many conservatives has been familiar here for a long time: "It's bound to come," as you put it, "and it is useless to resist," referring to complete democratization.

At the same time, the older stratum of workers is quite out of fashion, and people of assured position are more and more seldom found in office—that too is a phenomenon with which we are long familiar, and anyone who wants to see it on a really large scale need only look at France and its present governing personnel.

Your position in local government, my dear Sir, gives you an insight into the real ethos of the times which is entirely wanting to many a "man of the people," and which he would in any case forbid himself. One of the principal phenomena which you emphasize reveals itself as clearly as can be in Switzerland: a flight from the risks of business into the arms of the salary-paying State is manifest in the fact that the moment farming is in a bad way the numbers who want to enter classes for teachers increases. But where on earth is it to end—the enormous luxury of learning side by side with that of teaching? Here in Basle we are now faced again with disbursements of two millions for new school buildings! It's a single chain of related facts: free instruction, compulsory instruction, a maximum of thirty per class, a minimum of so and so many cubic metres per child, too many subjects taught, teachers obliged to have a superficial knowledge of too many subjects, etc. And, naturally, as a result: everyone dissatisfied with everything (as with you), a scramble for higher positions, which are of course very limited in number. Not to mention the absolutely insane insistence upon scholarship that goes on in girls' schools. A town is at the present time a place to which parents without resources want to move simply because there their children are taught all manner of pretentious things. And like many other bankruptcies, the schools will one day go bankrupt, because the whole thing will become impossible; but it may well be accompanied by other disasters, which it is better not to think about. It may even be that the present educational system has reached its peak, and is approaching its decline.

To **Nietzsche**

Basle, 13 September 1882

Your *Fröhliche Wissenschaft* reached me three days ago, and as you can well imagine, your book was the occasion of renewed wonder. First of all the unwonted, clear, Goethe-like tone of the poems, which no one would have expected of you—and then the whole book, and the conclusion, *Sanctus Januarius!* Do I deceive myself, or is this last section a special memorial to one of the last winters in the South?[90] It is so *all of a piece.* But what always gives me to think anew is the question: What would

90. It was written in Naples in the winter—hence the title—following on his "revelation" at Sils Maria.

come of it all if you taught history? Fundamentally, of course, you are always teaching history, and have opened up some astonishing historical perspectives in this book, but I mean—if you were to illuminate history *ex professo,* with your particular lights and from your particular angle of vision: by comparison with the present *consensus populorum* everything would be stood on its head in the most splendid fashion! How happy I am to have left the customary wishful thinking further and further behind, and to have contented myself with reporting what has happened without too many compliments or complaints. As for the rest, all too much of what you write (and, I fear, the best of it) is far above my poor old head; but where I can follow along, I am exhilarated by a feeling of admiration for the immense riches no less than for the concentrated form, and can clearly see what an advantage it would be for our science if one could see with your eyes. Unfortunately I must be content at my age, if I can collect new material without forgetting the old, and if the aged driver can drive along the usual streets without an accident, until at last the word comes to unharness.

It will be some time before I progress from a hasty glance to a careful reading of the volume, as has always been the case with your books. The leaning towards tyranny in certain circumstances, which you betray on p. 234, § 325, does not alter my feelings.[91]

To Max Alioth

Rome, 23 August 1883. Evening

I just want to give you a sign of life from Rome. What I have seen during these last eight days is indescribable, but what's the use, when one is

---

91. In § 325 Nietzsche speaks of "the strength to cause pain" as above the strength to bear pain and as a mark of "greatness." *Eine Anlage zu eventueller Tyrannei* is Burckhardt's oblique expression.

alone? What wouldn't I have given to have had you by me with your raptures and sarcasms, especially in front of Guido and Guercino and Caravaggio. The likes of us simply cannot deal with these things alone, one must have a practising artist with one, specially for Domenichino.

What none of you can do any more is the huge luscious Venetian stuff, for example Herodias by Pordenone in the Doria Gallery, which beats all Titians of the kind hollow. Further, this afternoon in the broiling heat I made a vain attempt—*par acquit de conscience*—to get into the Villa Ludovisi to see the statues again. Everything was hermetically sealed; so I sauntered out by Porta Salaria and Porta Pia, hung my jacket over my arm, went to S. Costanza and S. Agnese and had myself shown both old churches again, after thirty years, by a kind old monk; and then the glorious Campagna lay there, so characteristic—the battle-ground of Tramontana and Scirocco—and I walked out beyond Ponte Nomentano and saw the Teverone again as in the days of my youth. On the way home I was revived by a delicious Fiaschetto of Velletri in a country Osteria. How unchanged everything there looks compared with the damnable street, formerly the via Flaminia, running from the Porta del Popolo, where the lovely Rococo Casino on the right has vanished, all but a few remains, and one four-storied horror after another has arisen!

The Rome that has remained unchanged is still unspeakably beautiful, and in the new quarters one simply closes one's eyes. Once you reach the Porta Pia you only find what is old and magnificent. They have begun building on the Aventine, where I strolled yesterday evening, so I was able to enjoy its sublime loneliness as it was coming to an end. . . .

Rafael makes quite a different impression upon me now, and I see many marks of greatness in him that I never saw before.

To Max Alioth

Basle, 20 March 1885

The dinner-party at X's, where I found myself for drinks afterwards, was very pleasant, and as it was Friday, and I don't lecture on Saturday, I allowed myself an extension till two o'clock. On ordinary days I very much like to be between the sheets by half-past eleven.

Our local affairs are still in the hands of you know who. During the last few days it has been fashionable for the *Volksfreund* and the *Basler Nachrichten* to give the University some kicks under the table. But in this matter I am a hard-bitten fatalist: whether the University is destined to disappear, depends on higher decisions, not on newspaper articles; and if we are to last on, then it is written that these fellows are not to do us any harm. One little sign of improvement is that the radicals too are beginning to howl about the extravagance here, or what comes to the same, the tax prospects.

I still have a bone to pick with you over your idolisation of the Parisienne. For all their grace they are, after all, a spent, town-dwelling race, and if you want to convince yourself on the point, you have only to observe the smallness of their voices, and conclude from that the total physical neediness of the race. I am purposely not, for the moment, appealing to your eyes (which ought to reveal to you at once the insufficiency in shoulders, etc.). The conclusion of all this is: go and study where there are peasant women in considerable numbers. To study the very well-developed models who go there from all over the world betweenwhiles, is not enough to preserve you from the *culte de la femme Parisienne*. And then it may well be that other nations' respect for Paris is, as a whole, on its last legs. That is slanderous, I know, but I can't suppress it.

21 March

I am unable to better myself in this respect today, either. People pay too much court to Paris *chic*. It would be a stimulating undertaking for a future history of art (if such a thing were possible in the coming age of barbarism), to seize the whole phenomenon as a thing of the past, as historical, in descriptive words and revealing illustrations.

For months I have had rheumatism in the left ankle, and now must wait to see what the doctor orders for the holidays. They begin for me next Friday, and last three weeks, and then on with the dance again.

To Nietzsche

Basle, 26 September 1886

First of all my sincerest thanks for your latest work,[92] which came safely to hand, and my congratulations and best wishes on the unbroken power which lives in it.

Alas, you overestimate my capacities too much, as is shown by your letter, which has since arrived. I have never been capable of pursuing problems such as yours, nor even of understanding the premises clearly. I have never, my whole life long, been philosophically minded, and even the past history of philosophy is more or less a closed book to me. I am even very far from being able to make the claims which drew down upon the heads of some scholars the description on p. 135. Wherever more general intellectual facts stand in the way of a consideration of history, I have always simply done the unavoidably necessary about it, and referred people to better authorities. What I find easier to understand in your work are your historical judgments and, more particularly, your views on the present age; on the will of nations, and its periodic paralysis; on the

92. *Beyond Good and Evil.*

antithesis between the great security given by prosperity, and the need for education through danger; on hard work as the destroyer of religious instincts; on the herd man of the present day, and his claims; on democracy as the heir of Christianity; and quite specially on the powerful on earth of the future! On this point you define and describe their probable formation and the conditions of their existence in a manner which ought to arouse the highest interest. How embarrassed are the thoughts of people like us, by comparison, when they turn to the general fate of present-day European man! The book is far above my poor old head, and I feel quite stupid at the thought of your astonishing insight into all the spiritual and intellectual movements of the present day, and when I consider the power and the art and the *nuances* of your characterizations of the particular.

I should so much have liked to hear something about your health in your letter. For my part, I have laid down my professorship of history on account of my advancing years, and only retained the history of art.

To Max Alioth

Basle, 17 November 1886

Two of the Aula performances are, thank God, over; I really cannot describe my aversion to appearing before the public in my old age. Old actors who have to appear on the stage with steadily diminishing success, in order to earn their daily bread, have my deepest sympathy, as I can more or less put myself in their position. . . .

Idealism — Realism. As I wanted to begin thinking things over, I found that my whole intellectual capital on living art was entirely rusted up. But this much I still can feel, I can foresee the execration of a not far distant future for quite crude realism, however great the talent with which it is exhibited. Photography has a lot more talent for the reproduction of indifferent or repulsive objects.

Stick to the old idealistic line; only a scene that has somehow or other been loved by an artist can, in the long run, win other people's affection. Those are the only kind of works which one can meditate upon, whereas realism kills its clients outright. No one can marvel for long at the *rendu* of odious objects, whereas the disgust remains. One does not, of course, have to paint angels with wings in order to be an idealist.

To von Preen

Basle, Whitsunday 1887

The fact that I have delayed so long in replying has, funnily enough, been due for the last fortnight to the place-hunting crisis in France. I wanted to wait for the end — *avec ou sans Boulanger* — but it is still not over. In the meanwhile there are rumours of serious financial misdemeanours at the Ministry of War; but if the French nevertheless have this individual imposed upon them, then anything may happen, even a declaration of war. We know the inner weakness of democracies against impertinent factions only too well. But I think that this time Germany can safely let war come, for in France in the last few years they have taken good care that there should not be a capable man (such as Thiers, and in a certain sense even Jules Favre) in any decisively responsible position. If Boulanger's pertinacity should end by getting him to the Ministry of War, with the help of a Paris street-rising, then he would have to carry on with a declaration of war; but it is probable that the boundless confusion that would come to light on the call-up and mobilization would end with the whole business collapsing before one step had been taken against Germany.

To von Preen

Basle, 15 October 1887

While you were enjoying your summer holiday in Baden, I spent three wonderful hot weeks quite alone in Locarno, from the end of July, and identified myself as far as possible with the magnificent, beautiful landscape and the completely southern vegetation. And now I will disclose the motive which, quite apart from my preference for the south, drove me over the Alps. To the north of the Alps the *table d'hôte* tyrannically dominates all inns and pensions, an institution that utterly destroys my good health and my good spirits, and if one tries to eat *à la carte* in inns it is expensive and bad, and is out of the question during a stay of any length. In my glorious northern Italy, on the other hand, I am perfectly free, and everyone orders what he likes and what the kitchen happens to have. I ate the same thing almost every day with the greatest pleasure; at any rate my principal meal was *fedelini all'asciutto*. When you reach my age, you will perhaps adopt the same views.

When the three weeks were up some good, kind people came from Basle and Milan and fetched me for a trek through Novarra, Vercelli, Varallo, Milan, Como, etc., and thus another fortnight passed pleasantly. I went once more up the Sacro Monte near Varese, and from there looked once again over the plain of Lombardy like Moses on Mount Nebo. But next year, if I am still alive and in good health, I shall again go and anchor myself at the same inn in Locarno, and take a little work with me and eat *fedelini all'asciutto* daily. . . .

It always does one good to meet the sort of Frenchmen you met over the Red Cross affairs; a Frenchman in middle age, or in advanced years, really cultured and with his passions under control is, after all, the most perfect product of European humanity. But they are only a small minority, and even in the realm of taste they are being completely shouted down, which was certainly not the case under Louis Philippe. Now the masses are beginning to express their views in aesthetic matters, a thing that could be seen, for example, from the funeral of Victor Hugo! In politics the masses unquestionably want peace, but when vote-catching starts on the streets, and calls for war, everyone feels ashamed, and does likewise, so as at all costs not to be thought cowardly, and so that they should not seem cowardly to their womenfolk. Taking everything into consideration, one must therefore say that war may come any day now, and Crispi's visit has, on the whole, only opened our eyes to the fact that simultaneously with war in Lorraine and the Vosges a great war would break out in the Mediterranean. Crispi is certainly enormously popular in Italy now, simply because he has bargained in the North, though nothing is known about it; "when Cavour went to Plombières in 1858, we got Lombardy; when Govone went to Berlin in 1866, we got the Veneto; this time we're sure to get something more." The next item is an open fight with Boulanger, for if he merely retires to his lair growling, he's done for, for good.[93] Europe's greatest insurance, however, against war—and let us still hope, for peace—is the German army, and I congratulate you on the fine impression the autumn manoeuvres made. And ditto for your elections; the end of the *Kulturkampf* has done wonders. We too have just been visited by a revision of the Constitution, now on the carpet, though even the radicals regret it, but advocate it nevertheless, for fear of the workers, etc. Have pity on old Basle! We are in a poor way. Of course, I too try to avert my gaze from "disturbing things," but I don't quite succeed.

93. He retired without a growl, seen home after a banquet by the Chief of Police, who was able to reassure Grévy that there would be no rising: "Je l'ai couché" were the words which marked the end of his opportunity.

To   von Preen

Basle, 17 March 1888

What you wrote on Kaiser Wilhelm I, about whom you have so much more information and many more personal impressions than many who likewise knew him, was of the greatest interest to me. The mere existence of a man like that is a protest against the view, though the whole world held it, that one can make do with men who are raised up from below, by majorities, by the masses: he was, as you say, the exception. Democracy, to be sure, has no sense for the exception, and when it can't deny it or remove it, hates it from the bottom of its heart. Itself the product of mediocre minds and their envy, Democracy can only use mediocre men as tools, and the ordinary careerist gives it all the guarantees it can desire of common feeling. A new spirit then undoubtedly begins to penetrate down into the masses, and they once again begin to feel an obscure impulse to look for the exceptional, but in this they may be astonishingly badly advised, and capriciously fix on a Boulanger. The parallel happenings in France could be infinitely instructive for Germans if they were in the mood to attend to them. But people are turning from a corpse that is all too historic, to one who is marked for an early death.[94] I can think of no similar situation in the whole of history: in all other cases, when a ruler was succeeded by a man who was dying, little depended on the change, and the world did not, as it does now, feverishly reckon up the probabilities attached to it.

94. This refers to the death of the above-mentioned William I and his son Frederick III, who was succeeded, a year later, by William II.

To Ludwig von Pastor

Basle, 12 May 1889

For a long time now I owe you my thanks for the reiterated acknowledgments which you made to my work in your first volume,[95] but above all for the authoritative work itself, and for the agreeable prospect of the appearance of a second volume in the course of this year. You deserve great praise for combating the prejudice against the Renaissance which exists within your Church, at least in Germany. It has always pained me to hear sincere Catholics adopt an inimical tone, and when they failed to see that, within the artistic and literary Renaissance in Italy, one great, strong current served to promote respect for religion and the glorification of the holy, wherever the other current may have run. I can still remember quite distinctly the impression this phenomenon made on me in the course of my work, and only deplore that I did not pursue the point more vigorously; but thirty years ago one was very much alone with such thoughts, and the crowd of impressions of all that was new to me was so great that it was impossible to preserve one's sense of proportion in everything. And yet how little I knew compared with the vast extent which these studies have since attained, principally through your work.

To von Preen

Basle, 5 June 1889

Once again I give you notice of my arrival in Baden-Baden this year, at the end of July, being at the same time impertinent enough to picture to myself how agreeable it would be if you too were to be living in the

95. The first volume of Pastor's *History of the Popes.*

neighbourhood, or were to appear now and then to cheer me, as you did last year. Only I am somewhat less mobile than I was: legs and muscles behave as formerly, but unless I move as slowly as the hands of a clock I begin to pant and sweat immediately. My heart, the doctor says, is not yet affected, but in the meanwhile an emphysema of the lungs has declared itself, and it is only a matter of time, as I know perfectly well, before heart disease follows, two of my sisters having died of it, and my dear surviving sister suffering from it. Other complaints of age have followed. One after the other they arrive, quite quietly, saying Hallo! Good Evening, here I am. Fortunately I can still acquit myself passably in my five weekly lectures on the history of art, and can speak without any difficulty whatsoever, as long as I don't have to march along at the same time.

Of course I am talking of Baden-Baden as though it were certain that the frontier would not be closed within a few weeks, and as though historical events of a very different order were not to appear on the horizon before then, when very different people from the likes of us would have to give up their cures at watering-places. In the meanwhile it would be kind of you to send me a few words from the treasures of your knowledge, and reassure me with your soothing pen.

I go on working without pause, though without exerting myself particularly. Now this and now that section of my lectures and note-books are carefully revised, not with the idea of publication, but as a final settlement, for my own sake. In all this I remain the old author who cannot really do otherwise but who no longer fancies he must address the public. My continuing purchases of photographs and other reproductions for my course on art provide me with proof that I propose to go on living, and is really the only symptom of extravagance in which I have indulged for a long time back. Perhaps I ought also to inform you that yesterday, once again, I laid down wine for a year, the self-same Trentino that your son Wolfgang knows, so that I am acting on the assumption of living on. An *amicus jocosus*, it is true, said that if I did not drink the wine, my nephews would manage to finish it. The wine grows near Calliano, between Trent and Rovereto, under the auspices of a Count Martini, who behaves as though it were very precious, and as though he sold the drink out of pure charity.

On fine Sundays I now go in the afternoon to Rheinfelden or Frenkendorf and Haltingen, take an hour's stroll in the neighbourhood, have supper, and return. Most evenings from nine to eleven I am at the piano, and accompany it with the aforesaid Calliano. If only Paul or Wolfgang or you yourself would turn up one evening! I have not seen or heard of Kaiser for an age. Nor have I been to Lörrach for a whole year. Though the hostess of the "Lerche," the widow Senn (formerly Bäbeli Richter, of Grenzbach), is still a point of attraction. If I had as much money as I wanted, I should buy Frau Senn free from Lörrach, and move into a nice house and have myself looked after by her to the end of my days. But that is quite between ourselves! Those are but sportive thoughts which would not perhaps go down at all well with Frau Senn. (Though no, she would not take it badly from me.)

To   von Preen

Basle, 11 July 1889

I continue to receive author's copies from the most unexpected sources, history of art, history and specially poetry. I should like to know why I deserve the latter. On the assumption that I am still in the best of health, all kinds of people pack up their things and send them to me. I have now devised a formula to be used in returning them: "At my advanced age, and quite unable to be of any assistance to your admirable book, etc." Sending the packages back would not cause me any trouble if only I had not to tie them up and seal them with my old hands, and go on my old legs to the post office. In addition, there are the people of standing, where sending the book back is not at all suitable, and letters of thanks have to be devised, and the book in question run through, at least. What effect will the world crisis we are facing have on the enormous amount of printing? What sorts of literature are going to die a peaceful death? Those are some of the parenthetical ideas that occur to me from time to time.

To von Preen

Baden, Aargau. Hotel Verena-Hof. 24 July 1889

And so you too were destined to join the ranks of those suffering from heart disease. But compared with me you have the advantage of ten years of youth, and will—provided only you are very careful not to work too much—enjoy perfectly good health. For me, on the other hand, the winter season of life has definitely set in, I am easily tired, and must be grateful that eyes and ears hold out, and that I can read with complete comfort. I mean to be back in Basle on the 20th or 22nd at the latest, and all my hopes are fixed upon our meeting again in September. God grant it may be so!

There were special reasons why I decided in favour of Aargau-Baden; I am considerably nearer to an old sister who is very dear to me, and who has been lying between life and death for some time past, and I can get to her in two hours. . . . *Ma parliamo d'altra cosa!* After coffee I crawled along the streets of the town—crawled, so as not to sweat—to a really good bookshop, where one can lay in a stock of "Reclam's Universal Library." There I bought *Rochholz, Legend of the Aargau,* and must on this occasion confess that myths attract me more and more, and draw me away from history. It was not for nothing that the only book I took with me from Basle was the Greek Pausanias. Bit by bit I am acquiring really mythical eyes, perhaps they are those of an old man once again approaching childhood? I have to laugh when I think that I used to polish off twenty battles and wars, so and so many changes of territory, and whole series of genealogica in a single lecture. Wolfgang will bear me out in this.

Old legends are not my sole concern; like you I recapitulate my own varied past from time to time, only perhaps I have more cause to wonder than you, having made so many foolish decisions and done so many foolish things; who could describe how blind one has been in decisive matters, and the importance one has attached to inessentials, and the degree of emotion! On the whole I really cannot complain, it might all have gone much less well. What we both have in common on our earthly pilgrimage, at least since a certain year, has been the need to be satisfied with the moment through one's work, and what is more a varied and stimulating work. The leaden roller that flattens out so many people has not passed over us.

How the younger generation will survive, and build its nest, is something which, seeing the complete inconstancy of things, one ought really not to worry about too much. The young folk in my family, at any rate, look out on the world just as cheekily as we did in our day, and one of my principles is to conceal my fears for the future entirely from them. The forty-year-olds are of course beginning to notice things for themselves. The picture I have formed of the *terribles simplificateurs* who are going to descend upon poor old Europe is not an agreeable one; and here and there in imagination I can already see the fellows visibly before me, and will describe them to you over a glass of wine when we meet in September. Sometimes I meditate prophetically on how our learning and quisquilian researches will fare when these events are in their very early stages, and culture, in the interval, has only sunk a peg or two. Then, too, I picture to myself something of the lighter side of the great renovation: how the pale fear of death will come over all the careerists and climbers, because once again real naked power is on top and the general *consigne* is: "shut your mouth." In the meanwhile, what is the most grateful task for the moment? Obviously: to amuse people as intensively as possible. We have here a velocipede circus, though only till tonight, which has completely paralysed and emptied two theatres, the operetta in the *Kursaal* and the play at the *Theatre,* to the great aesthetic misery of the local rag. From the point of view of the history of culture, it is not yet quite clear to me how far this sort of display will damage the animal circus, or possibly drive it out of business. Does the spectacle of men perhaps really awaken more interest than the sight of horses? And then consider the minute capital sunk in steel wheels as compared with the purchase of horses, not counting their keep, the vet., hay, straw and oats. Such are the thoughts of my thermal leisure, you will say.

I take part in the social life of the watering-place to the extent that there are several people with whom I have a nodding acquaintance, and converse with my neighbour at the luncheon table, but take the greatest care not to tie myself down in any way for the evenings, and drink my glass of wine by myself. Baden, which is deserted in the Alpine season, is fairly full at the present time.

One of these afternoons I must go to Zürich, where I mean to hire a cab for a couple of hours and take a look at all the new buildings, specially the Quais, the neighbourhood of the Concert Hall, and one or two other things. These things are talked about in Basle, and I must be able to voice my opinion along with the others. But I much prefer to think of Lucerne, where I intend to go for a visit at the end of my cure. O, if only my health allows me to go for a fortnight to Locarno! My finances could stand it, and I should not regret it. I remain here in Baden, as far as I know, till the 12th or 14th August; first of all there are the ritual twenty-one baths to be undergone, and then a couple of days' rest. The real Bâlois, by the way, always take twenty-two baths — "just so that one shouldn't have anything to reproach oneself with afterwards."

I don't suppose you know "Goldwändler" by any chance? It is not a tramp or a ghost that wanders about in this district, but a light red wine which grows against the "golden wall" on the steep heights west of the baths. It is an excellent and fairly innocuous wine that the patients can stand, and has been growing there, without any doubt, since Roman times. The place I live in was called *castellum thermarum,* and is mentioned by Tacitus, an honour which Karlsruhe, beautiful Karlsruhe, cannot boast. We in Basle are at least mentioned in Ammianus Marcellinus.

To Paul Heyse

Basle, 13 January 1890

Your "Italian Poets," first of all the old ones, which I read in my earliest days, then Leopardi, thirdly Giusti, together with the supplement, arrived one after another as presents, and finally the volume of *Lyrical Poets and Popular Songs* drifted in with a friendly dedication to me, and with the 1860 passage repeated! How little I deserve anything of the kind! Almost seventy-two years old, and somewhat of an invalid, I have gradually weaned myself from many subjects and interests, and every time the University calendar is rustled, I have to ask myself if I shall be on my legs next term. Fortunately my sight has been preserved up to now, and I have read often and much in the first three volumes, and rejoice over the fourth, which promises so much that is new to me. I once again ventured as far as upper Italy a year and four months ago, and we in Basle live in constant communication with that bit of the south; but I could not say that I hope for anything very good where its future is concerned. Your heroes, who since the days of Parini and Alfieri have been crowned with laurels, all hoped for a very different Italy from the one which lies exploited in one way or another at the present time, and the real Garibaldians fought for a different one. There is something quite unusually pathetic about the way the poets believed that old institutions and the men of former times were all that stood in the way of the happiness of their people. Now we know who really wanted to get to the top, and who really got there. And looking round, one no longer wonders at the fact that a Nievo should have fallen into oblivion. You, dear friend, are doing your best, in the most charming way possible, to make the new Italy have a spiritual influence upon Germany. May God reward you.

Do not forget your rather dull old friend, who would give so much to be able to see you again.

To   von Preen

Basle, 25 March 1890

What times we live in, indeed! Men, interest and things may well come to the fore that will overturn our present antlike existence. Our dear 19th century has so accustomed people to the idea that everything new, however questionable in itself, is justified, that nothing can any longer hinder the process. It is quite incredible how empty-headed and defenceless even thoroughly decent people are when confronted by the spirit of the age. The Parties which have existed up to now seem to me like groups of actors gesticulating in front of the footlights, and illuminated hitherto by a strong light from above — and suddenly caught in their various attitudes and lit from below by a hard red light.

. . . Everyone reads the papers in his own way; the unrest in Köpenick, for example, made *one* impression upon me which was that the rioters followed a strictly military order, which means to say that a sense of duty and the accompanying sense of discipline may be beginning to move over to the other side. The usual rowdyism, which has been latent hitherto, will become more and more prominent, and increasingly difficult to keep down with the methods employed up till now. We had a little example of it here last Saturday among the Germans liable for military service and their defiant and threatening disturbances in the lower town, the like of which have never occurred previously on the same scale.

And in times like these they "shatter"[96] the Chancellor to pieces. Not that he had any medicine in his bag against serious dangers; but it would have been wise, outwardly at least, to do everything possible to preserve whatever looks like authority, or even recalls it. That article may one day become something of a rarity. A troublesome Reichstag can be sent packing, and they will probably be able to govern without it if only for a time. And then, no doubt as a result of some event or other, Ministries will be

96. The expression used by William II when Bismarck was retired.

forced upon the Government by the Parties, and with them you will get unrestrained opportunism, careerists and everything and everybody constantly changing, both personnel and tendencies. In the meanwhile those in the rest of Europe who have had to duck under, or have been elbowed into the gutter by the German Reich, will rise to a more or less courageous and impudent independence. One may, for example, be justifiably curious to see how Italy behaves when, owing to financial crashes, lack of discipline and a failure of authority will have made themselves felt.

All of which is very strange. All the same yesterday we had the last or almost the last sign of good fortune: by a large majority our "people" (δῆμος) scotched the Health Insurance Act which the Supreme Council had already accepted out of sheer exhaustion; it had been proposed by the most unruly demagogues and, at the same time, was calculated to promote the despotism of the State over the private life of individuals in its most extreme form (that is to say, through a Head of Department). Among the whole gang of promoters not one was Bâlois by origin, though one or t'other may have been born here. However, we old Bâlois are quite accustomed to swallowing a good deal of this kind of thing.

To von Preen

Basle, 25 September 1890

Yes, indeed, Authority is a mystery; how it comes into being is dark, but how it is gambled away is plain enough. The Bund came into being in 1847, after the *Sonderbundkrieg,* and as long as Louis Napoleon ruled in France people behaved fairly legally and tolerably objectively; since then, however, the German *Kulturkampf* has had a completely disintegrating effect upon us and at present we are being carried along on the wave of a general world movement. Individually these waves are called the rise of the world of the workers, the growing danger of World War, revolution imminent in Portugal and perhaps too in Spain, the McKinley laws in

North America, etc. And every month the pulse beat is a little faster. What an easy time the Radicals of the 'thirties had! Their "superficiality combined with ruthless indifference towards the established order" (I entirely endorse your admirable definition) fitted in perfectly with the continued existence of the general situation. Things are different now, and, as you say, our present age of universal unrest will in the future seem relatively calm and undisturbed. "Purely legal questions" have, of course, never existed once whole peoples were set in motion; but this time, to judge by the expression on the world's face, there will be neither Law nor process of Law in any shape or form.

26 September 1890

I entirely approve of your supporting the Bismarck memorial, however obnoxious I myself always found that individual, and in spite of the harm which his acts have done us in Switzerland; for his *Kulturkampf* (I must repeat), together with the doings of the French Radicals, has had the effect of encouraging every form of nihilism and disintegration. But where Germany was concerned, Bismarck was in fact the prop and banner of that mystery Authority, and you will have learnt to appreciate the immense value of such *imponderabilia* from many angles. Those who only esteemed and flattered the contingent element in his power can safely turn away from him now he is fallen; on the other hand, what you value is the creator and sustainer of Power itself, without which the individual powers in even the best of nations would probably paralyse one another mutually and cancel each other out. But as far as I am concerned I must beg you to look indulgently on the *Schadenfreude* with which I have noted the interviews given since then; no man has ever "raged" against his own fame like Bismarck. He has exonerated purely historical study from treating him with the least trace of piety — and then there is that *faux grand homme* Boulanger, and the revelations in the *coulisses* which are so enjoyable to follow! Only one must say that France has in fact withstood this crisis too, and that as a Republic it may gradually form an entirely new skin, *faire peau neuve,* as they say in France; even governments composed of the worst careerists are tolerated, and perhaps will be for a long time to come, till capital and credit are entirely eaten up. But if these Jacobins could come to some tolerable arrangement with the Church their position would be secure *in secula seculorum.* Everything hangs on such points, and on the chances of world war. Apart from that, France would simply be the country that had already been through the moult that others will have to go through. But one must be mediocre, or woe betide you! The incredible hatred of Ferry is due solely to the fact that he is somewhat, though by no means much, above the average.

To von Geymüller★

Basle, 8 May 1891

Very many thanks for your letter of the 1st of this month, and for the note that followed! But for a long time now there has been no question of a visit to Paris, to which you so kindly invite me; in my condition I have to take the greatest care of myself, and be thankful if I can crawl away to Oberbaden towards the end of July. Everyone here takes me for healthy, because I still go about and lecture five times a week, but the machine only just keeps going and is showing various defects. Death has not for me the hopes with which you, dear friend, are filled; nevertheless, I face it without fear or horror and hope for the undeserved.

In the realms which concern both of us particularly, things looked very different in the days when you were young from what they do now, and still more so when I was young; it was taken for granted that the aim of art was ideal beauty, and harmony was still one of the conditions of creation. But since then life has been influenced to an incalculable degree by life in large cities, and the spirit that formerly existed in small centres of influence has departed. In large towns, however, artists, musicians and poets grow nervous. A wild, pressing competition infects everything, and newspaper *Feuilletons* play their part in this. The actual amount and de-gree of gifts at the present time is very great, but it seems to me that with the exception of an occasional, and often fanatical, little circle of supporters nobody really enjoys individual works any more.

It is true that I see all this from a distance, and that after some expe-rience I withdrew almost entirely from contemporary art, so as to con-cern myself the more with the great past, and enjoy it. It is true, too, that the same nervousness tries to nestle down in this field in the form of violent quarrels about the history of art, especially about attributions, but these I avoid, and usually say that I know nothing about the matter. I still, today, agree with my old and long-departed friend Gioachino Curti, who used to say: *Purchè la roba sia buona, non dimandar il nome dell' autore.*

The spread of naturalism is typical of our *fin de siècle*. But what sort of patrons and Maecenases will the art of the twentieth century have, or perhaps they'll sink in a great general flood? Some very curious ideas sometimes occur to me about the questionable prosperity which is just beginning. In Italy, where forty or fifty years ago I almost had the illusion of a centuries-old way of life, the "present day" is forcing itself upon one in a horrifying way; careerists on top, and beneath them a nation that is gradually becoming appallingly disillusioned.

Seen from France, and reflected in the concave mirror of hatred, Italy may appear to be behaving thoroughly badly and, apart from the people speculating in old pictures, there are hardly any Frenchmen studying the old Italy.

To von Preen

Basle, 10 September 1891

Prompted by the quotation from Solomon, I once again glanced through that pessimist, and then read him again from beginning to end, and re-called too that some fifty-three years ago as a theological student I had begun to read him in Hebrew; but he was too difficult for me, and still is in some places for scholars, down to the present day. I do beg you to take up one of the correct translations, Dewette's for example, in the place of Luther's largely erroneous one; it is one of the most astonishing books, and at bottom pretty well godless. But if only something of the preacher's way of thought could be got into the heads of our socialists; the fact is, they are terribly dangerous because of their optimism, and the combination of a small mind and a huge mouth. There is no longer any question of *vanitas vanitatum!* — they see everything *couleur de rose.*

How much longer will bells be rung, even those of your city church? But do you know, my dear Sir, that on the occasion of Saturday's bell-ringing, you added a very pretty supplement to Schiller's *Glocke?* It is quite true, bells do not only accompany a single life on earth, but link the centuries together. Schiller only touches quite lightly on the idea:

Noch dauern wird's in späten Tagen, etc.

Though the thought would allow of really sublime treatment. The bell is the only sounding thing that outlasts the changing years, and whenever something serious or solemn happens they have always until now been called upon to express it. Unfortunately nobody would dare to write another verse claiming to be Schiller's.

To von Preen

Basle, 28 December 1891

Unfortunately I am no longer mobile, and fight shy of travelling. And that alone is enough to make me realize how far I am from my green days. I have heaps of photographs sent to me from the Italy I still love so deeply, but it is not the same thing as the sight of it that I once enjoyed so richly. I still lecture five times a week, but my portfolio of photographs is now carried to and fro by a servant, after I have been known for so long as *ce vieux Monsieur au portefeuille.* In such circumstances it is a good thing to have beings one loves in the growing world near to one, as you have in your flourishing descendants, and I in my growing family. Of course, one thinks now and then of the curious times which await youth, but they themselves will know how to grow up and fit into new conditions. A dear learned nephew of mine, and following him his eldest son, who is just ripening for his matriculation, and promises to be a very capable fellow—these are to be the heirs of my unpublished manuscripts; they were not in any sense written for publication; this branch of our house will therefore be in duty bound to witness to the fact that their uncle, or great-uncle, as the case may be, continued to work diligently, even when he no longer worked for the public, but simply for his own sake, and in order to tidy up a number of scholarly matters. Anyone who works officially at the history of art can never escape quarrels and disputes, and the same is true of ancient history; but I have an inborn tendency to arrange all that I have collected in the course of years.

The fact that your official position enables you to be helpful to the poor and unfortunate, and that it is known and recognized as a work of goodwill, is a matter for congratulation. I can imagine all the information and the decisions it must have called for, so that people should at least understand their situation. How few civil servants in any country do more than the strict necessary in these matters!

To von Preen

Basle, 2 July 1892

It is not without the selfish hope of obtaining a sign of life from you that I take up my pen. But quite apart from anything else, today is a day *boni ominis;* early today my doctor examined me thoroughly, as is the custom at the beginning of the holidays, and gave me a good mark, considering my seventy-five years. And next I must inform you in good time that I am changing my rooms at the beginning of September, and moving to the Aeschengraben, which *tempore suo* I will tell you more about. Perhaps you will think that after twenty-six years in the same rooms, your old friend might have finished the rest of his days in the same hole; only my relations persuaded me it was high time that I began to keep house for myself, and they are seeing to finding me a real Perpetua,[97] so I took the decision, and in my heart of hearts am really pleased to have certain things arranged according to my own fancy at last, instead of submitting to sacred routine. I really don't know whether the thought of moving my household things or my books and photographs fills me with greater horror!

To von Preen

Basle, 6 Aeschengraben, 26 December 1892

My best wishes for 1893, which will witness your entry into your seventieth year. You will simply have to prepare to act the part of a jubilee greybeard on the appointed day: I too had to do likewise, with the greatest reluctance, in the year 1888, after having begged in vain and on my knees to be let off, and although I had prohibited anything of the kind. People are possessed by a demon nowadays who drives them to "celebrate" something or other, quite regardless of what or who it is. On the other hand, it may comfort you if I tell you that I have had some very good times in the five years since then, although feeling a noticeable decline in my working powers. And now, as I am taking care of myself for the future, perhaps *l'huile à la lampe* will still last a little, and the best thing is not to think any more about it. My living-quarters, and the cooking and attentions of my Perpetua, have given me renewed courage. Yes-

97. Don Abbondio's servant in *I Promessi Sposi.*

terday and the day before I saw the younger members of our family *en résumé,* and there were faces full of hope and promise round the Christmas tree, and one or two exceptionally pretty children's heads with an expression of absolute and earnest wonder. . . . As regards the spiritual production of the present times in which you, my dear friend, miss the great individuals of the past, the twentieth century will probably show that, once the age of impoverishment and simplification has come, and production ceases to be orientated entirely in accordance with the desire of large towns and their press, really original and great powers can exist, capable of avoiding and outliving the universal falsification! Such, then, are my unauthoritative consolations.

In the said twentieth century those astonishing caricatures of so-called liberal clergymen and professors, who are still at the present time allowed to push themselves forward to the front of the scene, along with the most pressing questions of existence, will simply cease to exist. One fine day, the two above-named figures will all of a sudden look with amazement at one another, when there is no longer anyone there to nominate and pay them. They never, of course, existed on their own strength, they were merely installed to occupy the pulpit and sit in the seats of believers. There has never been so false a position, and when its time is up it will crash. It may be that on the whole this is really working for the Roman Catholics, and that has often been put to them; twenty years ago I said as much to a good friend of mine, who took part in it, and he answered: I know it perfectly well. We in Basle have known this so-called "Reform" for decades, and its party coincides more or less with that of political radicalism, only that the resistance of the positive believer is much more energetic and open than the resistance of the Conservatives in the State, though they are for the most part the same people. The Apostles' Creed was done away with here, *florente ecclesia,* some thirty years ago, because the great soul of a certain Parson Horler (who was a Hegelian, and believed nothing) felt constrained by it. But have no fears, all this will be powdered to dust the moment men are faced with a genuine need. . . .

To   von Geymüller

Basle, Thursday, 13 April 1893

It cannot, indeed, be denied that I handed in my resignation last week, but it happened unfortunately for perfectly good reasons. Almost three weeks ago I was attacked by a very painful go of sciatica in the left side and by a still more serious asthma, and the latter tipped the scales; though I can still speak connectedly, the least movement (unless done very slowly) makes me pant and sweat, and in that condition one cannot promise a course of lectures anymore. Added to that I have three-quarters of a century on my back.

You would never believe how lordly an old man feels when he becomes free from all obligations and responsibilities for the future. I have at once undertaken a little bit of work, and begun to busy myself with it; little things that one can easily drop. But nothing important or far-reaching again! The very thought of it makes me sweat.

The doctor has up to now been giving me Strophanthus drops against the conspiracy of heart and lungs, and I am massaged daily for my sciatica (successfully), but the trouble is that the whole machine is old, and three of my family died of heart disease, and *il faut bien qu'on meurt de quelque chose*. I won't complain much if at the end that now follows, both eyes and ears remain clear.

To   Georg Klebs

Basle, 2 May 1893

As we may not meet in the Reading Club during the next few days, I am writing to you confidentially.

If anything at all—whether on the part of the University, or of the Faculty, or of any particular School should be proposed in my honour on the occasion of my resignation, or my birthday — whatever it might be — I would ask you, as Rector Magnificus, and as an old friend, to decline it definitely and firmly in my name, for which purpose I herewith give you full authority. My wish for complete silence on my retirement from office is quite unconditional.

I am sure you will be good enough to help me in this matter as a friend.

To **Arnold von Salis**

Basle, Whit Monday 1893

During the last few days I have had many proofs of unexpected attachment from pupils and hearers of various generations; but your lines have moved and pleased me quite particularly. I must indeed confess that you describe my work more as it ought to have been and as I should like it to have been, than as it was; but you also recall the personal relationship which was granted us in such a friendly way, and I too remember some really delightful evenings which we spent together. Now that everything is over, I feel that all in all I ought to have been something more to many more pupils outside my class time; but it was always difficult to do, as you can well imagine. And now life has passed, and various complaints suddenly inform me that I have entered upon extreme old age.

My sincere thanks for your kindness and this mark of your friendship.

To **von Preen**

Basle, 2 June 1893

I go on arranging my notes, not as though something were to come of it, but because I cannot stand mere aimless reading, i.e., complete inac-

tivity. The beautiful position of my rooms and my comfortable arrangements are a great consolation, for which I am constantly grateful to my
sister; but for her I should never have been able to take the decision last
year, nor have managed the great exodus. In the dark trees which I look
down upon, the cheekiest birds, the blackbirds, are performing the purest
of songs.

And now I think of you once again, walking along the pavement of
the Karl-Friedrichstrasse, or on some Promenade or other, and daily gathering new strength, and not, what is more, for your desk, but for a happy
and comfortable rest, such as we asthmatics get. A very good sign is the
fact that you get eight hours' sleep, though I cannot complain as I still get
six to seven. Children and old people ought really to be able to sleep, and
what is more allowed to sleep, when they like. The extra glass of wine
you mean to drink on my liberation will be answered tonight with a
special gulp when I have my drink next to me at the open piano.

My successor Wölfflin, who comes from here, was fortunately
brought here at once from Munich, and given the post, so that there was
no gap in the course on the history of art. If weeks and months had gone
by in discussion and correspondence, the whole world would have got
mixed up in it and the devil would have got his finger in the pie.

To a Theological Student

Basle, 26 May 1895

I have still not answered your kind letter of 20th January, and am only
doing so now after having assured myself, through my nephew, that you
are still in Berlin.

I am now entering upon my seventy-eighth year and am not only old
but thoroughly tired, and attend quite objectively at the campaign which
my excellent and valued doctor (also a nephew) is fighting against my
illness with the help of frequent examinations and three alternating med-

icines. However, I have my eyes and my ears, sleep tolerably and will not complain.

Be true to art "in all its branches," to music, to poetry and to painting, and persevere in believing that it is not for nothing that it is given to one to have one's life exalted by these glorious things. There are of course admirable people who do without all these things and they will be granted an *Ersatz,* but it is better to have them. And how much better placed the youth of the present day is than ours was, when there were no cheap editions of music, no cheap books, no photographs, and no trains either, to make travelling easy. But one of the blessings of youth is a marvellous memory for everything seen and heard, and for things too, that one has only enjoyed once.

The art of today has long ago vanished almost entirely from my horizon and I hardly know, or don't know at all, what the catch-words mean. In great old age one only wants peace, and that is best found when one no longer hears anything about the quarrels in art and in literature. That only goes for very old people, for in one's youth one must know about such things, and must be able to adopt a position, for one's contemporaries and friends do the same.

But Berlin, even in my time (in 1839, under Frederick William III), was a very important place, because it was the best place in which to learn history and the history of the arts. The whole of the *Altes Museum* had been arranged in that sense and spirit; it was the only place where I received an indelible impression of Gluck's operas and (in a private choir) of old Church Music—at least to the extent of reaching the beginning of an understanding. Since then an incalculable amount has been added, put to use and employed as nowhere else in the world.

There are treasures in Berlin which are to be found nowhere else in the whole world; in sculpture, the Pergamon Altar, and among pictures, the van Eyck Altar from Ghent. Then in the *Neues Museum,* casts of everything important in the whole world. Now it is likely that as a country parson you will one day be thrown back entirely on the profound recollection and impressions which such things have made upon you, which will not, as I think, be in any way harmful to your spiritual office. If you come back home again, and I am still in the land of the living, I should very much like to thank you some time for the ticket which you left for me, for the last concert that I have been able to attend in Basle. And then I should also like to talk to you about art and all sorts of things.

To Heinrich Wölfflin

Basle, 18 September 1895

. . . I can well believe that *Classical Art in Italy*[98] is not an easy theme; still, that is the kind of question which one expects, Sir, to have answered by people such as you. And now that the weather is cooler, you are just in the right state for it.

But in the meanwhile: Who are *we*, indeed, that *we* should demand an unchanging idealism, constant *in secula seculorum,* from the Italy of the Cinquecento? Our present cult of colour makes us without further ado, *a priori,* into fairly limited fools. . . .

Moreover, whether you like it or not, your book or booklet will take on an historical character; you will have to note a number of transitions in quite general terms (so that a bit of genuine fatalism is greatly to be recommended). And in the Renaissance there is above all the life of beauty, of itself necessarily frail, which at bottom was only a ray of sunshine, brighter than usual, that combined on earth with a simplified or a higher economy of thought, as a result of which the realistic individualism of the Quattrocento, among other things, was avoided. It was inevitable, in that state of things, that the element which you call the formal, the schematic should appear among all the great masters of the second rank, and even among those of the first rank in moments of fatigue. Then

98. English trans. London (Phaidon Press), 1953.

the second stage was that the formal began to gesticulate, and what was supposed to be classical often turned into rodomontade. . . .

But throughout the whole of the Cinquecento you will have to bear in mind the nation standing by and encouraging the artists, and encouraging them to boast and brag.

But that is enough of my importunate interruptions. Be patient and kind and accept it as evidence of my interest.

To Ludwig von Pastor

Basle, 13 January 1896

Many thanks for your benevolent offer to set to rights the words which appeared in the *Historisch-Politischen Blättern*.[99] I think, nevertheless, that it will be best to allow it to pass by me.

First of all old and sick people willingly turn away from the noise of the day, keep peace with the whole world and prepare themselves for quite other things.

And then Nietzsche's name at the present time is not only in itself a sort of power, but a publicity stunt which asks for nothing more than discussions and explanations pro and contra. But anyone who like me began their studies when Hegel was still in the full limelight can view the rise and fall of very various reputations calmly and even learn to put up with the frailty of the greatest.

Moreover, since the philosophical vein is entirely wanting in me, I recognized from the time of his appointment here that my relations with him could not be of any help to him in his sense, and so they remained infrequent, though serious and friendly discussions.

99. Friedrich Nietzsches Geistesentwicklung und Geistesphilosophie. (Vol. 116, Munich 1895, p. 823 ff.)

I never had any dealings with him in respect of *Gewaltmenschen*, the power maniacs, and do not even know whether he clung to this idea at the time when I still saw him fairly often; [100] from the time when his illnesses began I only saw him very rarely.

I for my part have never been an admirer of *Gewaltmenschen* and *Outlaws* in history, and have on the contrary held them to be *Flagella Dei*, willingly leaving their precise psychological construction to others, a point on which one can be most astonishingly mistaken. I really interested myself more in the creative aspect of things and that which makes people happy, the vitalizing aspect, which I thought was to be found elsewhere. In the meanwhile I am reading various parts of your incredibly rich volume, and am more and more in your debt for the fullness of light which it radiates.

To **von Geymüller**

Basle, 6 April 1897

Unfortunately I can only reply to your twofold despatch with some pain, as my present state of health is going noticeably downhill. Sleep and other things are still tolerably good, but my breathing is very short; and there is no longer any question of work, and so I am utterly incapable of appreciating the great enquiry into the two styles about which you are speaking. The old times are quite past, and although a great many things still interest me a lot, I cannot any longer express myself connectedly. And so I am sadly returning your manuscript; for I should even be too weak to discuss things thoroughly, and even to get out such photographs as I still possess. [101]

I was very pleased to hear that His Royal Highness had such a friendly

---

100. See above, p. 220, Burckhardt's reaction to *Beyond Good and Evil*.
101. He gave his collection to Wölfflin.

recollection of the picture; my service in the matter was very slight. It was a question, moreover, not of a Garofalo, but of a very early Guido Reni, at the time when he was working under the influence of Albrecht Dürer which, in this case, was difficult to guess. The picture belongs to the Grand Duchess personally, and on the occasion I received a superb photograph of it.

And now, good-bye, and continue to be well disposed to your old "Cicerone," our lives having crossed and recrossed so often and in such a friendly fashion; and after my death, take me just a little (not too much) under your care; it is said to be a meritorious work!

—

BIOGRAPHICAL NOTES
on the principal correspondents in the order of their mention

RIGGENBACH, CHRISTOPH JOHANN, 1818–1890, after studying medicine in Basle, read theology in Berlin, where he shared rooms with Alois Biedermann (see below). In Berlin they came under the influence of Marheinecke and through him of Hegel. They were ordained in 1842 and married sisters. After espousing Biedermann's advanced theological views and his "Church of the Future," Riggenbach returned to a more conservative attitude and became lecturer in Dogmatic Theology at Basle University. He is the author of a number of articles on theological questions. See Introduction, p. xxviii.

BIEDERMANN, ALOIS EMANUEL, 1819–1885, to whom there are no letters extant. Biedermann, who was born in Winterthur, was sent to school in Basle, which was considered less liberal in theological matters than Zürich, where his father worked. An independent mind who influenced all who came in touch with him, Biedermann took charge of a parish in Basle on his return from Berlin, but he soon moved to Zürich, where he became the leader of the so-called *Reformtheologie* and made a name for himself as Professor of Theology. His work on dogmatic theology was deeply marked by Hegel and Strauss.

VON TSCHUDI, FRIEDRICH, 1820–1886, came of a family long resident in Glarus. Studied theology in Basle, Bonn and Berlin and, like Riggenbach, fell under Biedermann's influence and the spell of Hegel. For a short time he held a living in Toggenburg, but withdrew early in life from the Church and turned to politics. From his retirement in the neighbourhood of St. Gallen he published numerous articles and pamphlets during the Sonderbundkrieg which aroused attention, and continued to play a certain part in politics. His *Animal Life in the Alps* went into several editions and is still read.

SCHREIBER, HEINRICH, see Introduction, p. xxxi.

ZWICKI, CASPAR, 1820–1906, studied in Zürich and in Berlin, where he met B. through von Tschudi. He read theology and took Orders.

MEYER-MERIAN, 1818–1867, of an old Basle family, studied medicine in Berlin and practised all his life in Basle, where he did much to organize and improve the hospital system.

SCHAUENBURG, EDUARD, 1821–1901, the younger of the two brothers who played a large part in B.'s life in Germany. Born in Herford in Westphalia, of a family that came from Oldenburg, Schauenburg read philology in Bonn and Berlin, where B. met him through another Westphalian, Siegfried Nagel, mentioned in the letters. He became a schoolmaster and from 1866 to his retirement was director of the Gymnasium in Krefeld.

KINKEL, GOTTFRIED, see Introduction, p. xxxiv.

BEYSCHLAG, WILLIBALD, 1823–1900, took up his theological studies under the influence of the works of Schleiermacher and Neander, and was ordained. His violent opposition to the Roman Catholics in Trier led to a lawsuit and he moved to Halle, where he became Professor of Theology in 1860 until his retirement.

FRESENIUIS, KARL, 1819–1876, studied science and philosophy. Taught first in Weinheim and subsequently in Eisenach. A friend of Kinkel's whom he knew in Bonn.

WOLTERS, ALBRECHT, 1822–1876, a friend of Beyschlag's, through whose influence he was appointed Lecturer in Theology at Halle.

SCHAUENBURG, HERMANN, 1819–1876, brother of Eduard. Hermann S. studied medicine in Bonn and Berlin, but soon became absorbed in politics. His liberal views led him into trouble with the authorities and it was only after 1848 that he settled down to his profession and practised as a doctor. Hermann S. was the most politically minded of Burckhardt's friends during his years in Germany. Some of his medical works were well thought of and remained in print for a long period.

HEYSE, PAUL, 1830–1914, poet, dramatist and novelist, born in Berlin, brother-in-law of Bernhard Kugler, the son of Franz Kugler (see Introduction, p. xxxii), in whose house he first met Burckhardt in 1849. From 1854 to the end of his life he lived in Munich and was one of the group of writers who gathered round Maximilian of Bavaria. His translations from Italian poetry were dedicated to Burckhardt. He was awarded the Nobel Prize for literature in 1910.

MÜNDLER, OTTO, seven years younger than Burckhardt, an historian of art living mostly in Paris who assisted von Zahn with the revision of the second edition of Burckhardt's *Cicerone*.

VON PREEN, FRIEDRICH, 1823–1894, born in Mannheim, the son of an officer in the service of the Grand-Duchy of Baden. Studied law in Heidelberg where he became the life-long friend of Goethe's grandson Wolf Goethe. Entered the civil service and while stationed in Lörrach, near Basle, met Burckhardt through Dr. Kaiser mentioned in some of the letters. Preen was shortly after moved to Bruchsal and later to the capital, Stuttgart, where he died. See Introduction, p. xlvi.

ALIOTH, MAX, 1842–1892, came of a prosperous Basle family. Studied architecture and practised for a time in Paris and in Basle. In spite of considerable gifts he was unsuccessful and for a time tried his hand at painting. After some years in Paris he took up his profession again and joined an architect's office in Frankfort. A year or more before his death he returned to Basle in poor health. Until the end Burckhardt showed a lively interest and sympathy in all his undertakings. See Introduction, p. xlvi.

VON GEYMÜLLER, HEINRICH, 1839–1909, a cousin of Alioth's and an Austrian by nationality. Geymüller made his name as an historian of architecture with his work on St. Peter's. But though their friendship began in the same years as the correspondences with Preen and Alioth, the letters to Geymüller are of rather more special interest than the other two correspondences. This will explain why a life-long friendship is only represented by three letters.

PRINCIPAL EDITIONS OF
BURCKHARDT'S LETTERS

Jacob Burckhardt: Briefe, vol. 1, 1818–1843. Edited by Dr. Max Burckhardt. Benno Schwabe, Basle, 1949. (This edition will be completed in ten volumes.) [This note is from the 1955 edition.]

Burckhardt-Wölfflin Briefwechsel, und andere Dokumente ihrer Begegnung, 1882–1897. Edited by Joseph Gantner. Benno Schwabe, Basle, 1948.

Briefe Jacob Burckhardts an Gottfried und Johanna Kinkel. Edited by R. Meyer-Kraemer. Benno Schwabe, Basle, 1921.

Jacob Burckhardt, Briefwechsel mit Heinrich von Geymüller. Edited by Carl Neumann. Georg Müller, Munich, 1914.

Jacob Burckhardt, Briefe an einen Architekten, 1870–1889. Edited by Hans Trog. Georg Müller, Munich, 1912.

Jacob Burckhardt, Briefe an seinen Freund Friedrich von Preen, 1864–1893. Edited by Emil Strauss. Deutsche Verlags-Anstalt, 1922.

Jacob Burckhardt: Briefe und Gedichte an die Brüder Schauenburg. Edited by Dr. Julius Schwabe. Benno Schwabe, Basle, 1923.

INDEX

Photographs are indicated with italics. The initials JB refer to Jacob Burckhardt. All Germanic names are indexed under the primary name rather than the prefix. Entries with an underscore, e.g., Beck, _____, indicate unidentified first names.

Aargau-Baden letter, 229–31
Acton, Lord, xxiii, xxiv, xxv
Aeschengraben move, 240–41, 244
Age of Constantine, l, liii–liv
Aida, 167, 177–78
Alboni, _____, 133–34
Aldronvandi, Count, 187
ale/beer, English, 202
Ales Museum, 245
Alexander II, 137, 137n66
Alfieri, _____, 210
Alioth, Max: biography, xlvii, 253; letters to, 163–65, 167–70, 175–78, 180–89, 191–95, 209–10, 212–14, 217–20, 221–22
Alsace, 139, 151
Amiens Cathedral, 193
Ancien Régime (Taine), 173
Ancona, Italy, 186
Andromaque (Racine), 60
Animal Life in the Alps (Tschudi), 251
animals in Italy, 187–88
Apostles' Creed, 241

Architectural Journal, 10
architecture: Bologna, 182, 183, 184, 186–87, 188; Bruschal, 131, 131n60; Dresden, 169–70; Gravedona, 180–82; London, 192, 195, 197–98, 200; Munich, 21, 175–77; Paris, 61, 193; Ravenna, 84; Rome, 163, 165, 167–68, 218; Thann, 132; Zürich, 231. *See also* Kugler, Franz
Armide, xxxii, 207
Arnim, Bettina von, xxxv, 29–30, 40–43, 44, 52, 62, 62n35
Arnim dispatch, 161, 161n78
art: advice to youth, 107–8, 245–46; amateurism and, xliv; idealism vs. realism, 221–22; JB's historical orientation, xxxix–xl, 20–21, 73, 97; leisure and, 165–66, 196; purpose, lvi–lviii, 236–37. *See also* architecture; history; paintings/painters
art galleries. *See* paintings/painters
Art of the Renaissance (Burckhardt), 117–18, 122

Asia Minor, research decisions, 19–20, 23

asthma, JB's, xlv, 206–7, 242

authority/power traditions: cartoon discussed, 187; as financial guardians, 204–5; leadership inadequacies during democratization trends, 215, 225; progress and, 143–44, 233–34. *See also* socialism/democracy trends

authorship: advice about, 114, 119, 159–60; burdens of, xlvi, 228–29; criticisms of self, 126–28; expectations about, 122–24

"away sickness," 22–23, 48–49

Baden letter, 229–31

Baldung, Hans Grien, 21–22

Balfe, ——, 66–67

Bamberg Cathedral, 20

Basle letters, 3–17, 67–81, 83–84, 91–99, 114–19, 122–62, 170–74, 189–91, 204–10, 212–17, 219–29, 232–49

Basler Zeitung, xxxviii–xxxix, xl, 72, 74–75

Bauer, Bruno, 69, 69n38

beauty, yearnings for, 88, 89, 98–99, 102, 103

Beck, ——, 12, 174

beer/ale, English, 202

Beethoven, Ludwig van, 10

"Beiträge zum Cicerone," xlii, xlv n2, xlvi, 117, 118, 118 n52, 126–28, 132, 136, 166

Belgium, 36, 38 n27, 44

Bellini, ——, 211

Berlin: anticipation of, 15–17, 83; letters from, 17–30, 40–52, 54–57, 84–90; memories of, 245; overview of JB's residency, xxxii–xxxiv, xl–xli

Berlin Academy of Art, xl, 83

Berri, Melchior, 13 n14

Beyond Good and Evil (Nietzsche), 220–21, 220 n92

Beyschlag, Willibald: biography, 252; G. Kinkel and, 76, 76 n39; letters to, 48–49, 60–62, 68–71

Biedermann, Alois Emanuel: biography, xxviii, 251; JB's relationship, xxx; letters about, 5, 8, 12

Bishop's Palace (Bruchsal), 131, 131 n60

Bismarck, 135, 135 n64, 145, 148, 151, 161, 161 n78, 173, 235

Böcklin, Arnold, xliii

Bode, Wilhelm, xlvi, 160, 166

Bologna letters, 182–88

Bonn period, xxxiv, xxxvi–xxxvii, 39

book publishing. *See* authorship

botany, 174

Boulanger, Georges, 222, 224

Bourbaki, ——, 193, 193 n85

Bourgraves (Hugo), 60

Braunschweig letter, 36, 39–40

Brenner, Albert, letters to, 102–13

Brenner-Kron, Emma, letters to, 95–97

Bretano, Clemens, xxxv, 41 n28, 42 n29

bridges, 195, 195 n86

Bridgewater Gallery, 203

Brockhaus Encyclopedia, xxxviii, 67

Burckhardt, Jacob (biographical highlights): appearance, xliv, xlvi, 37, 120, 121; Basle period, xxxviii, xxxix–xl, xliv–xlvi; Berlin period, xxxii–xxxiv, xl–xli; Bonn period, xxxiv, xxxvi–xxxvii; family, xxvi–xxvii; friendships/relationships characterized, xxx–xxxi, xli, xliii–xliv, xlvii–xlix; holiday travels, xlvi–xlvii, li–lii; Italy periods, xl, xlii; journalism period, xxxviii–xxxix; letters characterized, xxv–

xxvi; life perspective, xxvii–xxviii; religious perspective, xxviii–xxx, xxxi, l; reputation, xxiii–xxv; Zürich period, xlii–xliii

Burckhardt, Louise (sister): JB's letters discussed, xxix, xxx; letters to, 25–27, 29–33, 36, 39–43; marriage, xxxii, 7n6, 36n26, 54

business world, 135–36, 147, 174, 215–16

Camposanto (Pisa), 165

Camuph (Johannes Jakob Oeri), xxiv, xxxii, 7, 7n6, 12, 15, 15n15, 23

Caracci, Ludovico, 184

Cassell (art gallery), 170

Catalogue Raisonné, 196

Caterina Cornaro (Lachner), 177

Catholic vs. Protestant Church, 119, 122

Centaurs (sculpture), 164–65

Chalard, ____, 177

Chambéry fountain, 168

le chapeau de paille, 197

character, advice about, 109–13

Christ, xxviii, 4, 69–70

Christianity: Beck's lectures, 12; Dewette's views, xxviii, 4, 12; JB's beliefs, xxviii–xxix, l, lii–lviii, lix–lx, 8–9, 17–18, 26, 68–70; JB's family conflict, 13–14, 16; optimism and, lii–lviii, 144; orthodoxy and doubt, 3–5; Pastor's book, 226; Protestant vs. Catholic, 119, 122; Schelling's perspective, 47–48; Schreiber's views, xxxi. *See also* theology profession

Church. *See* Christianity; theology profession

Cicerone, xlii, xlvn2, xlvi, 117, 118, 118n52, 126–28, 132, 136, 166

cigar varieties, 198

Civilization of the Renaissance in Italy

(Burckhardt), xxiii, xlii, xlvn2, liii–liv, 64n36, 114, 114n47, 115, 116–17, 116n50, 153, 153n74

Classical Art in Italy (Wölfflin), 246

Cleopatra's Needle, 192–93, 200

Clough, Mrs. A. H., 118n52

Club of Westphalians, 31

coffee/coffeehouses: Italian, 164, 180; London, 197–98, 202

Cologne, *38, 39,* 44, 55

community and selfishness, liv–lvi, 8–9

Como, Lake, letter from, 180–82

Concert Hall, Basle, 172

Conrad of Cologne, Archbishop (JB's book), 44, 54, 55

conservatives. *See* political issues

Constance, Lake, period, li–lii

Constitution of Cologne, 55

contemplation as study, li, lviii, 49–51

Cornelius, ____, 175, 175n81

Correggio, 203

Crespi, ____, 224

Creuzer of Heidelberg, xxxv, 41n28

Crippa, 168

Curti, Gioachino, 237

Curtius, Ernst, 149n72

La Dame Blanche, 66

dance music, 171

death, feelings about, l, 236

Decamerone, 136

democracy. *See* socialism/democracy trends

Dewette, ____, xxiii, xxviii, 4–5, 12

diary entries, London, 196–204

Dilthey, Wilhem, li, 124–25, 124n57

Dornach property, 73

drama/plays, 60

dreams of cathedrals, 10

Dresden letters, 53, 169–70

Droysen, ____, xxxii, 22, 24, 28

Dudley-Ward's gallery, Lord, 203

economic conditions, 174, 182, 204
educational system, 179, 216. *See also*
   teaching profession
Education Sentimentale (Flaubert), 133
E Hämpfeli Lieder (Burckhardt), xli
Ehrenberg, ____, 10
England: London letters, 191–95; po-
   litical philosophies, 143
English History (Ranke), 161
English language, 199
Ense, Varnhagen von, 30, 30 n25
Epoca, 187
Erlkönigs Mutter, 207
Eycks, Jan van, 203

faith. *See* Christianity; theology
   profession
Fallersleben, Hoffmann von, 63–64
Falsi Monetari (Rossi), 167
family: elderly years and, 229, 239,
   240, 241, 244; father, xxvii, xxxii,
   16, 27, 29, 44; overview, xxvi–
   xxvii, xxix; sister Margarethe, 13–
   14, 13 n14. *See also* Burckhardt,
   Louise (sister)
father, xxvii, xxxii, 16, 27, 29, 44
Faust, 104–5, 207
Faust period, 7, 7 n7
Filiberto statue, 168
Flaubert, Gustave, 133
Florence, 6–7, 11, 182
Focke, August, 35, 39, 40
food: England, 192, 201–2; Italy, 180,
   223
Förster-Nietzsche, Elisabeth, xlviii,
   xlviii n3
"Fortune and Misfortune in His-
   tory," 144
Fourment, Hélène, 197
France: Neuchâtel visit, xxviii; Paris
   letters, 57, 60–67. *See also* Paris
France, JB's political comments:
   Boulanger, Georges, 222, 224;
character of Frenchmen, 64, 223–
   24; foreign policy, 65; future of,
   235–36; Tunisia, 212; war and af-
   termath, 137–41, 145, 151, 214,
   222
Frankfurt letter, 30–33
Frantz, Konstantin, 146, 146 n71
Frauenkirche (Munich), 175
Frederick III, 225, 225 n94
freedom, 143–44
French History (Ranke), 161
Fresenius, Karl: biography, 252; let-
   ters to, 50–52, 81–82
Friedrich Wilhelm IV, 56–57
Fröhliche Wissenschaft (Nietzsche),
   216–17, 217 n91

Gabriel Affair, 150, 150 n73
Galli, Cardinal Tolomeo, 180
Gare du Nord (Paris), 193
Geersdorff, ____ von, xlviii
Geibel (poet), 53, 86, 87, 89, 125
Gelzer, Dr., 16
Genoa: letters from, 210–12; memories of, 7–8, 163
*German History in the Age of the Refor-
   mation* (Ranke), 161
Germany: anticipation of university
   studies, 15–17; Berlin letters, 17–
   30, 40–52, 54–57, 84–90; countryside letters / travels, 30–36, 36 n27,
   39–40; culture changes, 134, 140–
   41, 154–55; Dresden letters, 53,
   169–70; *Faust's* importance to,
   104–5; memories of, 245; Munich
   letters, 175–78; overview of JB's
   residencies, xxxii–xxxiv, xxxvi–
   xxxvii, xl–xli
Germany, JB's political comments:
   Arnim dispatch, 161–62, 161 n78;
   Bismarck, 135, 173, 208–9, 235;
   leadership changes, 225; Posnania
   petition, 56–57; socialism in

Rhineland, 77, 87; war and aftermath, 137–41, 145, 148–49, 151, 222
Geymüller, Heinrich von: biography, xlvi, 253; letters to, 236–37, 242, 248–49
Godet, Fritz, 8*n*8
Goethe, Johann Wolfgang von, xxxv, 9*n*9, 41
Goldwänder wine, 231
Gothic style, JB's opinion, 132
Gravedona letter, 180–82
Griechische Kulturgeschichte, xxiv, l, lv
Grillparzer, ——, 154
Grosvenor Gallery, 203
Grüninger, Robert, letters to, 162–63, 165–67
Gsell, ——, 12
Guide to the Artistic Treasures of Belgium (Burckhardt), 44, 45, 52
Günderode, Karoline, xxxv, 41–42

Habicht, ——, 55
Hagenbach, ——, 12
Handbuch der Kunstgeschichte (Ebner), 114*n*46, 115
Hartmann, Eduard von, 151
Harz mountain trip, 27–28
health in old age, JB's, 204, 206–7, 220, 227, 239, 242, 244–45, 248–49
Health Insurance Act, 234
hearing loss, JB's, 171
heart disease, JB's, 227, 242
Hebel, ——, 152, 178
Herostratus, 143*n*70
Herzen, ——, xxxvii
Heusler, Andreas, xxxviii, xl
Heyse, Paul: biography, 252; letters to, 97, 99, 102, 114–15, 116–17, 118–19, 122–24, 232
Hildesheim trip, 27–28
history: advice to young scholars, 128–31; career decision-making,

19–20; contemplation as study, li, lviii, 49–51; facts vs. culture, 141, 155; Nietzsche letters, 216–17, 220–21; poetry compared, 24–25, 51; religion and, 1*n*6; teaching principles, xlv, 156–57; writing styles, 45–46. *See also* teaching profession
History of Architecture (Kugler), 114–15, 123, 123*n*55, 124
History of the Popes (von Pastor), 226, 226*n*95
home-sickness, 22–23, 48–49, 60–62
honour, liii
Horler, Parson, 241
Hufeland, ——, 25–26, 29
Hugo, Victor, 60
Human, all-too-human (Nietzsche), 190, 190*n*84, 191

idealism and art, 107–8, 221–22
industrialization of the state, 148–49
Isteiner wine, 174
Italienische Liederbuch (Heyse), 116*n*49
Italy: anticipation of, 78–79, 85–87, 145; art losses to England, 196; Bologna letters, 182–88; Genoa letters, 210–12; Gravedona letter, 180–82; memories of, xl, 6–8, 9–11, 83–84, 169, 223; Milan letter, 188–89; overview of JB's residencies, xl, xlii; poets, 232; political issues, 189, 215, 224; Rome letters, 81–83, 162–68, 217–18; Wöfflin's art book, 246–47

Jews, 150, 205
Johann Parricida, 45
journalism: history compared, 129; JB's work, xxxviii–xxxix, xl, 63, 72, 75–76; poetry and, 109; rulers and, 161–62; socialism and, 184

Kaegi, Professor, xxix
Kaiser, Dr., 149 n72
Karlsruhe, von Preen's appointment,
    157, 157 n77
Karr, Alphons, 89
Kaufmann, Angelica, 174
Kaulbach's frescoes, 168
Kiel, 124, 124 n57
Kierkegaard, Sören, 47 n31
Kindermann, _____, 177
Kinkel, Gottfried: biography, xxxiv–
    xxxviii, xli; JB's opinion stated, 70,
    91, 92; letters to, 44–48, 53–57,
    60, 63–66, 67, 72–73, 74–78, 83–
    87; opinion of JB, xxxvi, xxxvii
Kinkel, Johanna Matthieux: biog-
    raphy, xxxv–xxxvi, xxxvii, xxxviii;
    compositions, 42; friendship with
    JB, 39, 41; letters to, 66–67, 71,
    81
Klebs, George, letter to, 242–43
Köbi, _____, 19 n18
Kölnische Zeitung, xxxviii, 89
Köpenick unrest, 233
Krefeld, lecture invitation, 125–26
Kritische Gänge, 135
Kugler, Bernhard: Heyse and, 252;
    JB's statement on his study, 118–
    19, 118 n54; letters to, 128–31, 152–
    54, 159–60
Kugler, Franz: architecture studies,
    21, 23, 114 n46, 117, 123 n55, 124;
    biography, xxxiii, 118 n54; Brock-
    haus work, 67; drawing of JB, 37;
    friendship with JB, xxxii–xxxiii, xl,
    23, 27, 44, 64, 86; Heyse's request
    of JB, 123; Kinkel and, 84–85
Kunst der Renaissance (Burckhardt),
    124

Lachmann, _____, 28
Lachner, _____, 177
Lake Como letter, 180–82

Lambert, _____, 213
Lansdowne, Earl of, 203
lectures. See teaching profession
Leipzig visit, 31–34
leisure, lvi, 165–66, 196
Lenau, _____, 112
liberalism. See political issues
Liège, 58
Liel, 174
life's purpose, advice about, 8–9,
    109–11
Liszt, Franz, 43
literature: businesspeople and, 135–
    36; mythology, 229–30; novels /
    poetry compared, 133; recom-
    mended, 136. See also poetry
Locarno, 223
lodgings in Basle, xlv–xlvi, 240–41
London: diary entries, 196–204; let-
    ters from, 191–95
loneliness: advice about, 3; complaints
    of, 22–23, 48–49, 60–62, 90
Loreto, 186
Lörrach, 131, 131 n61, 149 n72
Louis Philippe, 201, 201 n87
Lübke, _____, 114, 115, 117, 119, 124,
    132, 132 n63, 149
Ludwig I, 175
Lyrical Poets and Popular Songs
    (Heyse), 232

Macbeth (Chalard), 177
Magic Flute, 10
"malism," 171
Männerlied (Kinkel), 84–85, 87
Manzer, _____, 23
Marches, Signor, 187
marriage, opinions on, xxx–xxxi,
    xxxviii, xli, lix, 25–26, 25 n20, 71,
    88, 94
Martel, Charles (JB's writing), 44
Martha, 190
Martini, Count, 228

masses, the. *See* socialism/democracy trends

Matthieux, Johanna. *See* Kinkel, Johanna Matthieux

Maximiliane, Fräulein, 42

Maximilianeum, 176

melancholy and artists, 51–52. *See also* loneliness

memorials, undeserved, 178

Merlin (Immermann), 105

Meyerbeer, Giacomo, 66–67

Meyer-Merian, Theodor, 252; letter from, 19*n*18; letter to, 22–23

Middle Ages: art history, 73; career decision-making, 19–20; JB's opinion of, 90

Milan: letter from, 188–89; memory of, 9–10

militarization of the state, 148–49

Missa posthuma (Rossini), 133–34

Monte Imperiali, Italy, 186–87

Mörike, ____, 133

mother, xxvi, xxvii, 13, 14

move in elderly years, 240–41

Müller, Johannes von, 66

Mündler, Otto: biography, 132, 253; letters to, 117–18, 126–28

Munich: art/architecture, 21; letters from, 175–78

Murrillo, 203

Museo Capitolino, 164

music: Basle performances, 10, 133–34, 172, 190, 207–8; Berlin period, xxxii, 245; Bologna experiences, 182–83, 185–86; Genoa trip, 211; hearing loss and, 171; Heyse's book, 116, 116*n*49; JB's compositions/performances, xlvii, 10, 31, 42, 45; Liszt's recital, 43; Munich opera, 177–78; Paris opera, 66–67; Rome opera, 167; solitude and, 190; Wagner's, 154–55, 182

mythology, 229–30

Nachbauer, ____, 177

Nagel, Siegfried, xxxiii, 31, 252

Napoleon, 137, 137*n*66

National Gallery, 196, 199

Natural History Museum (England), 192

nature, 22–23, 162, 173–74

Neuchâtel, France, xxviii

newspapers. *See* journalism

Nicordi, ____, 167

Nietzsche, Friedrich: JB's opinion of, xlvii–xlviii; letters about, 140, 140*n*68, 146–47, 190, 190*n*84, 247–48; letters to, 156–57, 191, 216–17, 220–21; opinion of JB, xlii, xlviii–xlx, li

Nike of Samothrace, 213–14

Norma, 182–83

Northbrook's gallery, Lord, 203

novels/poetry compared, 133

Novi, 4, 4*n*5

Oeri, Johannes Jakob (Camuph), xxiv, xxxii, 7, 7*n*6, 12, 15, 15*n*15, 23

Offenbach, Jacques, 171

Ofionide (Picchinoni), 64, 64*n*36, 117, 117*n*51

Ollivier, ____, 135, 135*n*65

opera: Basle performances, 10, 133–34, 172, 190, 207–8; Bologna conversation, 185–86; French performances, 66–67; Italian performances, 167, 182–83; Munich, 177–78

optimism/progress, xxv, liii, lvii–lviii, lix–lx, 143–44, 170–71, 187, 212–13, 233–35, 238

Les Orgines de la France Contemporaine (Taine), 173

orthodoxy, xxix, 3–5. *See also* Christianity; theology profession

Oser, Maria, xxx–xxxi, 25–26

Otto der Schütz (Kinkel), 45, 92

paintings/painters: Baldung, 21–22; Böcklin, ——, xliii; Caracci, 184; Cassell gallery, 170; Cornelius, 175, 175 n81; JB's purchase, 118 n53; Lambert, 213; lectures on, xxxix–xl, 77; modern, 209–10; Moors in National Gallery, 199; portraits at Ludwig I residence, 176, 176 n83; Rafael, 105, 192, 202, 203, 218; Rubens, lix, 197; Stähelin-led tour in London, 203–4

Palazzo del Magnifico, 163

Palazzo Publico, 165

Palazzo Sauli, 7–8

Palazzo Zuchinni, 188

Paris: architecture, 193; letters from, 57, 60–67; people of, 219; visit to, 158

Parliament Houses (England), 200

Pastor, Ludwig von: letters to, 226, 247–48; Renaissance/Zarthustra comparison, xlviii

Pergamon Altar, 214

Pero, ——, 181–82

Perponcher household, 52, 53

Peter the Great, 206

Philip II, 161

philosophy. See history

photographs, xlvi, 165, 168, 201, 213, 221, 227, 238–39

Piazza di Spagna, 168

Picchioni, —— (Ofionide), 64, 64 n36, 117, 117 n51

Pindar, 136–37

Piombo, Sebstian del, 199

Pisa, 6–7, 165

Platen, ——, 11, 11 n11, 85

plays/drama, 60

Podesti's frescoes, 168

Poems (Mörike), 133

poetry: advice about, 95–97, 106–9, 112–13; Faust's importance, 104–5; H. Schauenburg's, 32, 33; Heyse's

book, 232; history compared, 24–25, 51; JB's, xxviii, xli, 9, 45, 49, 74, 86, 188–89; novels compared, 133; Pindar's, 136–37

political issues: H. Schauenburg discussions, 32–33; Italy, 184, 187, 189, 215, 224; JB's decision to not participate, 78–80, 88–89; liberalism, 71–72; Russia, 206; theology and, xxix–xxx, xxxix, liii–lvi, 70–71, 241; war and aftermath, 137–41, 146, 148–49, 214–15, 222. See also France, JB's political comments; Germany, JB's political comments; socialism/democracy trends; Switzerland

Pont des Arches, 58

Ponte Rotto, 59

Popes (Ranke), 161

Pordenone, 203

Preen, Friedrich von: biography, xlvi–xlvii, 253; letters to, 131–46, 148–52, 154–55, 157–58, 161–62, 170–74, 178–80, 189–90, 204–7, 208–9, 210–12, 214–16, 222–25, 226–31, 233–36, 237–41, 243–44

professorship. See teaching profession

progress/optimism, xxv, liii, lvii–lviii, lix–lx, 143–44, 170–71, 187, 212–13, 233–35, 238

Protestant vs. Catholic Church, 119, 122

Providence. See Christianity

Prussia. See Germany

Prussian History (Ranke), 161

Prutz, Robert, 97

Puits d'Armour (Balfe), 66–67

radicalism, Swiss, xxxix, 72, 172, 209. See also socialism/democracy trends; Switzerland

Rafael (Raphael), 105, 192, 202, 203, 218

Ranke, ____: Bettina meeting, 29–30; colleague relationships, 29, 44; history books, 161; JB's poetry, 45; lectures, xxxii, 19, 20, 28; Paris meeting, 62–63; reputation, xxiii–xxiv, xxxii

Raumer, ____, 28, 29

Ravenna, Italy, 84

realism in art, 221–22

Recollections of Rubens (Burckhardt), lix

Reflections on History (Burckhardt), xxiii, xxiv, xliv, l, li–lii, liii, lvii n11, lix–lx

Regensburg, 20

Régime noveau (Taine), 173

religion. *See* Christianity; theology profession

Rembrandt, 210

Renaissance-related books, (Burckhardt), xxiii, xlii, xlv n2, liii–liv, 64 n36, 114, 114 n47, 115, 116–18, 122, 124, 153, 153 n74

Renan, ____, 145

Reni, Guido, 249

Reno baths, 183

resignation as attribute, 8–9, 11, 11 n11, 26

retirement, xlv, lviii–lix, 242–44

revelation, l, l n6. *See also* Christianity

Révolution (Taine), 173

Rhineland: population characterized, 87; socialism, 77; travels through, 33–35

Ribbeck, Otto: Kiel residency, 124 n57; letter to, 124–25

Ricordi, ____, 167

Riggenbach, Johannes (Christoph Johann): biography, 251; JB's relationship, xxviii, xxx; letters to, 3–12

Rimini, Italy, 186

Rome, 59, 101; anticipation of, 78–79; historical perspective, lvii n11; letters from, 81–83, 162–68, 217–18; memories of, xl, 83–84, 169

Rossi, ____, 167

Royal Aquarium, 201

Rubens, lix, 197

Rubinstein, Arthur, 207

Russia, 137–39, 206, 215

sadness, 51–52

St. Catherine's (Sienna), 163

Saint-Denis church, 61

St. Jacob, 20

St. Martin's Cathedral, 35–36

St. Michael's (Munich), 175

St. Peter's, 100

Salis, Arnold von, letters to, 146–47, 243

Salome, Margarethe, 13–14, 13 n14

Sancta Colonia letter, 33–36

San Paolo, 165

San Salvatore, 183

Sarasate, ____, 207

Sarasin, Felix, 118 n53

Savigny, Frau von, xxxv, 42

Savigny, Friedrich von, 42 n29

Schauenburg, Anna, 207–8, 208 n89

Schauenburg, Eduard: biography, xxxiii, 208 n89, 252; letter about, 31; letters to, 33–36, 68, 71–72, 93–95, 125–26, 207–8

Schauenburg, Hermann: biography, xxxiii–xxxiv, xxxvii, 252; letters to, 74, 78–80, 87–88, 89–93; meeting JB, 32–33

Schelling, ____, 47–48

Schiller, ____, 238

Schnaase, Karl, 64, 64 n37

school systems, 179, 216. *See also* teaching profession

Schopenhauer, Arthur, 140, 140 n67, 170

Schorndorff family background, xxvi
Schreiber, Heinrich: biography, xxxi–xxxii; letters to, 15–17, 19–22, 27–28, 43–44, 52, 98–99, 115
Schütz, Carl, xxxvii
sciatica, JB's, 242
sculpture/statues: London, 192–93, 203; Rome, 164–65, 168
Seeman, 153
selfishness and community, liv–lvi, 8–9
Senn, Frau, 228
sentiment decision, xxx, 6
Sienna, 163, 165
silk spinners, 181
sisters: elderly years and, 229, 244; Margarethe, 13–14, 13n14. See also Burckhardt, Louise (sister)
socialism/democracy trends: authority/power traditions and, 46–47, 187, 204–5, 215, 225; progress ideals and, 143–44, 170–71, 212–13, 238; tyranny of, 74–75, 80, 92–93, 209, 215, 223–24, 233–35. See also political issues
Solomon, 237–38
South Kensington Museum, 191–92, 196
speculation/contemplation compared, li, 50–51
Spezia, 163
Spiers and Pond, 197–98
spitting in Italy, 183
Stähelin, J. J., 3–4, 3n3, 12, 202–3
statues/sculpture: London, 192–93, 203; Rome, 164–65, 168
la Stella, 184
Strauss, David Friedrich, xxix–xxx
Switzerland: Burgundian invasion, 66; economic conditions, 174; German culture and, 39–40; Radicalism, xxxix, 72, 74–75, 172, 209. See also Zürich

Taine, Hippolyte, 173
Talleyrand, 190
teaching profession: advice about, lviii, 108–9, 159; appointments/invitations, xxiii–xxiv, xxxix, xl, xliv, 76, 149; business compared, 179, 215–16; decision for, 3; elderly years, 213, 221, 227, 238–39; JB's approach, 156–57; lecture plans/preparations, 67–68, 73, 144, 149–50, 158, 160; overview of lectures, xxiv, xxxix–xl, xlv; political issues, 219; resignation/retirement, xlv, lviii–lix, 242–44; Talleyrand lectures, 190
Thann, 132
Theatinerkirche, 175
theology profession: deciding against, 3–4, 15; faith and, xxxi, 16, 179–80; overview of JB's perspective, xxviii–xxx; politics and, xxxix, 70–71, 76–77, 241. See also Christianity
Thoughts out of Season (Nietzsche), 156–57
"Three Poor Devils," 45
Tibaldi, Pellegrino, 180–81
Titian, 203
tortoise in Bologna, 187
Treitschke, _____, xxiv, 149
Trentino wine, 227–28
Trublet, Abbé, 184
Tschudi, Friedrich von: biography, 251; JB's relationship, xxviii; letters to, 13–15, 17–18, 24–25
Tübingen, B. Kugler's appointment, 152
Tunisia, 212
Turin, 162, 168
Twelve Apostles, Ravenna, 84

Vasari, _____, 136
velocipede circus, 230–31

Verdi's *Aida,* 167, 177–78
Vico, ____, 1n6
Victoria Tower, 200
Vienna visit, 149, 150
Vinet, Alexandre, xxviii
Vischer, Wilhelm, 130
Vogel, ____, 207
Vögelin, Friedrich Salomon, letter
   to, 119, 122

Waagen, ____, 132–33
Wackernagel, Wilhelm, 10, 10n10,
   63–64, 71–72
Wagner, Richard, 154–55, 182
war and aftermath, xlix, 137–41, 146,
   148–49, 151, 222, 224
Wellington's gallery, Duke of, 203
Werity, ____, 198
Westminster, Marquis of, 196–97
Westminster Abbey, 201
Westphalian Club, 31
Wilhelm I, 137, 137n66, 225
Wilken, ____, 28
William I, 225, 225n94
William II, 225, 225n94

wine, 164, 174, 185, 194, 202, 227–28,
   231
Winterfeld, Frau von, 27, 27n22
Winterfeld, Karl August von, 27n
   22
Wölfflin, Heinrich: biography, xlv,
   lviii–lix, 244, 248n101; letters to,
   246–47
Wolter, Ferdinand, 28, 28n23
Wolters, Albrecht: biography, 252;
   letter to, 62–63
women, JB's opinions, 78, 81, 96, 216
worldliness vs. unworldliness theme,
   lii–lviii
writing styles: history, 45–46; JB's
   described, xxv–xxvi

Zahn, Herrn von, 126, 126n59
Zarathustra (Nietzsche), xlviii, xlix
Zürich: architecture, 231; JB's plans
   for, 99, 100; letters from, 102–13;
   overview of JB's residency, xlii–
   xliii; uprising, xxix–xxx, 15–16,
   15n16
Zwicki, Caspar, 18, 18n17, 252

The typeface used in this book is Dante, designed by Giovanni Mardersteig and hand-cut by Charles Malin at Stamperia Valedonega in Verona in the early and mid-1950s. Dante was adapted as a Monotype face in 1957 and subsequently redrawn for digital composition by Ron Carpenter of Monotype in 1991.

This book is printed on paper that is acid-free and meets the requirements of the American National Standard for Permanence of Paper for Printed Library Materials, Z39.48-1992. ∞

Book design by Mark McGarry, Texas Type and Book Works, Inc., Dallas, Texas

Typography by G & S Typesetters, Austin, Texas

Printed and bound by Edwards Brothers, Inc., Ann Arbor, Michigan